Between Parentheses

Roberto Bolaño was born in Santiago, Chile, in 1953. He grew up in Chile and Mexico City. He is the author of *The Savage Detectives*, which received the Herralde Prize and the Rómulo Gallegos Prize, and *2666*, which won the National Book Critics Circle Award. He died in Blanes, Spain, at the age of fifty.

Between Parentheses

ESSAYS, ARTICLES, AND SPEECHES, 1998–2003

ROBERTO BOLAÑO

Edited by Ignacio Echevarría
Translated from the Spanish by Natasha Wimmer

PICADOR

First published 2011 by New Directions Publishing Corporation, New York, and simultaneously in Canada by Penguin Books Canada

First published in Great Britain 2012 by Picador
an imprint of Pan Macmillan, a division of Macmillan Publishers Limited
Pan Macmillan, 20 New Wharf Road, London N1 9RR
Basingstoke and Oxford
Associated companies throughout the world
www.panmacmillan.com

ISBN 978-0-330-51068-4

Originally published in 2004 as *Entre parentesis* by Editorial Anagrama, Spain. Published by arrangement with the Heirs of Roberto Bolaño and Carmen Balcells Agencia Literaria, Barcelona.

Grateful acknowledgement is made to the magazines where some of these essays originally appeared: the *Nation*, *Newsweek*, the *Hudson Review*, *Granta*, and the *New York Review of Books*.

1 3 5 7 9 8 6 4 2

A CIP catalogue record for this book is available from the British Library.

Printed and bound by CPI Group (UK) Ltd, Croydon CR0 4YY

CONTENTS

3. Between Parentheses

INTRODUCTION

This volume collects most of the newspaper columns and articles that Roberto Bolaño published between 1998 and 2003. Also included are a few scattered prefaces, as well as the texts of some talks or speeches given by Bolaño during the same period. Taken together, they make up a surprisingly rounded whole, offering in their entirety a personal cartography of the writer: the closest thing, among all his writings, to a kind of fragmented "autobiography."

The starting date, 1998, isn't arbitrary. Up until then (and despite the critical success of *Nazi Literature in the Americas* and *Distant Star*, in 1996, and the short-story collection *Llamadas telefónicas* [Phone Calls], in 1997), Roberto was a little-known writer who lived in relative isolation in Blanes, a coastal town in the Spanish province of Gerona, north of Barcelona. It was after the publication of *The Savage Detectives*, in 1998, and the powerful response the novel elicited, that

Roberto was given the opportunity to write for various Spanish and Latin American publications, and he began to be called upon to give lectures, write prefaces, preside at book launches, and participate in conferences.

Today, it's hard to grasp how quickly all of this happened. In fact, the oldest of the pieces collected here—"Who Would Dare?"—is an isolated article that appeared in *Babelia*, the literary supplement of the Spanish newspaper *El País*, in January 1998. Less than a year later, Bolaño agreed to write a more or less weekly column for the *Diari de Girona*. The first was published in January 1999, and from then on, Bolaño—who had begun to acquire a taste for this new kind of writing—continued to publish articles on a fairly regular basis, and also to field a growing number of requests for his presence at different events.

As a result, all of the texts collected here were written in the short span of about five years. It makes sense, then, that the tone should be consistent, that multiple internal resonances should be revealed, and that the pieces should fit together in a natural way, with surprising neatness. In assembling the volume, a strict chronological order might have been adopted. But in the end this was rejected in favor of a more deliberate scheme, according to which the different materials are grouped in six main sections, preceded by a brief "Self-Portrait" and concluding with one of the last interviews that Bolaño gave shortly before he died.

First come three talks or speeches (either term is better than *lectures*) delivered by Roberto on very different occasions. The adjective "insufferable" has been attached to all three, deliberately: to underscore the close relationship of these speeches with the two that Roberto himself included at the end of his posthumous collection, *El gaucho insufrible* (2003) [The Insufferable Gaucho]. "Literatura + enfermedad = enfermedad" [Literature + Illness = Illness] and "Los mitos de Cthulhu" [The Myths of Cthulhu] were surprising because of their aggressive stance, provocatively full of categorical statements. "The Vagaries of the Literature of Doom," the first of the "three insufferable speeches" gathered here, continues in the same provocative vein; it begins with a discussion of *Martín Fierro*, the ultimate insufferable gaucho, and is dedicated to the patron saints of post-Borgesian Argentine literature. The other two speeches are somewhat different in character, much more personal. The "Caracas Address" is the text that Bolaño read in Venezuela when his novel *The Savage Detectives* won the 1999 Rómulo Gallegos Prize. It's an unexpectedly confessional speech, in which Bolaño makes a public profession of his literary faith and comes to state, with moving seriousness, that "everything I've written is a love letter or farewell letter to my own generation." "Literature and Exile," meanwhile, reflects on a subject as crucial to Bolaño's work as to his life; very shortly after giving this speech he faced the intense experience of returning, for the first time in twenty-five years, to Chile, the country of his birth.

"Fragments of a Return to the Native Land" is the title of a long piece that Bolaño wrote upon his return from the first of two trips he made to Chile, at the end of 1998. The same title heads the block of texts that serve as the backbone of this volume. The first was written—like the speech "Literature and Exile"—just before Bolaño's return to Chile. His first impressions of this trip are very clearly described in the piece cited above, which is wary yet warm in tone, full of humor. Shortly afterward, however, Bolaño published a much darker, more bitter piece in the Barcelona magazine *Ajoblanco*. It's the account of a dinner to which he was invited by the Chilean writer Diamela Eltit and her husband, the socialist minister Jorge Arrate, spokesman of the Frei government. The story— recast later in *By Night in Chile*—was soon making the rounds in Chile and, not surprisingly, feelings were hurt. As a result, when Bolaño traveled to Chile for the second time, in December 1999, the atmosphere was stormy, and even hostile, and Bolaño was shut out by the country's cultural establishment. This had to happen sooner or later, given Bolaño's visceral response to Chilean politics and society, as well as culture, and, more specifically, poetry. The texts collected in this section give a good sense of this response. Among them, special mention should be made of the piece on Nicanor Parra, a crucial influence on Bolaño's work, as is evident in many places. It's impossible to explain Bolaño's poetry (and Bolaño, of course, was first and foremost a poet) without keeping in mind Parra's influence. But the deep effect of the great Chilean poet is also recognizable in Bolaño's more or less insufferable speeches and his increasingly cantankerous, irreverent, and havoc-wreaking public persona.

The bulk of this volume consists of the columns that, under the heading "Between Parentheses," Bolaño wrote for the Chilean newspaper *Las Últimas Noticias*. Their forerunner was the column that Bolaño wrote regularly for more than a year for the *Diari de Girona*, of the Catalan city of the same name. The staff there, particularly Salvador Cargol, the editor of the arts section, deserve credit for having been the first to think of him as a columnist, when such a thing had never crossed Bolaño's mind. Starting in January 1999, Bolaño wrote for the *Diari de Girona* as noted, and continued to write for it for almost a year and a half, until the spring of 2000. Bolaño's column usually ran alongside the paper's editorial. There was something humorous, it must be said, about Bolaño sharing space with the

Catholic writer Josep María Gironella, once-renowned author of *The Cypresses Believe in God* and *One Million Dead*, among many other books. In the end, Bolaño published nearly fifty articles in the *Diari de Girona*, as well as a number of reviews. The pieces were translated at the newspaper's offices. Some of the Spanish originals were never found, and as a result those articles are not included here.

Soon after he stopped writing regularly for the *Diari de Girona*, it was Bolaño himself who, in reponse to an invitation to write a piece for his friend Andrés Braithwaite at *Las Últimas Noticias* (a venerable Chilean newspaper with a large circulation), proposed a weekly column. Roberto's correspondence with Braithwaite, full of nudges and in-jokes, makes it possible to follow their planning step by step. It's worth noting Bolaño's original proposal, as he described it to Braithwaite in July 2000: "On a different subject: I've been thinking that we might publish (emphasis on *might*) my one-page articles that have only appeared in Catalan, along with some other completely new things. These are pieces on writers, occasionally on European and American movies and artists. They're yours if you want them. Let me know if you're interested [. . .] I could make it a weekly column (there are more than forty already written)."

The next day, Roberto specifies: "I'd like to have a column where I can talk about everything from the most obscure Provençal poet to the most celebrated Polish novelist, which will all sound like the same gibberish in Santiago. The truth is, these pieces will be collected into a book at some point, and that's why I want to get in the ones that were already published in Catalan. To be perfectly clear: this would be an essentially literary column."

Andrés Braithwaite accepted Bolaño's proposal, and the two immediately began trying to come up with a good title for the column. "I think it *should* have a title," says Bolaño, and he suggests, tongue in cheek: "HELLO, GOD SPEAKING? THUS SPAKE ZARATHUSTRA? THE ORACLE OF DELPHI? THE DIVINE SCOURGE?... I'm joking. I repeat: joking. The truth is I can't come up with anything. page gues is a bad title, but that's the idea. Or: NOTES. Something along those lines." The matter was resolved after some back and forth around a list of suggestions sent by Braithwaite that caused Bolaño "considerable amusement." Among them was "Between Parentheses," which they both liked.

As this demonstrates, the idea of collecting Bolaño's newspaper columns in a book was very much a part of his own plans. The long section into which they're gathered is divided into three parts. I) In the first are the pieces that Bolaño didn't reclaim for his column in *Las Últimas Noticias*. Not all are included, since, as noted, the Spanish originals of some couldn't be found. II) The columns in the second part were all published in *Las Últimas Noticias* but many were previously published in the *Diari de Girona*. III) As for the pieces in the third part, almost all were originally published in *Las Últimas Noticias*.

In the case of the columns that were first published in the *Diari de Girona* and then in *Las Últimas Noticias* (about twenty), it was decided to follow the sequence that Bolaño established for the Chilean newspaper. This makes sense considering the greater care that Bolaño seems to have taken in his second stint as a columnist, when he was beginning to be a well-known writer and to contemplate the possibility of collecting his journalistic writings in a book. In any case, it's important to stress the periodic nature of the columns gathered in this section, written at weekly or bi-weekly intervals, all more or less similar in length and linked to one another in the manner of diary entries, in which the author expresses his likes, loves, infatuations, and obsessions.

The next section, titled "Scenes," collects some travel articles and other occasional pieces whose common denominator is the evocation of places that were familiar to Bolaño, or that he visited occasionally. The Catalan town of Blanes, a strong presence in a number of Bolaño's columns, naturally takes center stage. Bolaño always felt very comfortable in this seaside town, which he encountered for the first time—as he explains in "Town Crier of Blanes"—in *Últimas tardes con Teresa* [Last Evenings with Teresa], the novel by Juan Marsé, which he read avidly while he was still living in Mexico. The Blanes beach, meanwhile, is the setting for "Beach," a purely fictional piece that might have been included in any of Bolaño's story collections.

In this regard, it should be stressed that Bolaño's books, from very early on, displayed a marked tendency to flow easily from one genre to another. In his last two "story" collections, this translated into the grouping together, without any sort of distinction, of texts of very different types. In the collection *Putas asesinas* [Killer Whores] (2001), a piece like "Dance Card" already has an unequivocally autobiographical slant. And in the collection *El gaucho insufrible* Bolaño planned to include what were originally two talks or speeches that, as we've seen, bear a clear resemblance to those included in the first section of this book. At the start of *El gaucho insufrible*, too, comes "Jim," which Bolaño originally wrote as a column for *Las Últimas Noticias* and which the reader will find here again, so that it remains part of the series to which it first belonged. Like so many of the other pieces gathered here, "Jim" is ambiguous in nature, midway between autobiographical sketch and fiction. Meanwhile, "Beach," whose narrator is an ex-junkie, belongs fully to the genre of fiction, though it clearly has its origins in another column by Bolaño: "Sun and Skull," first published in the *Diari de Girona*, in 1999, and republished a year later, with slight modifications, in *Las Últimas*

Noticias. All of which leads to the conclusion that this book sits naturally alongside the books that Bolaño himself published before his death, making it possible to speculate that, far from trying to conceal its very miscellaneous character, Bolaño himself would have underscored it, assigning the book to the same category as *Putas asesinas* and *El gaucho insufrible.*

The fifth section deals entirely with writers and books. Again, these are occasional pieces, written on assignment, mostly prefaces and the odd review, as well as a few stray obituaries (like Camilo José Cela's) and pieces written to celebrate the publication of a book (like "Notes on Jaime Bayly"). At the end comes what is certainly one of Bolaño's last pieces, "Sevilla Kills Me," a fragment of an unfinished speech that he planned to read at the first Encuentro de Escritores Latinoamericanos [Conference of Latin American Writers], organized by the publishing house Seix Barral and held in Sevilla in June 2003. Bolaño traveled to Sevilla without having finished the speech, reading instead "Los mitos de Cthulhu," which was already written. It's clear that if finished, "Sevilla Kills Me" would join the company of the "insufferable speeches." Its content, in any case, makes plain the context in which one must view the back-slaps and knuckle-raps, the winks and cuffs that Bolaño deals his contemporaries, particularly the young Latin American writers who, justifiably or not, constantly cite him as an influence.

"The Private Life of a Novelist," the last of the sections into which this volume is divided, consists of four short pieces in which Bolaño recalls his education as a reader and reflects on his "literary kitchen," permitting himself to offer some "advice on the art of writing stories" and providing some clues to *The Savage Detectives.*

The book ends with one of the last interviews that Bolaño

gave, if not the last. The interview was conducted by Mónica Maristain, for the Mexican edition of *Playboy*, and it came out on the day he died. Bolaño sent written answers, and claimed he'd had fun with it. The result is a kind of sketch, for which Bolaño posed with characteristic openness and irony.

In putting together this book, it was necessary to overcome some scruples about doing so without the express consent of the writer. But, as we've seen, Bolaño himself more than once announced his intention of preparing a collection of his journalistic pieces, which provides an initial alibi for proceeding in his stead. There's room nevertheless, for reasonable doubt as to which pieces Bolaño might or might not have decided to include, what his selection criteria might have been, and how he might have ordered the pieces. In these matters there's no guidance to be had, so an attempt has been made to proceed as neutrally as possible, without relinquishing minimal standards of organization. There has been no "censorship," nor were any pieces automatically ruled out (with the exception, previously noted, of those published in Catalan that couldn't be located in the original version). Another matter are the undiscovered pieces that will doubtless surface here and there once this volume has been published. There are unlikely to be many of them. In any case, this volume isn't defined by its zeal for exhaustiveness, particularly since it was decided at the outset not to reprint a number of very old pieces, published during the years when Bolaño lived in Mexico. To include them in this volume would have meant disrupting the notable harmony of the elements of which it is presently composed. Also, there was some hurry to get these pieces into readers' hands. This haste was motivated by a wish that they be read while the memory of the writer was still fresh, and as I write these lines, a year has not yet passed since his death.

At the end of the volume, the source for each piece is provided, along with a few explanatory notes. It can be seen here that only in exceptional cases, when a piece is of particular interest, has it been included without definite proof of publication. Our aim has been simply to gather Bolaño's scattered writings, not to provide a place for unpublished pieces, or to pretend to make inroads into his posthumous body of work, which is immense.

At this point, it seems unnecessary to justify our choice of title—he chose it. All of the collected pieces were written by Roberto Bolaño during pauses in his incessant creative labors, or "between parentheses," and that urgency inevitably shines through in this volume, most of its pieces written in the course of the writer's increasingly desperate struggle with death to finish the monumental *2666*, which will surely confirm him as an utterly exceptional novelist, an essential figure.

We began by saying that this volume amounts to something like a personal cartography of Roberto Bolaño and comes closest, of everything he wrote, to being a kind of fragmented "autobiography." That the pieces it contains are—as the author stressed—of a "basically literary" nature, doesn't contradict this assertion. Borges boasted more about the books he'd read than the ones he'd written. In the "self-portrait" at the start of this volume, Bolaño, assiduous reader of Borges, claims to be "much happier reading than writing."

"Criticism is the modern form of autobiography," says Ricardo Piglia in *Formas breves* [Short Forms]. And he adds: "Writing fiction changes how we read, and a writer's criticism is the secret mirror of his work." Sergio Pitol says something similar in *El arte de la fuga* [The Art of Escape], a book that, like Piglia's, bears a certain family resemblance to *Between Parentheses*. One might suggest other precedents for this kind of confessional writing through reading, understood as an autobiographical approach to the fiction writer, but what has been said will suffice to justify the guiding role that this book is called to play in the proper reception of Roberto Bolaño as an author whose influence in the realms of Spanish and Latin American literature has only just begun to be felt.

IGNACIO ECHEVARRÍA
Barcelona, May 2004

Of what is lost, irretrievably lost, all I wish to recover is the daily availability of my writing, lines capable of grasping me by the hair and lifting me up when I'm at the end of my strength.

ROBERTO BOLAÑO, Antwerp

PREFACE: SELF-PORTRAIT

I was born in 1953, the year that Stalin and Dylan Thomas died. In 1973 I was detained for eight days by the military, which had staged a coup in my country, and in the gym where the political prisoners were held I found an English magazine with pictures of Dylan Thomas's house in Wales. I had thought that Dylan Thomas died poor, but the house looked wonderful, almost like a fairytale cottage in the woods. There was no story about Stalin. But that night I dreamed of Stalin and Dylan Thomas: the two of them were at a bar in Mexico City, sitting at a little round table, a table for arm wrestling, but instead of wrestling they were competing to see who could hold his liquor better. The Welsh poet was drinking whiskey and the Soviet dictator was drinking vodka. As the dream went on, however, I was the only one who seemed to feel queasier and queasier, ever closer to the verge of nausea. Well there you have the story of my birth. As for my books, I should say that I've published five collections of poetry, one book of short stories, and seven novels. Almost no one has read my poems, which is probably a good thing. My books of prose have some loyal readers, probably undeservedly. In *Consejos de un discípulo de Morrison a un fanático de Joyce* [Advice from a Morrison Disciple to a Joyce Fanatic] (1984), written in collaboration with Antoni García Porta, I talk about violence. In *The Skating Rink* (1993), I talk about beauty, which is fleeting and usually meets a disastrous end. In *Nazi Literature in the Americas* (1996), I talk about the pathos and grandeur of the writing career. In *Distant Star* (1996), I attempt a very modest approximation of absolute evil. In *The Savage Detectives* (1998), I talk about adventure, which is always unexpected. In *Amulet* (1999), I try to give the reader the impassioned voice of a Uruguayan woman who should have been born in ancient Greece. I omit my third novel, *Monsieur Pain*, whose plot is indecipherable. Though I've lived in Europe for more than twenty years, my only nationality is Chilean, which in no way prevents me from feeling deeply Spanish and Latin American. In my life I've lived in three countries: Chile, Mexico, and Spain. I've worked at every job in the world, except the three or four that anybody with a little pride would turn down. My wife is Carolina López* and my son is Lautaro Bolaño. They're both Catalan. In Catalonia, I learned the difficult art of tolerance. I'm much happier reading than writing.

*In March 2001, after this piece was written, Alexandra, the second child of Carolina and Roberto, was born.

I.
THREE INSUFFERABLE
SPEECHES

THE VAGARIES OF THE LITERATURE
OF DOOM

It's odd that it was bourgeois writers who transported José Hernández's *Martín Fierro* to the center of the Argentine canon. The point is debatable, of course, but the truth is that Fierro, the gaucho, paradigm of the dispossessed, of the brave man (but also of the thug), presides over a canon, the Argentine canon, that only keeps getting stranger. As a poem, *Martín Fierro* is nothing out of this world. As a novel, however, it's alive, full of meanings to explore, which means that the wind still gusts (or blasts) through it, it still smells of the out-of-doors, it still cheerfully accepts the blows of fate. Nevertheless, it's a novel of freedom and squalor, not of good breeding and manners. It's a novel about bravery rather than intelligence, let alone morality.

If *Martín Fierro* dominates Argentine literature and its place is in the center of the canon, the work of Borges, probably the greatest writer born in Latin America, is only a footnote.

It's odd that Borges wrote so much and so well about *Martín Fierro*. Not just the young Borges, who can be nationalistic at times, if only on the page, but also the adult Borges, who is occasionally thrown into ecstasies (strange ecstasies, as if he were contemplating the gestures of the Sphinx) by the four most memorable scenes in Hernández's work, and who sometimes even writes perfect, listless stories with plots imitative of Hernández's. When Borges recalls Hernández, it's not with the affection and admiration with which he refers to Güiraldes, or with the surprise and resignation evoked by Evaristo Carriego, that familiar bogeyman. With Hernández, or with *Martín Fierro*, Borges seems to be acting, acting to perfection, in fact, but in a play that strikes him from the beginning as not so much odious as wrongheaded. And yet, odious or wrongheaded, it also seems to him inevitable. In this sense, his silent death in Geneva is highly eloquent. More than eloquent. In fact, his death in Geneva talks a blue streak.

With Borges alive, Argentine literature becomes what most readers think of as Argentine literature. That is: there's Macedonio Fernández, who at times resembles the Valéry of Buenos Aires; there's Güiraldes, who's rich and ailing; there's Ezequiel Martínez Estrada; there's Marechal, who later turns Peronist; there's Mujica Láinez; there's Bioy Casares, who writes Latin America's first and best fantastic novel, though all the writers of Latin America rush to deny it; there's Bianco; there's Mallea, the pedant; there's Silvina Ocampo; there's Sábato; there's Cortázar, best of them all; there's Roberto Arlt, most hard done by. When Borges dies, everything suddenly comes to an end. It's as if Merlin had died, though Buenos Aires' literary circles aren't exactly Camelot. Gone, most of all, is the reign of balance. Apollonian intelligence gives way to Dionysian desperation. Sleep, an often hypocritical, false, accommodating, cowardly sleep, becomes nightmare, a nightmare that's often honest, loyal, brave, a nightmare that operates without a safety net, but a nightmare in the end, and, what's worse, a literary nightmare, literary suicide, a literary dead end.

And yet with the passage of the years it's fair to ask whether the nightmare, or the skin of the nightmare, is really as radical as its exponents proclaimed. Many of them live much better than I do. In this sense, I can say that I'm an Apollonian rat and they're starting to look more and more like angora or Siamese cats neatly defleaed by a collar labeled Acme or Dionysius, which at this point in history amounts to the same thing.

Regrettably, Argentine literature today has three reference points. Two are public. The third is secret. All three are in some sense reactions against Borges. All three ultimately represent a step backward and are conservative, not revolutionary, although all three, or at least two of them, have set themselves up as leftist alternatives.

The first is the fiefdom of Osvaldo Soriano, who was a good minor novelist. When it comes to Soriano, you have to have a brain full of fecal matter to see him as someone around whom a literary movement can be built. I don't mean he's bad. As I've said: he's good, he's fun, he's essentially an author of crime novels or something vaguely like crime novels, whose main virtue—praised at length by the always perceptive Spanish critical establishment—is his sparing use of adjectives, a restraint lost, in any case, after his fourth or fifth book. Hardly the basis for a school. Apart from Soriano's kindness and generosity, which are said to be great, I suspect that his sway is due to sales, to his accessibility, his mass readership, although to speak of a mass readership when we're really talking about twenty thousand people is clearly an exaggeration. What Argentine writers have learned from Soriano is that they, too, can make money. No need to write original books, like Cortázar or Bioy, or total novels, like Cortázar or Marechal, or perfect stories, like Cortázar or Bioy, and no need, especially, to squander your time and health in a lousy library when you're never going to win a Nobel Prize anyway. All you have to do is write like Soriano. A little bit of humor, lots of Buenos Aires solidarity and camaraderie, a dash of tango, a worn-out boxer or two, an old but solid Marlowe. But, sobbing, I ask myself on my knees, solid where? Solid in heaven, solid in the toilet of your literary agent? What kind of nobody are you, anyway? You have an agent? And an Argentine agent, no less?

If the Argentine writer answers this last question in the affirmative, we can be sure that he won't write like Soriano but like Thomas Mann, like the Thomas Mann of *Faust*. Or, dizzied by the vastness of the pampa, like Goethe himself.

The second line of descent is more complex. It begins with Roberto Arlt, though it's likely that Arlt is totally innocent of this mess. Let's say, to put it modestly, that Arlt is Jesus Christ. Argentina is Israel, of course, and Buenos Aires is Jerusalem. Arlt is born and lives a rather short life, dying at forty-two, if I'm not mistaken. He's a contemporary of Borges. Borges is born in 1899 and Arlt in 1900. But unlike Borges, Arlt grows up poor, and as an adolescent he goes to work instead of to Geneva. Arlt's most frequently held job was as a reporter, and it's in the light of the newspaper trade that one views many of his virtues, as well as his defects. Arlt is quick, bold, malleable, a born survivor, but he's also an autodidact, though not an autodidact in the sense that Borges was: Arlt's apprenticeship proceeds in disorder and chaos, through the reading of terrible translations, in the gutter rather than the library. Arlt is a Russian, a character out of Dostoyevsky, whereas Borges is an Englishman, a character out of Chesterton or Shaw or Stevenson. Sometimes, despite himself, Borges even seems like a character out of Kipling. In the war between the literary factions of Boedo and Florida, Arlt is with Boedo, although my impression is that his thirst for battle was never excessive. His oeuvre consists of two story collections and three novels, though in fact he wrote four novels, and his uncollected stories, stories that appeared in newspapers and magazines and that Arlt could write while he talked about women with his fellow reporters, would fill at least two more books. He's also the author of a volume of newspaper columns called *Aguafuertes porteños* [Etchings from Buenos Aires], in the best French impressionist tradition, and *Aguafuertes españoles* [Etchings from Spain], sketches of daily life in Spain in the 1930s, which are full of gypsies, the poor, and the benevolent. He tried to get rich through deals that had nothing to do with the Argentine literature of the day, though they did have something to do with science fiction, and they were always categorical failures. Then he died and, as he would have said, that was the end of everything.

But it wasn't the end of everything, because like Jesus Christ, Arlt had his St. Paul. Arlt's St. Paul, the founder of his church, is Ricardo Piglia. I often ask myself: What would have happened if Piglia, instead of falling in love with Arlt, had fallen in love with Gombrowicz? Why didn't Piglia devote himself to spreading the Gombrowiczian good news, or specialize in Juan Emar, the Chilean writer who bears a marked resemblance to the monument to the unknown soldier? A mystery. In any case, it's Piglia who raises up Arlt in his own coffin soaring over Buenos Aires, in a very Piglian or Arltian scene, though one that takes place only in Piglia's imagination, not in reality. It wasn't a crane that lowered Arlt's coffin. The stairs were wide enough for the job. The body in the box wasn't a heavyweight champion's.

By this I don't mean to say that Arlt is a bad writer, because in fact he's an excellent writer, nor do I mean to say that Piglia is a bad writer, because I think Piglia is one of the best Latin American novelists writing today. The problem is, I find it hard to stand the nonsense—thuggish nonsense, doomy nonsense—that Piglia knits around Arlt, who's probably the only innocent person in this whole business. I can in no way condone bad translators of Russian, as Nabokov said to Edmund Wilson while mixing his third martini, and I can't accept plagiarism as one of the arts. Seen as a closet or a basement, Arlt's work is fine. Seen as the main room of the house, it's a macabre joke. Seen as the kitchen, it promises food poisoning. Seen as the bathroom, it'll end up giving us scabies. Seen as the library, it's a guarantee of the destruction of literature.

Or in other words: the literature of doom has to exist, but if nothing else exists, it's the end of literature.

Like solipsistic literature—so in vogue in Europe now that the young Henry James is again roaming about at will—a literature of the I, of extreme subjectivity, of course must and should exist. But if all writers were solipsists, literature would turn into the obligatory military service of the mini-me or into a river of autobiographies, memoirs, journals that would soon become a cesspit, and then, again, literature would cease to exist. Because who really cares about the sentimental meanderings of a professor? Who can say, without lying through his teeth, that the daily routine of a dreary professor in Madrid, no matter how distinguished, is more interesting than the nightmares and dreams and ambitions of the celebrated and ridiculous Carlos Argentino Daneri? No one with half a brain. Listen: I don't have anything against autobiographies, so long as the writer has a penis that's twelve inches long when erect. So long as the writer is a woman who was once a whore and is moderately wealthy in her old age. So long as the author of the tome in question has lived a remarkable life. It goes without saying that if I had to choose between the solipsists and the bad boys of the literature of doom I'd take the latter. But only as a lesser evil.

The third lineage in play in contemporary or post-Borgesian Argentine literature is the one that begins with Osvaldo Lamborghini. This is the secret current. It's as secret as the life of Lamborghini, who died in Barcelona in 1985, if I'm not mistaken, and who left as literary executor his most beloved disciple, César Aira, which is like a rat naming a hungry cat as executor.

If Arlt, who as a writer is the best of the three, is the basement of the house that is Argentine literature, and Soriano is a vase in the guest room, Lamborghini is a little box on a shelf in the basement. A little cardboard box, covered in dust. And if you open the box, what you find inside is hell. Forgive me for being so melodramatic. I always have the same problem with Lamborghini. There's no way to describe his work without falling into hyperbole. The word *cruelty* fits it like a glove. *Harshness* does too, but especially *cruelty.* The unsuspecting reader may glimpse the sort of sadomasochistic game of writing workshops that charitable souls with pedagogical inclinations organize in insane asylums. Perhaps, but that doesn't go far enough. Lamborghini is always two steps ahead of (or behind) his pursuers.

It's strange to think about Lamborghini now. He died at forty-five, which means that I'm four years older than he was then. Sometimes I pick up one of his two books, edited by Aira—which is only a figure of speech, since they might just as well have been edited by the linotypist or by the doorman at his publishing house in Barcelona, Serbal—and I can hardly read it, not because I think it's bad but because it scares me, especially all of *Tadeys*, an excruciating novel, which I read (two or three pages at a time, not a page more) only when I feel especially brave. Few books can be said to smell of blood, spilled guts, bodily fluids, unpardonable acts.

Today, when it's so fashionable to talk about nihilists (although what's usually meant by this is Islamic terrorists, who aren't nihilists at all), it isn't a bad idea to take a look at the work of a real nihilist. The problem with Lamborghini is that he ended up in the wrong profession. He should have gone to work as a hit man, or a prostitute, or a gravedigger, which are less complicated jobs than trying to destroy literature. Literature is an armor-plated machine. It doesn't care about writers. Sometimes it doesn't even notice they exist. Literature's enemy is something else, something much bigger and more powerful, that in the end will conquer it. But that's another story.

Lamborghini's friends are fated to plagiarize him ad nauseam, something that might—if he could see them vomit—make Lamborghini himself happy. They're also fated to write badly, horribly, except for Aira, who maintains a gray, uniform prose that, sometimes, when he's faithful to Lamborghini, crystallizes into memorable works, like the story "Cecil Taylor" or the novella *How I Became a Nun*, but that in its neo-avantgarde and Rousselian (and utterly acritical) drift, is mostly just boring. Prose that devours itself without finding a way to move forward. Acriticism that translates into the acceptance—qualified, of course—of that tropical figure, the professional Latin American writer, who always has a word of praise for anyone who asks for it.

Of these three lineages—the three strongest in Argentine literature, the three departure points of the literature of doom—I'm afraid that the one which will triumph is the one that most faithfully represents the sentimental rabble, in the words of Borges. The sentimental rabble is no longer the Right (largely because the Right busies itself with publicity and the joys of cocaine and the plotting of currency devaluations and starvation, and in literary matters is functionally illiterate or settles for reciting lines from *Martín Fierro*) but the Left, and what the Left demands of its intellectuals is soma, which is exactly what it receives from its masters. Soma, soma, soma Soriano, forgive me, yours is the kingdom.

Arlt and Piglia are another story. Let's call theirs a love affair and leave them in peace. Both of them—Arlt without a doubt—are an important part of Argentine and Latin American literature, and their fate is to ride alone across the ghost-ridden pampa. But that's no basis for a school.

Corollary. One must reread Borges.

CARACAS ADDRESS

This preface or prologue or introduction to my Caracas Speech *is dedicated to Domingo Miliani, who for me is the incarnation of the classic Latin American intellectual, someone who has read everything and lived everything, and, on top of it all, is a good man. He's the perfect illustration of the phrase "to know him is to love him." But I would go even further: to see him is to love him. What do I see when I see Domingo Miliani? I see a brave and intelligent man, I see a good man. You don't even need to hear him speak. Miliani is part of the generation that is our common legacy. For Latin Americans it's a luxury—and I say* luxury *in full consciousness of what I'm saying—to have men like these. A few years ago I wrote a novel about a pilot who was the incarnation of near-absolute evil and who personified in some way the terrible fate of our continent. Domingo Miliani, who has also flown planes, is the incarnation of the good part of our story. He's one of those men who tried in vain to educate us. We—my turbulent generation—*

*ignored them completely. Among other reasons because we ignored
everyone, except for Rimbaud and Lautréamont. But we loved
them and each time one of them vanished it was as if a distant
uncle had vanished, our mother's crazy brother, or the forgotten
grandfather who leaves an incalculable, intangible inheritance.
It has been a joy and a privilege for me to meet him. And that's
the end of this preface.*

I've always had a problem with Venezuela. A silly problem,
fruit of my haphazard education, the most inconsequential of
problems, but a problem nonetheless. At its heart, the problem is verbal and geographic. It's also probably due to a kind
of undiagnosed dyslexia. Though by this I don't mean to say
that my mother never took me to the doctor. In fact, until I
was ten I was a frequent visitor of doctors' offices and even
hospitals, but after that my mother thought I was strong
enough to handle anything. But to get back to my problem.
When I was little I played soccer. My number was 11, the same
as Pepe and Zagallo in the Sweden World Cup, and I was an
enthusiastic but pretty bad player, though my shooting foot
was my left foot, and the conventional wisdom is that lefties
are always useful to have in a match. In my case that wasn't
true, I was almost never useful, although sometimes—once
every six months, say—I made a good play and won back at
least a fraction of all the credit I'd lost. At night, as is only
natural, I would lie awake thinking, and reflect on the sad state
of my soccer career. And it was then that I had the first conscious glimpse of my dyslexia. I was left-footed, but right-
handed. That was a fact. I would have liked to be left-handed,
but I was right-handed. And that was the problem. For example, when the coach said: pass to the right, Bolaño, I didn't
know where I was supposed to pass the ball. And sometimes,
playing on the left side of the field, at the coach's hoarse shout

I even had to stop and think: left-right. Right was the soccer field, to shoot left was to kick the ball out of bounds, toward the few spectators, kids like me, or toward the scrubby vacant lots that surrounded the soccer fields of Quilpué, or Cauquenes, or the province of Bío-Bío. In time, of course, I learned to consult a reference point whenever anyone asked me directions or told me about a street to the right or left, and that reference point wasn't my writing hand but my shooting foot. And more or less around the same time, or in other words until just yesterday, I had a similar problem with Venezuela. The problem was its capital. For me it was only logical that the capital of Venezuela should be Bogotá. And that the capital of Colombia should be Caracas. Why? Well, on the basis of verbal or alphabetical logic. The *v* of Venezuela bears a resemblance, almost a family resemblance, to the *b* of Bogotá.* And the *c* of Colombia is first cousin to the *c* of Caracas. This may seem trivial, and it probably is, but for me it became a major problem, so that once, in Mexico, during a lecture I was giving on the urban poets of Colombia, I talked about the force of the Caracas poets, and the audience, people as nice and polite as all of you, were quiet, waiting for me to end this digression on the poets of Caracas and move on to the poets of Bogotá, but I kept talking about the Caracas poets, about their aesthetic of destruction, and I even compared them to the Italian futurists, though without taking the comparison too far, of course, and to the first Lettrists, the group of Isidore Isou and Maurice Lemaître, the group where the seed of Guy Debord's situationism was planted, and at this point the people in the audience began to wonder, I think, speculating whether the Bogotá poets had all moved together to Caracas, or whether the Caracas poets had played a key role in the development of

*In Spanish, *v* and *b* have almost the same pronunciation.—tr.

this new group of Bogotá poets, and when I ended the talk, abruptly, as I liked to end things back then, people got up, clapped timidly, and hurried out to check the flyer at the door, and when I emerged, accompanied by the Mexican poet Mario Santiago, who was always with me and who had surely noticed my mistake, though he didn't say so because for Mario mistakes and misunderstandings were like Baudelaire's clouds drifting across the sky, in other words something to be gazed at, not corrected, and on our way out, as I was saying, we bumped into an old Venezuelan poet—and when I say old I think back and he was probably younger than I am now—who said to us with tears in his eyes that there must be some mistake, that he had never heard a word about these mysterious poets from Caracas. At this point in my speech I get the sense that Don Rómulo Gallegos must be turning over in his grave. Who is this person who's won my prize, he must be thinking. Forgive me, Don Rómulo. But even his Doña Bárbara, with a *b*, sounds like Venezuela, and Bolívar sounds like Venezuela and Doña Bárbara, too, Bolívar and Bárbara, what a great pair they would have made, although Don Rómulo's other two great novels, *Cantaclaro* and *Canaima*, could easily be Colombian, which leads me to think that they might be, and that there might be a method hidden in my dyslexia, a bastard semiotic or graphological or metasyntactic or phonemic method, or simply a poetic method, and that the underlying truth is that Caracas is the capital of Colombia just as Bogotá is the capital of Venezuela, in the same way that Bolívar, who is Venezuelan, died in Colombia, which is also Venezuela and Mexico and Chile. I don't know whether you're following me. *Pobre negro* [Poor Black], for example, by Don Rómulo, is an essentially Peruvian novel. *La casa verde,* or *The Green House*, by Vargas Llosa, is a Colombian-Venezuelan novel. *Terra Nostra*, by Fuentes, is an Argentine novel, and I should warn you that it's best not to inquire as to my reasoning here because the answer would be long and boring. In its extremely mysterious way, the pataphysical school teaches the science of imaginary solutions, which is, as you know, the study of the laws that regulate exceptions. And this confusion of letters is in some sense an imaginary solution that demands an imaginary solution. But let's get back to Don Rómulo before we take on Jarry, and meanwhile let's reflect on some strange portents. I've just been awarded the eleventh Rómulo Gallegos Prize. The 11th. My jersey number was 11. You'll think this is a coincidence, but it gives me the shivers. The 11 who didn't know how to tell left from right and who therefore mixed up Caracas with Bogotá has just won (and parenthetically, let me once more thank the jury, especially Ángeles Mastretta, for this distinction) the 11th Rómulo Gallegos Prize. What would Don Rómulo think? On the phone the other day, Pere Gimferrer, who is a great poet and who also knows everything and has read everything, told me that there are two commemorative plaques in Barcelona on different buildings where Don Rómulo lived. According to Gimferrer, although he wouldn't swear to this, it was in one of these two places that the great Venezuelan writer started *Canaima*. I really do have complete faith in 99.9 percent of the things Gimferrer tells me (though one of the buildings with a plaque on it was a bank, not a house, which planted a series of doubts: for example, whether during Don Rómulo's stay in Barcelona—I say stay and not exile because a Latin American is never an exile in Spain—he had worked at a bank or whether the bank had later moved into the house where he once lived), and then, while Gimferrer was talking, I started to think about my walks around the Eixample, long-ago walks that were exhausting then and are no less exhausting now to remember, and I saw myself there again, knocking around in 1977, 1978, maybe

1982, and all of a sudden I thought I saw a street at dusk, near Muntaner, and I saw a number, I saw the number 11, and then I walked a little farther, a few more steps, and there was the plaque. That's how I imagined it. But it's also likely that when I lived in Barcelona I walked along that street and spotted the plaque, a plaque that says something like "Here lived Rómulo Gallegos, novelist and politician, b. Caracas 1884, d. Caracas 1969," and then, in smaller letters, other things, titles of books, coats of arms, etc., and it's possible that I thought, without stopping to take a closer look, about another famous Colombian writer, though if I had stopped, I never would have thought such a thing, I swear, because I really had read Don Rómulo in school, whether early on in Chile or later in Mexico I don't know, and I liked *Doña Bárbara*, although according to Gimferrer, *Canaima* is better, and of course I knew that Don Rómulo was Venezuelan and not Colombian. Not that it really matters whether one is Venezuelan or Colombian, which brings us back at lightning speed to the *b* of Bolívar, who wasn't dyslexic and who wouldn't have been displeased by a united Latin America, which is a sentiment that I share with the Liberator, since it doesn't matter to me whether people say I'm Chilean, although some of my Chilean fellow writers would rather see me as Mexican, or whether they say I'm Mexican, although some of my Mexican fellow writers would rather see me as Spanish, or simply as lost in combat, and I don't even care whether people think of me as Spanish, although some of my Spanish fellow writers might protest and decide from now on to call me Venezuelan, born in Caracas or Bogotá, which wouldn't bother me either, in fact on the contrary. The truth is that I'm Chilean and I'm also many other things. And at this point I have to abandon Jarry and Bolívar and try to remember who it was who said that a writer's homeland is his language. I don't remember his name.

Maybe it was someone who wrote in Spanish. Maybe it was someone who wrote in English or French. The homeland of a writer, he said, is his language. It sounds a little demagogic but I completely agree with him, and I know that sometimes we have no choice but to be demagogic, just as sometimes we have no choice but to dance a bolero under a streetlight or a red moon. Though it's also true that a writer's homeland isn't his language or isn't only his language but the people he loves. And sometimes a writer's homeland isn't the people he loves but his memory. And other times a writer's only homeland is his steadfastness and his courage. In fact, a writer can have many homelands, and sometimes the identity of that homeland depends greatly on what he's writing at the moment. It's possible to have many homelands, it occurs to me now, but only one passport, and that passport is obviously the quality of one's writing. Which doesn't mean writing well, because anyone can do that, but writing incredibly well, and not even that, because anyone can write incredibly well. So what is topnotch writing? The same thing it's always been: the ability to peer into the darkness, to leap into the void, to know that literature is basically a dangerous undertaking. The ability to sprint along the edge of the precipice: to one side the bottomless abyss and to the other the faces you love, the smiling faces you love, and books and friends and food. And the ability to accept what you find, even though it may be heavier than the stones over the graves of all dead writers. Literature, as an Andalusian folk singer would put it, is danger. And as I return now at last to the number 11, which is the number of those who play the wing, and having mentioned danger, I'm reminded of the passage from *Don Quixote* in which the relative merits of military service and poetry are argued, and I guess the real argument is about the degree of danger, which is also an argument about the intrinsic value of each pursuit. And

Cervantes, who was a soldier, makes military service win out, makes the task of the soldier triumph over the honorable work of being a poet, and if we read the passage carefully (which I'm not doing as I write this speech, although from the desk where I'm writing I can see my two editions of *Don Quixote*) we get a strong whiff of melancholy, because Cervantes makes his own youth, the ghost of his lost youth, triumph over the reality of his labors in prose and poetry, so thankless thus far. And I'm reminded of this because to a great extent everything that I've written is a love letter or a farewell letter to my own generation, those of us who were born in the 1950s and who at a certain moment chose military service, though in this case it would be more accurate to say militancy, and we gave the little we had—the great deal that we had, which was our youth—to a cause that we thought was the most generous cause in the world and in a certain way it was, but in reality it wasn't. It goes without saying that we fought our hardest, but we had corrupt leaders, cowardly leaders with a propaganda apparatus that was worse than a leper colony, we fought for parties that if they had won would have sent us straight to labor camps, we fought for and put all our generosity into an ideal that had been dead for more than fifty years, and some of us knew it, and how could we not when we'd read Trotsky or were Trotskyites, but we did it anyway, because we were stupid and generous, as young people are, giving everything and asking for nothing in return, and now those young people are gone, because those who didn't die in Bolivia died in Argentina or Peru, and those who survived went on to die in Chile or Mexico, and those who weren't killed there were killed later in Nicaragua, Colombia, or El Salvador. All of Latin America is sown with the bones of these forgotten youths. And that's what moves Cervantes to choose military service over poetry. His companions were dead too. Or old and forgotten, poor and weary. To choose was to choose youth and to choose the defeated and to choose those who were stripped of everything. And that's what Cervantes does, he chooses youth. And even in this melancholy weakness, in this sense of loss, Cervantes is clear-sighted, because he realizes that writers don't need anyone to sing the praises of their work. We sing its praises ourselves. Our way of praising it is often to curse the evil hour that we decided to become writers, but most of the time we clap and dance when we're alone, because this is a solitary pursuit, and we read aloud what we've written and that's our way of singing our own praises and we don't need anyone to tell us what to do, much less a survey to show us that ours is the most honorable profession. Cervantes, who wasn't dyslexic but who lost an arm in the service, knew perfectly well what he was talking about. Literature is a dangerous game. Which leads us straight to Alfred Jarry, who had a gun and liked to shoot, and to number 11, the left-winger who, as plaque and house whizz by, gets a glimpse out of the corner of his eye of the former residence of Don Rómulo, who by now I hope isn't quite so angry with me, and who hopefully won't turn up in Domingo Miliani's dreams to ask why I was given the prize that bears his name, a prize that means so much to me, I'm the first Chilean to win it, a prize that doubles the challenge, if that were possible, if the challenge by its very nature, by virtue of its inherent worth, weren't already doubled or tripled. In this case, the awarding of a prize would be a gratuitous act, and now that I think about it, there is something gratuitous about it. It's a gratuitous act that says less about my novel and its merits than about the generosity of the jury. (Incidentally, until yesterday I hadn't met any of its members.) Let me be clear: like Cervantes's veterans of Lepanto and like the veterans of the ceremonial wars of Latin America, all I have is my honor. I read this and I can't believe it. Me talking about honor. Maybe the spirit of Don Rómulo will appear in my dreams instead of Domingo Miliani's. The words I've just read were written in Caracas (Venezuela) and one thing is clear: Don Rómulo can't appear in my dreams for the simple reason that I can't sleep. Outside, the crickets are chirping. At best guess, I calculate that there must be ten or twenty thousand of them. Maybe the song of one of those crickets is the voice of Don Rómulo, bewildered, happily bewildered, in the Venezuelan night, in the American night, in the night that belongs to all of us, to those who're asleep and to those who can't sleep. I feel like Pinocchio.

LITERATURE AND EXILE

I've been invited to talk about exile. The invitation I received was in English, and I don't speak English. There was a time when I did or thought I did, or at least there was a time, in my adolescence, when I thought I could read English almost as well, or as poorly, as Spanish. Sadly, that time has passed. I can't read English. By what I could gather from the letter, I think I was supposed to talk about exile. Literature and exile. But it's very possible that I'm completely mistaken, which, thinking about it, would actually be an advantage, since I don't believe in exile, especially not when the word sits next to the word *literature*.

It's a pleasure for me, I should say right away, to be with you here in the celebrated city of Vienna. For me Vienna is strongly associated with literature and with the lives of some people very near to me who understood exile in the way I sometimes understand it myself, which is to say, as life or as an attitude toward life. In 1978, or maybe 1979, the Mexican poet Mario Santiago spent a few days here on his way back to Israel. As he told it himself, one day the police arrested him and then he was expelled. In the deportation order, he was instructed not to return to Austria before 1984, a date that struck Mario as significant and funny and that today strikes me the same way. George Orwell isn't just one of the great writers of the twentieth century, he's also first and foremost a good man, and a brave one. So to Mario, back in the now distant year of 1978 or 1979, it seemed funny to be expelled from Austria like that, to be punished by being forbidden to set foot on Austrian soil for six years, until the date of the novel had arrived, a date that for many was the symbol of ignominy and darkness and the moral collapse of humankind. And here, leaving aside the significance of the date and the hidden messages that fate—or chance, that even fiercer beast—had sent the Mexican poet and through him sent me, we can discuss or return to the possible topic of exile or banishment: the Austrian Ministry of the Interior or the Austrian police or the Austrian security service issues a deportation order and consigns my friend Mario Santiago to limbo, to a *no-man's-land*, which frankly sounds better in Spanish than in English, because in Spanish *tierra de nadie* means precisely that, barren land, dead land, land where nothing lives, while in English the suggestion is that there are simply no men there, though there are other creatures, animals or insects, which makes it much nicer, I don't mean very nice, but infinitely nicer than in the Spanish sense, although probably my understanding of both terms is affected by my increasing ignorance of English and also by my increasing ignorance of Spanish (the term *tierra de nadie* isn't in the dictionary of the Royal Spanish Academy, which is no surprise; either that or I missed it).

But the point is that my Mexican friend was expelled and

set down in no-man's-land. I imagine the scene like this: some Austrian clerk stamps Mario's passport with an indelible seal signifying that he can't set foot on Austrian soil until Orwell's fateful date and then they put him on a train and ship him off, with a free ticket paid for by the Austrian state, into a temporal exile or a certain banishment of five years, at the end of which my friend, if he so desired, could request a visa and once again tread the lovely streets of Vienna. If Mario Santiago had been a devotee of the music festivals of Salzburg, he would surely have left Austria with tears in his eyes. But Mario never made it to Salzburg. He got on the train and didn't get off until Paris, and, after living in Paris for a few months, he got on a plane to Mexico, and when the fateful or happy—depending on how you look at it—year of 1984 arrived, Mario was still living in Mexico and writing poems in Mexico that nobody wanted to publish and that may rank among the best of late-twentieth century Mexican poetry, and he had accidents, and he traveled, and he fell in love, and he had children, and he lived a good life or a bad life, a life in any case far from the center of Mexican power, and in 1998 he was hit by a car under murky circumstances, a car that drove away while Mario lay dying alone on a street at night in one of the outlying neighborhoods of Mexico City, a city that at some point in its history was a kind of heaven and today is a kind of hell, but not just any hell—the special hell of the Marx brothers, the hell of Guy Debord, the hell of Sam Peckinpah, or in other words the most singular kind of hell—and that's where Mario died, the way poets die, unconscious and with no identification on him, which meant that when an ambulance came for his broken body no one knew who he was and the body lay in the morgue for several days, with no family to claim it, in a final stage of development or revelation, a kind of negative epiphany, I mean, like the photographic negative of an epiphany, which is also the story of our lives in Latin America. And among the many things that were left unresolved, one of them was the return to Vienna, the return to Austria, this Austria that for me, it goes without saying, isn't the Austria of Haider but the Austria of the youth who oppose Haider and who take to the streets in protest, the Austria of Mario Santiago, Mexican poet expelled from Austria in 1978 and forbidden to return to Austria until 1984, that is to say banished from Austria to the no-man's-land of the wide world, and who, anyway, could care less about Austria and Mexico and the United States and the happily defunct Soviet Union and Chile and China, among other reasons because he didn't believe in countries and the only borders he respected were the borders of dreams, the misty borders of love and indifference, the borders of courage and fear, the golden borders of ethics.

And now I think I've said all I had to say about litera-ture and exile or literature and banishment, but the letter I received, which was long and detailed, emphasized the fact that I should talk for twenty minutes, something for which I'm sure none of you will thank me and that for me could become a ordeal, especially because I'm not sure I read that wretched letter correctly, and also because I've always believed that the best speeches are short. Literature and exile, I think, are two sides of the same coin, our fate placed in the hands of chance. "I don't have to leave my house to see the world," says the *Tao Te Ching*, yet even when one doesn't leave one's house, exile and banishment make their presence felt from the start. Kafka's oeuvre, the most illuminating and terrible (and also the humblest) of the twentieth century, proves this exhaus-tively. Of course, a refrain is heard throughout Europe and it's the refrain of the suffering of exiles, a music composed of complaints and lamentations and a baffling nostalgia. Can one feel nostalgia for the land where one nearly died? Can one feel nostalgia for poverty, intolerance, arrogance, injustice? The refrain, intoned by Latin Americans and also by writers from other impoverished or traumatized regions, insists on nostalgia, on the return to the native land, and to me this refrain has always sounded like a lie. Books are the only homeland of the true writer, books that may sit on shelves or in the memory. The politician can and should feel nostalgia. It's hard for a politician to thrive abroad. The working man neither can nor should: his hands are his homeland.

So who sings this horrid nostalgic refrain? The first few times I heard it I thought it was the masochists. If you're locked up in prison in Thailand and you're Swiss, it's natural to want to serve your sentence in a Swiss prison. The reverse—in other words, if you're a Thai locked up in Switzerland and you still want to serve the rest of your sentence in a Thai prison—isn't natural, unless that perverse nostalgia is dictated by loneliness. Loneliness is certainly capable of producing desires with no connection to common sense or reality. But I was talking about writers, or in other words, about myself, so I can say that my homeland consists of my son and my books. A modest collection of books that I've lost twice, in two drastic and disastrous moves, and that I've patiently rebuilt. And at this point, talking about books, I can't help but recall a poem by Nicanor Parra, a poem that comes in handy in the discussion of literature, especially Chilean literature and exile or banishment. The poem starts with an argument about the four great poets of Chile, a thoroughly Chilean debate that any non-Chileans, in other words 99.99 percent of the literary critics of planet Earth, politely and somewhat wearily ignore. There are those who say that the four great poets of Chile are Gabriela Mistral, Pablo Neruda, Vicente Huidobro, and Pablo de Rokha; others, that they are Pablo Neruda, Nicanor Parra, Vicente Huidobro, and Gabriela Mistral; basically, the order varies depending on the source, but there are always four chairs and five poets, when the logical thing would simply be to talk about the five great poets of Chile, instead of the four great poets. Then came the poem by Nicanor Parra, which goes like this:

> Chile's four great poets
> are three:
> Alonso de Ercilla and Rubén Darío.

As you know, Alonso de Ercilla was a Spanish soldier, noble and dashing, who fought in the colonial wars against the Araucanians and upon his return to his native Castilla wrote *La Araucana*, which for Chileans is our foundational fiction and for lovers of poetry and history is a wonderful book, full of daring and generosity. Rubén Darío, as you also know, and if you don't it doesn't matter—we know so little, even about ourselves—was the creator of modernism and one of the most important Spanish-language poets of the twentieth century, probably the most important, a poet who was born in Nicaragua in 1867 and died in Nicaragua in 1916, and who arrived in Chile at the end of the nineteenth century, where he made good friends and read good books, but where he was also treated as an Indian or a *cabecita negra* by a Chilean ruling class that has always boasted of belonging 100 percent to the white race. So when Parra says that the best Chilean poets are Ercilla and Darío, who both spent time in Chile and had formative experiences in Chile (Alonso de Ercilla in the war and Darío in drawing room skirmishes), and who wrote in Chile and about Chile and in the lingua franca of Spanish, he's telling the truth, and not only does he resolve the by now boring question of the four greats, he also raises new questions, blazes new paths, and meanwhile his poem or *artifact*, which is what Parra calls these short texts, is a variation or spoof on the Huidobro poem that goes like this:

The four cardinal points
Are three
South and north.

Huidobro's poem is excellent and I like it very much—it's aerial verse, like much of Huidobro's poetry—but I like Parra's variation/spoof even better. It's like an explosive device set there to open our eyes and shake the nonsense out of us Chileans, it's a poem that explores the fourth dimension, as Huidobro intended, but a fourth dimension of the national consciousness, and although at first glance it seems like a joke, and it actually *is* a joke, at second glance it's revealed to be a declaration of human rights. It's a poem that tells the truth, at least to us contrite and hardworking Chileans, in other words that our four great poets are Ercilla and Darío, the first of whom died in his native Castilla in 1594, after a life as an inveterate traveler (he was page to Philip II and traveled through Europe and then fought in Chile under Alderete and in Peru under García Hurtado de Mendoza), and the second of whom died in 1916 (two years after the death of Trakl) in his native Nicaragua after having lived practically his entire life abroad.

And now that I've mentioned Trakl, let me digress, because it occurs to me that when Trakl gave up his studies and went to work as a druggist's apprentice, at the tender but no longer innocent age of eighteen, he was also choosing exile—and choosing it in a *natural* way—because going to work for a druggist at eighteen is a form of exile, just as drug addiction is a form of exile, and incest another, as the Ancient Greeks knew very well. So we've got Rubén Darío and we've got Alonso de Ercilla, who are the four great Chilean poets, and we've got the first thing that Parra's poem teaches us, which is that we don't *have* Darío or Ercilla, that we can't appropriate them, only read them, which is enough.

The second thing that Parra's poem teaches us is that nationalism is wretched and collapses under its own weight. If the expression "collapses under its own weight" doesn't make sense to you, imagine a statue made of shit slowly sinking into the desert: well, that's what it means for something to collapse under its own weight. And the third thing that Parra's poem teaches us is that probably our two best poets, Chile's best poets, were a Spaniard and a Nicaraguan who swung through these southern lands, one as a soldier and a person of great intellectual curiosity, the other as an immigrant, a penniless young man eager to make a name for himself, neither of them with any intention of staying, neither with any intention of becoming a great Chilean poet, simply two people, two travelers. And now I'd say it's clear what I think about literature and exile, or literature and banishment.

2.
FRAGMENTS
OF A RETURN
TO THE NATIVE LAND

EXILES

To be exiled is not to disappear but to shrink, to slowly or quickly get smaller and smaller until we reach our real height, the true height of the self. Swift, master of exile, knew this. For him *exile* was the secret word for *journey*. Many of the exiled, freighted with more suffering than reasons to leave, would reject this statement.

All literature carries exile within it, whether the writer has had to pick up and go at the age of twenty or has never left home.

Probably the first exiles on record were Adam and Eve. This is indisputable and it raises a few questions: Can it be that we're all exiles? Is it possible that all of us are wandering strange lands?

The concept of "strange lands" (like that of "home ground") has some holes in it, presents new questions. Are "strange lands" an objective geographic reality, or a mental construct in constant flux?

Let's recall Alonso de Ercilla.

After a few trips through Europe, Ercilla, soldier and nobleman, travels to Chile and fights the Araucanians under Alderete. In 1561, when he's not yet thirty, he returns and settles in Madrid. Twenty years later he publishes *La Araucana*, the best epic poem of his age, in which he relates the clash between Araucanians and Spaniards, with clear sympathy for the former. Was Ercilla in exile during his American ramblings through the lands of Chile and Peru? Or did he feel exiled when he returned to court, and is *La Araucana* the fruit of that *morbus melancholicus*, of his keen awareness of a kingdom lost? And if this is so, which I can't say for sure, what has Ercilla lost in 1589, just five years before his death, but youth? And with his youth, the arduous journeys, the human experience of being exposed to the elements of an enormous and unknown continent, the long rides on horseback, the skirmishes with the Indians, the battles, the shadows of Lautaro and Caupolicán that, as time passes, loom large and speak to him, to Ercilla, the only poet and the only survivor of something that, when set down on paper, will be a poem, but that in the memory of the old poet is just a life or many lives, which amounts to the same thing.

And what is Ercilla left with before he writes *La Araucana* and dies? Ercilla is left with something—if in its most extreme and bizarre form—that all great poets possess. He's left with courage. A courage worth nothing in old age, just as, incidentally, it's worth nothing in youth, but that keeps poets from throwing themselves off a cliff or shooting themselves in the head, and that, in the presence of a blank page, serves the humble purpose of writing.

Exile is courage. True exile is the true measure of each writer.

At this point I should say that at least where literature is concerned, I don't believe in exile. Exile is a question of tastes, personalities, likes, dislikes. For some writers exile means leaving the family home; for others, leaving the childhood town or city; for others, more radically, growing up. There are exiles that last a lifetime and others that last a weekend. Bartleby, who prefers not to, is an absolute exile, an alien on planet Earth. Melville, who was always leaving, didn't experience— or wasn't adversely affected by—the chilliness of the word *exile*. Philip K. Dick knew better than anyone how to recognize the disturbances of exile. William Burroughs was the incarnation of every one of those disturbances.

Probably all of us, writers and readers alike, set out into exile, or at least into a certain kind of exile, when we leave childhood behind. Which would lead to the conclusion that the exiled person or the category of exile doesn't exist, especially in regards to literature. The immigrant, the nomad, the traveler, the sleepwalker all exist, but not the exile, since every writer becomes an exile simply by venturing into literature, and every reader becomes an exile simply by opening a book.

The country that I come from, according to some of its native writers, is an island, the strangest island in the southern hemisphere. It's bordered to the north by the Atacama Desert, which Chileans say with utter conviction is the most inhospitable in the world; to the east by the Andes, which, according to the same native writers, is the highest and most impassable mountain range on earth (though occasionally news comes from the other side of a fearsome and infuriating tribe called "the Argentines"); to the west by the Pacific Ocean, the largest stretch of water on the planet; and to the south by the deadly white lands of Arthur Gordon Pym, traveler and exile *ad honorem*. The country that I come from is an island. But that isn't the worst of it. The country that I come from is or believes itself to be Easter Island (and a sovereign nation, too). And, like the old Easter Islanders, the natives of my country believe that they're the navel of the world, to a ridiculous degree.

The moai of Chile are the Chileans themselves who, bewildered, face out toward the four cardinal points.

Just a few years ago, a gay dance club in Valparaíso burned down. The club—maybe it was just a pub or a bar—was in a wooden building and the fire was quite large; more than twenty people died. The story was reported by a few news agencies. Soon after hearing about it, a Chilean living in Paris remarked to a friend of mine how surprised he was: there were no homosexuals in Chile, according to him, so it was impossible for a bar of that description to have caught fire. The only possible explanation was either that the news agency had made a mistake, or that the story was a conscious attempt to injure the country. This Chilean, bless his soul, was no peasant from Chillán or lumberjack from Aysén, but someone who lived in the capital of France, where he even had a job and was a legal resident. He went to the movies from time to time, and from time to time he slept with a woman. Occasionally he read books in Spanish and he frequently read the newspaper in French. On top of it all, I think he was on the left politically, though that doesn't have much to do with this story. Still, he couldn't believe that in Valparaíso, a port city celebrated by Darío and Neruda, more than twenty homosexuals could gather in a bar. Probably occupying a key place in his vast unconscious was the information we received in our childhood, which is that in Chile everyone is brave, no tears are shed, and all hearts are pure.

In 1973, when I returned to Los Ángeles, capital of the province of Bío-Bío, I was told that the *only* homosexual in town, whose name I've forgotten but who even back then wasn't the only one, had been sought out by a group of soldiers, lifelong clients, who took him out by the river and killed him. From that moment on, Los Ángeles was liberated of faggots. Now everyone was brave, no one shed a tear, and all were pure of heart.

Almost all Chilean writers, at some point in their lives, have gone into exile. Many have been followed doggedly by the ghost of Chile, and have been caught and returned to the fold. Others have managed to shake the ghost and gone into hiding; still others have changed their names and their ways and Chile has luckily forgotten them.

When I was fifteen, in 1968, I left Chile for Mexico. For me, back then, Mexico City was like the Border, that vast nonexistent territory where freedom and metamorphosis are common currency.

Despite everything, the shadow of my native land wasn't erased and in the depths of my stupid heart the certainty persisted that it was there that my destiny lay.

I returned to Chile when I was twenty to take part in the Revolution, with such bad luck that a few days after I got to Santiago the coup came and the army seized power. My trip to Chile was long, and sometimes I've thought that if I'd spent more time in Honduras, for example, or waited a little before shipping out from Panama, the coup would've come before I got to Chile and my fate would have been different.

In any case, and despite the collective disasters and my small personal misfortunes, I remember the days after the coup as full days, crammed with energy, crammed with eroticism, days and nights in which anything could happen. There's no way I'd wish a twentieth year like that on my son, but I should also acknowledge that it was an unforgettable year. The experience of love, black humor, friendship, prison, and the threat of death were condensed into no more than five interminable months that I lived in a state of amazement and urgency. During that time, I wrote one poem, which wasn't just bad like the other poems I wrote back then, but excruciatingly bad. When those five months were up, I left Chile again and I haven't been back since.

That was the beginning of my exile, or what is commonly known as exile, although the truth is I didn't see it that way.

Sometimes exile simply means that Chileans tell me I talk like a Spaniard, Mexicans tell me I talk like a Chilean, and Spaniards tell me I talk like an Argentine: it's a question of accents.

As it happens, Argentine transplants—who are as likely to be writers as soccer players—have occasionally faced the dichotomy of exile with success. They've been naturalized and they've adopted the languages of their new places of residence with an ease that leads us to wonder whether they're aliens, not Argentines. Copi and Bianciotti are cases in point.

But Argentina isn't just a country, or at least at one time it wasn't: it's also a way station for immigrants. An immigrant factory. I'm thinking, for example, about Di Stéfano, an older example, and about Che Guevara, another older example, and about the much stranger case of Cantatore, coach of the Real Valladolid in Spain, who was born in Argentina and talks like an Argentine, but is a naturalized Chilean, which comes as a surprise. But he's not the only one : Manuel Rojas, one of the founders of the contemporary Chilean novel, was also born in Argentina and left for Chile as an adolescent, never to return.

Able to see in Argentina that quality of exile and capacity for exile, Gombrowicz recognized it as a land where Form is constantly dismantled, a land whose history remains unwritten, which is to say a land with room for freedom and immaturity.

Strange cases of exile are fairly easy to turn up, if we dig a little. One Argentine novelist, whose name, I believe, was Cataño, author of the notable and now forgotten novel *Las*

Varonesas [The Man-Ladies], published by Seix Barral at the end of the 1970s, left for Costa Rica, where he lived until the triumph of the Sandinista revolution, after which he moved to Managua. What took Cataño to Costa Rica? Political repression in Argentina? Probably. It's also possible that his wife was Costa Rican. Why not? Or that he wanted to live in the tropics. Or maybe he was offered a more interesting job in Costa Rica than anything he could find in Argentina. In any case, imagine that you have to go into exile and you're offered three destinations: France, Italy, and Senegal. Cataño chose Senegal. Where is Cataño now? I have no idea. I've only read one novel by him. I hope he's still writing. I hope he's still alive.

The fates chosen by those who go into exile are often strange. After the Chilean coup in 1973, I remember that few political refugees made their way to the embassies of Bulgaria or Romania, for example, with France or Italy preferred by many, although as I recall, top honors went to Mexico, and also Sweden, two very different countries that must have stood for two opposite manifestations of desire in the Chilean collective unconscious, although it's true that in time the balance tilted toward the Mexican side and many of those who went into exile in Sweden began to turn up in Mexico. Many others, however, remained in Stockholm or Göteborg, and when I was living in Spain I ran into them every summer on vacation, speaking a Spanish that to me, at least, was startling, because it was the Spanish that was spoken in Chile in 1973, and that now is spoken nowhere but in Sweden.

Enrique Vila-Matas told me a story. A while ago he attended a conference on exile. The participants were Mario Benedetti, Cristina Peri Rossi, and Augusto Monterroso. Probably a few others, I don't know. The point is that Benedetti and Peri Rossi talked about exile as something terrible, horrible, etc., and when it was Monterroso's turn, he said that for him exile had been a delightful, happy experience. In other words, he was satisfied with everything that had happened to him during his long stay in Mexico. I wasn't at this conference, and Vila-Matas didn't say much else about it, but I'm absolutely in agreement with Monterroso's account. In even the worst case, going into exile is better than needing to go into exile and not being able to. And exile, in most cases, is a voluntary decision. No one forced Thomas Mann to go into exile. No one forced James Joyce to go into exile. Back in Joyce's day, the Irish probably couldn't have cared less whether he stayed in Dublin or left, whether he became a priest or killed himself. In the best case, exile is a literary option, similar to the option of writing. No one forces you to write. The writer enters the labyrinth voluntarily—for many reasons, of course: because he doesn't want to die, because he wants to be loved, etc.—but he isn't forced into it. In the final instance he's no more forced than a politician is forced into politics or a lawyer is forced into law school. With the great advantage for the writer that the lawyer or politician, outside his country of origin, tends to flounder like a fish out of water, at least for a while—whereas a writer outside his native country seems to grow wings. The same thing applies to other situations. What does a politician do in prison? What does a lawyer do in the hospital? Anything but work. What, on the other hand, does a writer do in prison or in the hospital? He works. Sometimes he even works a lot. (Not to mention poets.) Of course the claim can be made that in prison the libraries are no good and that in hospitals there often are no libraries. It can be argued that in most cases exile means the loss of the writer's books, among other material losses, and in some cases even the loss of his papers, his unfinished manuscripts, projects, letters. It doesn't matter. Better to lose manuscripts than to lose your life. In any case, the point is that the writer works wherever he is, even while he sleeps, which isn't true of those in other professions. Actors, it can be said, are always working, but it isn't the same: the writer writes and is conscious of writing, whereas the actor, under great duress, only howls. Policemen are always policemen, but that isn't the same either, because it's one thing to *be* and another to *work*. The writer is and works in any situation. The policeman only is. And the same is true of the professional assassin, the soldier, the banker. Whores, perhaps, come closest in the exercise of their profession to the practice of literature.

Archilochus, Greek poet of the seventh century BC, is a perfect example of this phenomenon. Born on the island of Paros, he was a mercenary, and, according to legend, he died in combat. We can imagine his life spent wandering the cities of Greece.

In one fragment, Archilochus doesn't hesitate to admit that in the midst of battle, probably a skirmish, he drops his weapons and runs away, which for the Greeks was undoubtedly the greatest mark of shame, let alone for a soldier who has to earn his daily bread by his courage in combat. Archilochus says:

> Some Saian mountaineer
> Struts today with my shield.
> I threw it down behind a bush and ran
> When the fighting got hot.
> Life seemed somehow more precious.
> It was a beautiful shield.
> I know where I can buy another
> Exactly like it, just as round.*

*All translations from Archilochus are by Guy Davenport, from *Archilochus, Sappho, Alkman: Three Lyric Poets of the Late Greek Bronze Age*, U. Cal Press, 1980.—tr.

According to the classical scholar Carlos García Gual, Archilochus had to leave the island where he was born to earn a living with his lance, as a soldier of fortune: he knew war only as a toilsome chore, not as a field of heroic deeds. He won renown for his cynicism in a few lines of verse that tell how he flees the battlefield after he throws away his shield. His openness in confessing such a shameful act is striking. (In hoplite tactics, the shield is the weapon that protects the flank of the next soldier, symbol of courage, something never to be lost. "Return with the shield or on the shield," it was said in Sparta.) All the pragmatic poet cared about was saving his own life. He cared nothing for glory or the code of honor.

Another fragment: "Hang iambics. / This is no time / for poetry." And: "Father Zeus, / I've had / No wedding feast." And: "His mane the infantry / cropped down to stubble." And: "Balanced on the keen edge / Now of the wind's sword, / Now of the wave's blade." And this, which could only have been written by someone buffeted by fate:

> Attribute all to the gods.
> They pick a man up,
> Stretched on the black loam,
> And set him on his two feet,
> Firm, and then again
> Shake solid men until
> They fall backward
> Into the worst of luck,
> Wandering hungry,
> Wild of mind.

And this, spotlessly cruel and clear:

Seven of the enemy
    were cut down in that encounter
And a thousand of us,
    mark you,
Ran them through.

And:

Soul, soul,
Torn by perplexity,
On your feet now!
Throw forward your chest
To the enemy;
Keep close in the attack;
Move back not an inch.
But never crow in victory,
Nor mope hangdog in loss.
Overdo neither sorrow nor joy:
A measured motion governs man.

And this, sad and pragmatic:

The heart of mortal man,
Glaukos, son of Leptines,
Is what Zeus makes it,
Day after day,
And what the world makes it,
That passes before our eyes.

And this, in which the human condition shines:

Hear me here,
Hugging your knees,
Hephaistos Lord.
My battle mate,
My good luck be;
That famous grace
Be my grace too.

And this, in which Archilochus gives us a portrait of himself and then vanishes into immortality, an immortality in which he didn't happen to believe: "My ash spear is my barley bread, / My ash spear is my Ismarian wine. / I lean on my spear and drink."

FRAGMENTS OF A RETURN
TO THE NATIVE LAND

THE INVITATION

Twenty days in Chile that shook the (mental) world that I inhabit. Twenty days that were like twenty sessions of humanity falling with a thud. Twenty days that would make anyone weep or roll on the floor laughing. But let's start from the beginning. I left Chile in January 1974. The last time I flew anywhere was in 1977. I thought I'd never go back to Chile again. I thought I'd never get on a plane again. One day a girl called me from *Paula Magazine* and asked if I wanted to be on the jury for a story contest that the magazine organizes. Right away I said yes. I don't know what I was thinking. Maybe I was thinking about the glorious sunsets of Los Angeles, though not the Los Ángeles of Bío-Bío, in Chile, but the Los Angeles of California, the sunsets of the city that sprang up from nothing and from whose rooftops you can see see the radiance that oozes from every inch of the planet. I might have been thinking about that. I might have been making love. Yes, now I remember, that was it. Then the phone rang and I got out of bed and answered and a female voice asked if I'd like to come to Chile and then the city of Los Angeles full of sky-scrapers and palm trees became the city of Los Ángeles full of one-story buildings and dirt roads. Los Ángeles, the capital of the province of Bío-Bío, the city where Fernando Fernández played foosball in yards that were like something dreamed up by deranged adolescents, the city where Lebert and Cárcamo were constant companions and where tolerant Cárdenas was class president at a boys' school designed by some petty demon and where El Pescado suddenly went underground. City of evening raids. Savage city whose sunsets were like the aphasic commentary of privilege. So I said yes in the same tone that I might have said no. The room was dark; I was expecting a phone call, but not this one; the voice that spoke to me from the other side of the world was sweet. At that moment I could have said no. But I said yes because like a mountain cat, the capital of the province of Bío-Bío suddenly leaped onto the map of the city of happiness and was clawing at it, and in those (invisible) claw marks it was written that I had to return to Chile and I had to get back on a plane.

THE TRIP

So I went back to Chile. I got on a plane. I don't know how planes manage to stay up in the air. Turbulence over the Atlan-tic, turbulence over the Amazon. Turbulence over Argentina and just before crossing the Andes. On top of it all, Lautaro, my eight-year-old son, couldn't play his Game Boy during the flight. But it's okay. We're flying. My son is sleeping peacefully. My wife, Carolina López, is sleeping peacefully. The two of them are Spanish and it's their first trip to America. I'm not asleep. I was born in America. I'm Chilean. I'm awake and I'm holding up the wings of the plane mentally. I listen to the other passengers talk. Most of them are asleep but they're talking in their sleep. They have nightmares or recurring dreams. They're Chilean. The Spanish stewardesses glance at them as they walk back and forth down the aisles, sometimes parallel to each other and sometimes in opposite directions. When it's the latter and their paths intersect, the stewardesses raise their eyebrows in the dark and continue on unperturbed. Wonderful, the women of Spain. Would you like a glass of water, orange juice? they ask when they pass me. No, thanks very much, I say. No, many thanks, I say, as the jet engines drill through the night, the night itself a plane flying inside another plane. The ancients depicted this as a fish eating a fish eating another fish. Meanwhile, the real night, outside the plane, is huge and the moon is very small, like Pezoa Véliz's moon. I'm on my way to Chile. Every once in a while I drop off to sleep, too, and I have strange and vivid dreams. Brief dreams in black and white that take me back to lives I'll never live. If people slept during the day they'd dream in color, my son said to me once. Fuck, I'm approaching Chile at more than five hundred miles an hour. And finally dawn begins to break and the plane crosses the Andes and now we're back and here's the first change: the last time I left Chile, on a Santiago-Buenos Aires flight, the Andes seemed much bigger and whiter; now they don't seem so big and the snow is striking for its absence. But they're still pretty. They seem wilder, more lost, less sleepy. Then the plane is over a dusty stretch of ground, and with no time even to think "Pure, Chile, are your blue skies," it lands.

I'm back home. No problem. The passengers get up out of their seats: I don't see any especially happy faces. Instead everyone seems worried, except for the woman sitting directly behind me. During the night I heard her talking. From what she says I deduce that she's a hooker. A Chilean hooker who works in Europe and is returning to Chile after a more or less extended absence to buy real estate, although it's not clear to me where: sometimes she seems to say the south and other times she talks about abandoned buildings in Santiago. In any case, she's a woman with a nice face and dyed blonde hair, her body still lovely, and—surprise—she talks in her sleep too. Unintelligible words in Spanish and Italian and German. For a few minutes, I heard her snoring almost as loudly as the engines of the plane that had miraculously brought us to Chile. When I heard her, I thought those exaggerated snores might be a bad omen. I thought about saying something. But in the end I decided not to do anything and the snoring stopped all of a sudden, as if it were simply the physical manifestation of a nightmare she'd had, this hooker with a heart of gold, and then moved beyond, just as one leaves behind bad days and illnesses.

A while ago I met a Chilean who was always having a hard time. No matter where he was or what he was doing, he was having a hard time. This Chilean, a drifter, sometimes reminisced about his native country and he always ended his ramblings in the same way: I'm going to kiss the ground, he'd say. When I get back to Chile the first thing I'll do is kiss the ground. He had forgotten the terror, the injustice, the folly. Baffled and amused, we made fun of him, but he didn't care. Go ahead and laugh, he'd say, but the first thing I'll do when I get back is kiss Chilean soil. I think he died in some South or Central American country, and if he had returned, I imagine his face would look just like the faces of the other Chilean passengers (except the hooker), deadly serious, worried, as if seen from several angles at once, mutating in seconds from Cézanne to Picasso to Basquiat, the usual face of the natives of this long and narrow country, this island-corridor. Of course, I didn't kiss my native soil. I tried not to trip on the way out of the plane and I tried to light one of my last Spanish cigarettes with a steady hand. Then I breathed the air of Santiago and we headed toward Customs.

THE FACES

And all of a sudden, there were the Chilean faces, the faces of my childhood and adolescence, everywhere, streaming, I was surrounded by Chileans, Chileans who looked like Chileans, Chileans who looked like Martians, Chileans walking around with nothing to do in an airport that I guess wasn't the old Pudahuel Airport though at moments it seemed like it, and also Chileans waiting for passengers and waving white handkerchiefs, and even Chileans crying (a common sight, as I remembered, Chileans cry a lot, sometimes for no reason, sometimes even when they don't feel like crying), and also Chileans laughing as if the world were about to end and they were the only ones who knew it. But most of all what I saw in those first few moments were Chileans standing still and silent, Chileans staring at the floor as if they were floating over an uncertain abyss, as if the airport were a specter and all of us were suspended over a kind of nothing that miraculously (or inevitably) kept us aloft and that demanded in return a mysterious and unspeakable tribute, a tribute that no one was prepared to pay, but that no one was prepared to say they wouldn't pay, either.

Getting through Customs was simple. It's been years since they let me into a country so easily. My wife had to fill out a form and I think she had to pay something. When I asked what forms I had to fill out, a round, friendly little customs agent told me I didn't have to fill out anything. That was the first welcome. The second came from a second customs agent, who decided not to search any of our suitcases. You're all right, she said, go ahead. The third came from my grandmother and Alexandra Edwards and Totó Romero and Carlos Orellana and La Malala Ansieta, who greeted us as if we were lifelong friends. By now we were outside the airport and we were waiting for a taxi to take us to the hotel and everything was going fine, but somehow I wasn't back in Chile yet. Or to put it another way, I was there, surrounded by Chileans, which was something I hadn't experienced since January 1974, but I still wasn't back, in the real sense of the word. I was still on the plane, I was still sprinting down the corridors of the airport in Madrid, I was still in bed in my house on Calle del Loro, in Blanes, I was still dreaming that I was about to go somewhere.

YOU CAN'T GO HOME AGAIN

It was Samuel Valenzuela, of *Las Últimas Noticias*, who really let me know that I was back. We talked for a while. I didn't have much to say. So what I did was ask questions and Samuel Valenzuela answered them all. Samuel Valenzuela looks like someone out of a Manuel Rojas novel. I think he paints in his spare time. It was the first day, I was still jet-lagged, and we were at a ranch that they'd brought me to, an agrarian nightmare as painted by Miquel Barceló. Vicente Huidobro used to spend his vacations here, someone said behind me. This ranch—where one hundred and twenty patriots or maybe two hundred and twenty, or maybe just twenty or maybe even only two took refuge during the War of Independence, and which is now a vineyard, museum, and restaurant—is the dadaist setting of my first event on native soil. I look around and the ghosts of those patriots appear and disappear, fading into the whitewashed walls and the huge, sad trees of the great park that surrounds the ranch, in one corner of which there's a Roman bath built by a previous owner that gave me the shivers when it was pointed out to me. The tweeness of Chileans has no equal on the planet. Neither does Chilean hospitality, and in my case it's unceasing. Until Samuel Valenzuela takes me aside for an interview. We talk about Chilean wine. Wine that I can no longer drink. We also talk about empanadas. What does it feel like to be back? he asks. I tell him I don't know. Nothing, I say, it doesn't feel like anything. The next day our interview is in the paper. The headline reads: "Bolaño Can't Go Home Again." When I read it, I think: it's true! With that headline, Samuel Valenzuela told me everything that he could humanly, metaphysically, ontologically, or tellurically tell me. That was when I knew I was back in Chile.

PHONE CONVERSATIONS WITH PEDRO LEMEBEL

The first thing Lemebel asked me was how old I was when I left Chile. Twenty, I said. So how could you lose your Chilean accent? he asked. I don't know, but I lost it. You can't have lost it, he said, by the time you're twenty you can't lose anything. You can lose lots of things, I said. But not your accent, he said. Well, I lost it, I said. Impossible, he said. That might have been the end of everything: the conversation didn't seem to be going anywhere. But Lemebel is the greatest poet of my generation and from Spain I had already admired the glorious and provocative wake left by his performance art duo Las Yeguas del Apocalipsis (The Mares of the Apocalypse). So I took the plunge and we went to eat at a Peruvian restaurant and I talked to all the other people we were with—Soledad Bianchi, Lina Meruane, Alejandra Costamagna, the poet Sergio Parra—and meanwhile Lemebel lapsed into a state of general melancholy and was silent for the rest of the evening, which was too bad. No one speaks a more Chilean Spanish than Lemebel. Lemebel doesn't need to write poetry to be the best poet of my generation. No one goes deeper than Lemebel. And also, as if that weren't enough, Lemebel is brave. That is, he understands how to open his eyes in the darkness, in those lands where no one dares to tread. How do I know all this? Easy. By reading his books. And after reading them, in exhilaration, in hilarity, in dread, I called him on the phone and we talked for a long time, a long conversation of golden howls, during which I recognized in Lemebel the indomitable spirit of the Mexican poet Mario Santiago, dead, and the blazing images of *La Araucana*, dead, forgotten, which Lemebel brought back to life and then I knew that this queer writer, my hero, might be on the side of the losers but that victory, the sad victory offered by Literature (capitalized, as it is here), was surely his. When everyone who has treated him like dirt is lost in the cesspit or in nothingness, Pedro Lemebel will still be a star.

THE FAT REPORTER

One day a fat reporter came to interview me. He wasn't as young as the others. He might have been my age, maybe a bit younger, and he was from La Serena. He gave me a copy of his paper, a La Serena paper, and then he sat down in a chair, panting, and he spotted my cigarettes and asked for one. He didn't buy them anymore because he had stopped smoking, but that morning he was in the mood for one.

There was no photographer with him, so he took my picture. Do you know how these cameras work? he asked. I looked at the camera and said I had no idea. For a while we stood there studying the camera. A photographer colleague at La Serena had loaned it to him. His indecisiveness, I soon realized, was greater than mine. Let's take the pictures on the balcony, he said, there's more light. I don't know why, but I didn't like the idea. I have a sore throat, I said, I don't want to go outside. The problem is you smoke too much, he said, leaving his cigarette in the ashtray. Finally I sat in a chair and I said take the pictures now or never. He sighed and took three or four pictures. Being a local reporter is boring, he said. But there must be interesting parts too, I said. The guys on the police beat have more fun, he said. Yes, there are interesting parts. Like in any life.

CHILEAN LITERATURE

This is what Chilean literature taught me. Ask for nothing, because you'll be given nothing. Don't get sick because no one will help you. Don't ask to be included in any anthology because your name will always be omitted. Don't fight because you'll always be defeated. Don't turn your back on power because power is everything. Don't be stinting in your praise for idiots, the dogmatic, the mediocre, if you don't want to live a season in hell. Life here goes on more or less unchanged.

A writer sometimes has absolutely solid hunches. One of my few hunches is Rodrigo Pinto. There can't be many critics like him in Chile. He's a priceless character: every pore of Rodrigo Pinto speaks to us of his love for literature, his humor, his wisdom.

Rodrigo Pinto is that mythical Chilean, the one who has read everything or is prepared to read everything. And on top of it all, he's a good person. Rodrigo Pinto can go from Wittgenstein to Juan Emar, from Stendhal to Claude Simon without blinking. I thought readers like that had disappeared, or were holed up in Viña, or Villa Alemana, or Valdivia. But Rodrigo Pinto lives in Santiago and is still young, which means it's possible to suppose that he'll keep up the fight for a long time in this valley of tears. The last time I saw him, in Santiago, he had a stunning woman on each arm, one dark-haired and the other a redhead, and he was on his way to a Japanese restaurant for sushi.

WOMEN WRITERS

I'm not sure whether it's under the reproving eye of Gabriela Mistral, Violeta Parra, María Luisa Bombal or Diamela Eltit, but there's a generation of women writers out there who promise to be insatiable. Two among them clearly stand out. They are Lina Meruane and Alejandra Costamagna, followed by Nona Fernández and five or six other young women armed with all the tools of good literature. Lina and Alejandra, both born in 1970, have already published books, which I've read. They write very differently from each another. Or rather: the forms to which their writing adheres are very different. And yet they resemble each other in the force of their writing. When they write, the reader has no choice but to follow them through the ruins of this waning century or through the apparently no-exit blaze of the coming millennium. Their prose issues from the hammer blows of conscience, but also from the intangible, and from pain. Stylistically, Lina Meruane can be associated with a certain French school (I'm thinking of Marguerite Duras, Nathalie Sarraute), more subjective and introspective, whereas Alejandra Costamagna works in the North American tradition, objective, faster-paced, less ornate. One writes in shades of gray and the other in black and white. *Las Infantas* [The Princesses], by Lina Meruane, and *En voz baja* [In a Low Voice] and *Ciudadano en retiro* [Citizen in Retirement], by Alejandra Costamagna, are achievements in themselves, but above all they are the firm promise of a literature that refuses to relinquish anything. The young female writers of Chile write like women possessed.

SANTIAGO

Santiago is still the same. Twenty-five years doesn't change a city. People still eat empanadas in Chile. The empanadas of Chile are called *empanadas chilenas* and they can be sampled at the Nacional or the Rápido (recommended by Germán Marín). People still eat the sandwiches called *barros-luco* or *barros-jarpa* or *chacareros*, ergo the city hasn't changed. The new buildings, the new streets, mean nothing. The streets of Santiago are still the same as they were ninety-eight years ago. Santiago is the same as it was when Teófilo Cid and Carlos de Rokha walked its streets. We still live in the age of the French Revolution. Our cycles are much longer and more crowded and twenty-five years is nothing.

In Chile everybody writes. I realized this one night when I was waiting to do a live television interview. A girl who had been Miss Chile, or something like that, was on before me. Maybe she'd only been Miss Santiago or Miss Burst Into Flames. Anyway, she was a tall, pretty girl, who talked with the empty poise of all Misses. She was introduced to me. When she found out that I had been a juror for the *Paula* contest she said that she had almost sent in a story but in the end she hadn't been able to, and that she would submit something next year. Her confidence was impressive. I hope she'll have time to type up her story for the 1999 contest. I wish her the best of luck. Sometimes the fact that everyone in the world writes can be wonderful, because you find fellow-writers everywhere, and sometimes it can be a drag because illiterate jerks strut around sporting all the defects and none of the virtues of a real writer. As Nicanor Parra said: it might be a good idea to do a little more reading.

NICANOR PARRA AND GOODBYE TO CHILE

My friend Marcial Cortés-Monroy takes me to visit Nicanor Parra. As far as I'm concerned, Parra has long been the best living poet in the Spanish language. So the visit makes me nervous. It makes no sense when you think about it, but the truth is that I'm nervous: at last I'm going to meet the great man, the poet who sleeps sitting in a chair, though his chair is sometimes a flying chair, jet-propelled, and sometimes a chair that drills down into the earth, but anyway, I'm going to meet the author of *Poems and Antipoems*, the most clear-sighted resident of this island-corridor that is strolled from end to end by the ghosts of Huidobro, Gabriela Mistral, Neruda, de Rokha, and Violeta Parra, looking in vain for a way out.

We're met at the door by Corita. A bit wary, Corita, though you can see she isn't a bad person. Then we're left alone and soon we hear footsteps approaching the living room. Nicanor comes in. His first words, after he greets us, are in English. It's the welcome Hamlet receives from some peasants of Denmark. Then Nicanor talks about old age, about Shakespeare's fate, about cats, about his first house in Las Cruces, which burned down, about Ernesto Cardenal, about Paz, whom he values more as an essayist than a poet, about his father, who was a musician, and about his mother, who was a seamstress and made shirts out of scraps for him and his siblings, about Huidobro, whose tomb on the other side of the bay, above a forest, is visible from the balcony, a white spot like bird shit, about his sister Violeta and her daughter Colombina, about loneliness, about a few afternoons in New York, about car accidents, about India, about dead friends, about his childhood in the south, about Corita's mussels, which really are very good, about Corita's fish with mashed potatoes, which is also very good, about Mexico, about Dutch Chile and the Mapuches who fought on the side of the Spanish crown, about the university in Chile, about Pinochet (Nicanor is prophetic regarding the judgment of the House of Lords), about new Chilean fiction (he speaks highly of Pablo Azócar and I'm in complete agreement), about his old friend Tomás Lago, about Gonzalo de Berceo, about Shakespeare's ghosts and Shakespeare's madness (always visible, always circumstantial), and I listen to him talk—live—and then I watch a video of him talking about Luis Oyarzún and I feel like I'm falling into an asymmetrical well, the well of the great poets, where all that can be heard is his voice gradually mingling with other voices, and I don't know who those other voices belong to, and I also hear footsteps echoing through that wooden house as Corita listens to the radio in the kitchen and hoots with laughter, and Nicanor goes up to the second floor and then comes down with a book for me (the first edition of which I've owned for years; Nicanor gives me the sixth) that he inscribes, and then I thank him for everything, for the book that I don't tell him I already have, for the food, for the very pleasant few hours that I've spent with him and Marcial, and we say *hasta luego* though we know it isn't *hasta luego*, and then the best thing is to get the fuck out of there, the best thing is to find a way out of the asymetrical well and hurry silently away as Nicanor's steps echo up and down the corridor.

THE CORRIDOR WITH NO APPARENT
WAY OUT

It's strange to come back to Chile, the corridor country, but when you think twice (or even three times) about it, it's strange to come back anywhere. Assuming, of course, that you're really back, and not dreaming that you're back. It was twenty-five years before I came back. The streets actually seemed the same as always. The faces, too. Which can spell deadly boredom or madness. So this time, for a change, I decided to keep calm and wait and see what would happen, sitting in a chair, which is the best place to keep a corridor from surprising you.

One day I was invited to dinner at the house of a government minister. The chance of a lifetime to write an in-depth article on power. Actually, I was invited to dinner at the house of the writer Diamela Eltit, whose lover or partner, or anyway the man she lived with, was the Socialist minister Jorge Arrate, spokesman of the Frei government. That was enough to make anybody nervous. Our friend Lina Meruane came to pick us up at eight at the hotel where we were staying and off we went.

First surprise: the neighborhood where Eltit and Arrate live is a middle-middle class neighborhood, not upper class or upper-middle class. The kind of neighborhood that produced the illustrious (and not so illustrious) gladiators of the seventies. Second surprise: the house is relatively small and not ostentatious at all, not the kind of house where one expects a Chilean minister to live. Third surprise: when we get out of the car I scan the street for the unmarked car driven by the minister's bodyguard and I don't see it.

Many hours later, when I ask Jorge about his bodyguards, he says he doesn't have any. What do you mean you don't have any? I ask. I just don't, he says, Diamela doesn't like bodyguards and anyway they're a nuisance. But is it safe? I ask. Jorge Arrate is well-acquainted with persecution and exile and he knows that no one is ever safe. Diamela glances at him. We're at the table, eating the dinner that Jorge personally prepared. There's no meat. Someone in the house is a vegetarian and presumably he or she has imposed the diet on everyone else. In any case, it's Jorge who cooks and he does a fine job. I enjoy vegetarian food the way I enjoy a kick in the stomach, but I eat what they put in front of me. Diamela looks at Jorge and then she looks at my wife, Carolina, and then at Lina and at the novelist Pablo Azócar, the fifth guest, and she doesn't look at me. I get the sense she doesn't like me. Or maybe she's very shy. Anyway. The truth is, all I can think about right now is a band of Nazis bursting into the house to kill the minister and along the way killing my wife and my son, Lautaro (who hasn't come to the table and is asleep in a room with the TV on). And what if those bastards from Patria y Libertad turn up? I ask. I hope they don't, says Jorge, so calmly it makes my hair stand on end.

This is no country for me, I think.

That morning, Jorge Arrate went out all by himself to shop for provisions for dinner. It's clear at a glance that he hasn't gotten rich as a minister under Frei. I think he was a minister in the Aylwin government too. I'm not sure. What I do know is that he hasn't gotten rich. Still, as he waited patiently in line to pay for his lettuce and tomatoes, some kids who probably weren't even born when he was already a political exile started chanting "yellow, yellow, yellow." Other times, of course, what they yell (different kids, horribly vulgar women) is "red, red." So what did you do when they called you yellow? I asked. Nothing, what could I do? said Jorge. Take the two slurs together, I tell him, and you'd have the Spanish flag. Jorge doesn't hear me. He's telling my wife the story of an independent candidate in the first democratic elections who, in the name of equal opportunity, was allotted fifteen seconds of free advertising space on television. The candidate had decided to say only her name. But then she wasn't even given enough time for that. She said her name, but so fast that you could hardly understand her, the whole thing reduced to a short and desperate squawk.

The surprising thing is that the candidate won, which gave the big party strategists and advertising people much food for thought. Anyway, says Jorge, as if to play down this—and any other story—the point is that soon afterward the independent candidate joined a party on the far right.

And so any fantasy about a heroic or at least eccentric woman taking a solitary stance was shattered, as everything is shattered in Chile, and herein perhaps lies the country's charm, its strength: in its insistence on sinking when it could soar and soaring when it's hopelessly sunk. In its taste for bloody paradoxes. In its schizophrenic reactions.

Maybe that's why there are so many writers in Chile, I say

to myself. Because here, as I confirm on a daily basis, every-body writes. A writer publishes just one collection of stories at a bottom-tier publishing house and he's got an ad in one of the newspapers or magazines, and out of nothing comes another writing workshop, full of young people and people no longer so young, all eager to face up to the mystery of the blank page. This is how writers make a living, of course. Most don't make much, but there are some who rake it in. People flock to these workshops (it scares me to think how many there must be up and down the Republic) in the same frame of mind in which some New Yorkers go to see a therapist. Not desperate, but close. Not calm, but close. They aren't tightrope walkers, but when it comes to teetering on the brink of the abyss—an abyss that seems more Latin American every day—they manage to keep their balance, a precarious balance that is in some sense deeply pathetic, but also heroic.

Of course, not everybody limits themselves to attending workshops. Some are also in therapy. One very dear friend, during dinner at a restaurant, told me about her psychoana-lyst, who turned out to be none other than Norman Mailer's daughter. Another friend (a writer, and not a bad one, either) was listening and said that he was in therapy with Norman Mailer's daughter too. Almost instantly, another girl jumps in and says the same thing. For a moment I thought they were kidding me. Everyone had drunk lots of pisco and I hadn't touched anything because I can't drink anymore, but the sense I got was that I was the only drunk person in the room. Norman Mailer's daughter is a psychoanalyst and she lives in Chile? Hard to believe. But it's true. What could possibly bring Norman Mailer's daughter to Chile? If we were in Mexico, it would make more sense: there's a tradition of outrageousness there that encompasses a sub-genre of bizarre visitors. But not in Chile. And yet Norman Mailer's daughter lives here and has been seeing these people for a while now. So is she any good? I ask. My friend says she's very good, although I don't think she sounds very convinced. The writer says sometimes she's good and sometimes she has no clue. But why did she come to live in Chile? I ask, on the verge of tears. No one knows.

Jorge Arrate, as far as I know, isn't in therapy. But he hasn't been able to avoid writing workshops. Somebody told me the story of how he met Diamela Eltit. She ran a workshop and he decided to enroll. At first he came at the scheduled time, like everyone else in the group, except that Arrate had a chauffeur and an official car since he was already a minister. Then one day he came half an hour early. And another day he came an hour early. And finally he came three hours early. And while they were waiting for the workshop to begin—while Diamela, I suppose, wrote or cooked or ironed her son's clothes—Arrate would sit himself down in a chair in her house, which is where writers hold their workshops, and talk to her about literature. I like to imagine them like that, Jorge sitting and Diamela ironing and every so often giving him one of those Diamelian looks, at once brooding and innocent, and talking about her writing, which is as complex as anything you'll come across in Spanish today, and probably also about other people's work, books by women, avant-garde texts, works that Arrate, a socialist and an exile forged in fights where such things had no place, wasn't familiar with and that from then on he set to reading with passion and humor—the same passion and humor that he brings to everything he does—and also with the boldness of love. After a while he was dating Diamela, contemporary Chilean literature's most *maudit* writer, and then, basically, as sometimes happens, they moved in together.

Then the bodyguards disappeared. But what if one night you're attacked by some group from Patria y Libertad? I asked for the hundredth time, ready to eat my dessert and go. I can only hope they don't have my address, says Arrate. Never had a house seemed more vulnerable to me. The room where Diamela writes overlooks the yard and is big and full of books. Arrate's office, meanwhile, is small, with photographs on the walls: most are of two kids, Jorge's children, who live in Holland, others are of legendary leftist figures, a brief frozen history of lost dreams. At some point during the night we talk about Carson McCullers and her unhappy husband who wanted to write and couldn't. Diamela knows McCullers's work very well. Arrate, joking, says that he, a former writing workshop participant, has something in common with McCullers's husband. I suppose he's referring to his literary efforts. I don't know. I've never read anything by Arrate and I probably never will. But he's right about one thing: Carson McCullers's husband fought in World War II and he was brave, and Arrate fought in the disastrous little wars of Latin America and he's brave. Brave like Allende's former comrades. In other words, stoically brave. But I don't tell him that.

Chilean writers, real or aspiring, are hopeless. That's what I'm thinking as, late that night, I leave the house where Diamela and the minister live, and outside we say goodbye to Pablo Azócar, who wants to leave Chile as soon as possible and never quite manages to go and finally is lost; that's what I'm thinking as Lina, Carolina, and I wave goodbye on a dark street in the neighborhood that produced so many illustrious gladiators.

And that's what I'm thinking when I talk late one night to Pedro Lemebel, one of Chile's most brilliant writers. It's his birthday. Lemebel—born in the mid-fifties, according to him, although I think he was born in the early fifties—has published four books (*Incontables* [Countless], 1986; *La esquina es mi corazón* [The Corner Is My Heart], 1995; *Loco afán* [Wild Desire], 1996; and *De perlas y cicatrices* [Of Pearls and Scars], 1998), and for some time, a pretty shitty time, as it happens, he was one of two members of the group Las Yeguas del Apocalipsis or The Mares of the Apocalypse, whose name is an accomplishment in itself and whose survival was something like a miracle.

Who were the Yeguas? First and foremost, the Yeguas were two penniless homosexuals, which in a homophobic and hierarchical country (where being poor is an embarrassment, and being poor and an artist is a crime) was almost an invitation to abuse, in every sense of the word. Much of the honor of the real Republic and the Republic of Letters was saved by the Yeguas. Then came the rift and Lemebel began his solo career. There is no battlefield on which Lemebel—cross-dresser, militant, third-world champion, anarchist, Mapuche Indian by adoption, a man reviled by an establishment that rejects the truth he speaks, possessor of a painfully long memory—hasn't fought and lost.

In my opinion, Lemebel is one of Chile's best writers and the best poet of my generation, though he doesn't write poetry. Lemebel is one of those few who doesn't seek respectability (the respectability for which Chilean writers would sell their own asses) but freedom. His contemporaries, the hordes of right-leaning and left-leaning mediocrities, glance at him over their shoulders and try to smile. He isn't the first homosexual, god knows, of the Chilean Parnassus, with all its closeted queers, but he's the first cross-dresser to appear on stage alone in the glare of the footlights, addressing a literally stupefied crowd.

They can't forgive me for having a voice, Robert, says Lemebel at the other end of the line. Santiago glitters in the night. It looks like the last great city of the southern hemisphere. Cars pass under my balcony and Pinochet is in prison in London. How many years has it been since the last curfew? How many years will it be until the next? They can't forgive me for remembering all the things they did, says Lemebel. But you want to know what they really can't forgive, Robert? They can't forgive me for not forgiving them.

I have the sense that Lemebel and Jorge Arrate wouldn't get along. Anywhere in Europe, this would be a pity, but in Chile it's a tragedy too.

And last of all, a true story. I repeat: this isn't fiction, it's real, it happened in Chile during the Pinochet dictatorship and more or less everybody (the small and remote "everybody" that is Chile) knows it. A right-wing young woman sets up house with a right-wing American, or marries him. The two of them aren't just young, they're good-looking and proud. He's a DINA (National Intelligence Directorate) agent, possibly also a CIA agent. She loves literature and loves her man. They rent or buy a big house in the suburbs of Santiago. In the cellars of this house the American interrogates and tortures political prisoners who are later moved on to other detention centers or added to the list of the disappeared. She writes, and she attends writing workshops. In those days, I suppose, there weren't as many workshops as there are today, but there were some. In Santiago people have grown accustomed to the curfew. At night there aren't many places to go for fun, and the winters are long. So every weekend or every few nights she has a group of writers over to her house. It isn't a set group. The guests vary. Some come only once, others several times. At the house there's always whiskey, good wine, and sometimes the gatherings turn into dinners. One night a guest goes looking for the bathroom and gets lost. It's his first time there and he doesn't know the house. Probably he's a bit tipsy or maybe he's already lost in the alcoholic haze of the weekend. In any case, instead of turning right he turns left and then he goes down a flight of stairs that he shouldn't have gone down and he opens a door at the end of a long hallway, long like Chile. The room is dark but even so he can make out a bound figure, in pain or possibly drugged. He knows what he's seeing. He closes the door and returns to the party. He isn't drunk anymore. He's terrified, but he doesn't say anything. "Surely the people who attended those post-coup, culturally stilted soireés will remember the annoyance of the flickering current that made lamps blink and music stop, interrupting the dancing. Just as surely, they knew nothing about another parallel dance, in which the jab of the prod tensed the tortured back of the knee in a voltaic arc. They might not have heard the cries over the blare of disco, which was all the rage back then," says Pedro Lemebel. Whatever the case, the writers leave. But they come back for the next party. She, the hostess, even wins a short story or poetry prize from the only literary journal still in existence back then, a left-wing journal.

And this is how the literature of every country is built.

WORDS FROM OUTER SPACE

So what is *Secret Interference*? It's a clandestinely recorded tape. It's voices talking and transmitting orders and counter-orders on September 11, 1973. Voices we've vaguely heard at some point in our lives, but to which we aren't able to attach a body, as if they issued from forms without substance. Voices that are echoes of a nebulous fear located in some part of our bodies. Imaginary ghosts. A real fear, and also a vulgar fear.

Some orders are unequivocal: there's talk about killing on sight, arrests, bombings. Sometimes the men who're talking make jokes: this doesn't bring them any closer to us, in fact, it sinks them deeper into an abyss, they're men who emerge from invisible and imperceptible pits and who, in vaguely military terms, promise to establish order. Despite it all, the humor they flaunt is familiar. A humor that one recognizes and would rather not recognize.

The man who's talking could be my father or grandfather.

The man who's giving orders could be an old school friend, the bully or the teacher's pet, the kid no one remembers or the kid we played with just once. In those familiar voices we can contemplate ourselves, at a remove, as if watching ourselves in a mirror. It isn't Stendhal's mirror, the mirror that strolls along a path, but it could be, and for many who hear the tape it surely will be precisely that.

At first the voices are indistinguishable. Gradually, however, each begins to acquire a personality, a unique character, though they all bear the common stamp of Chileanness, that is, the common stamp of a childhood wreathed in mist and in something that for lack of a better word we can call happiness. The voices that reach us from outer space aren't just redesigning the childhood island called Chile: they're teaching us our reality with the teacher's rod, they're asking us to open our eyes and also our ears. They're the voices of real men. Some—to judge by the way they talk, by their moments of hesitation—are scared, nervous. Others control their emotions and maintain their composure with impressive coldbloodedness. The tape rolls and little by little the voices become familiar, as if they'd always been there, talking to us, threatening us. The image is redundant. In fact, they were always there. They're the men who ordered a father to sodomize his own son if he didn't want them both to be killed, the bosses who put live rats into the vagina of a twenty-two-year-old Mirista they called a whore.

And yet it all seems like a game. The voices creep in from our childhood like prankster guardian spirits: anything is possible if God doesn't exist, anything can be done if it's in the name of Chile. Some voices raise doubts. Most comply, hesitant. Sometimes their ignorance is staggering. A top commander, in direct communication with another commander, says that from now on, given the importance of the information he has to transmit, he'll speak in English. As if English were a dead language, or as if no one on the other side spoke English.

There's no getting around it: these are the voices of our childhood. Chilean voices, as if smuggled into a movie too big for them, voices that relay a message that the speakers themselves don't quite understand. A conversation on the far side of reality, where conversation is impossible. And yet no matter how many extraordinary deeds are accumulated, the picture we're left with is tinged with a familiar vulgarity, taken to a sickening degree. At some point in our lives we knew the people who're talking. The voices are performing for us, as if in a radio serial, but mostly they're performing for themselves. Pornography, snuff movies. At last they've found the roles of their lives. Finally, the soldiers have their war, their great war: before them we stand, unarmed but watching and listening.

A MODEST PROPOSAL

Everything would suggest that we're entering the new millennium under the glowering word *abject*, which comes from the Latin *abjectus*, which means lowly or humble, according to Joan Corominas, the sage who spent his last years on the Mediterranean coast, in a town just a few miles from mine.

September 11, 1973, glides over us like the penultimate Chilean condor or even like a winged *huemul*, a beast from the *Book of Imaginary Beings*, written by Borges in collaboration with María Guerrero in 1967, in which there is a chapter, "An Animal Dreamed by Kafka," that literally transcribes the words of the Prague writer. It goes like this: "It is the animal with the big tail, a tail many yards long and like a fox's brush. How I should like to get my hands on this tail some time, but it is impossible, the animal is constantly moving about, the tail is constantly being flung this way and that. The animal resembles a kangaroo, but not as to the face, which is flat almost like a human face, and small and oval; only its teeth have any power of expression, whether they are concealed or bared. Sometimes I have the feeling that the animal is trying to tame me. What other purpose could it have in withdrawing its tail when I snatch at it, and then again, waiting calmly until I am tempted again, and then leaping away once more?"

Sometimes I get the feeling that September 11 wants to break us. Sometimes I get the feeling that September 11 has already irrevocably broken us.

What would have happened if September 11 had never existed? It's a silly question, but sometimes it's necessary to ask silly questions, or it's inevitable, or it suits our natural laziness. What would have happened? Many things, of course. The history of Latin America would be different. But on a basic level, I think everything would be the same, in Chile and in Latin America. It can be argued: there would be no disappeared. True. And there would be no caravan of death. Or firing squads. In Mexico, I met a Mirista who was tortured by having rats put into her vagina. She was a young girl, just a little older than me, which means she must have been twenty-two or twenty-three, and later I was told that she died of sadness, like in a nineteenth-century novel. Without September 11, that wouldn't have happened. What would we have seen? A different kind of repression, maybe. Instead of meeting that Mirista in Mexico, maybe I would've met her at a concentration camp in the south of Chile, where she was sent for her leftist views, that "childhood malady" (for *childhood*, read childish), and I was sent for being a writer with no class consciousness or sense of history. Would that have been better? I think so. Such a bath of horror, you might say, would be less sticky than the real historic bath of horror into which we were plunged.

A little while ago I was in Chile, where I happened to

watch two or three televised conversations among politicians of different views. The conversations, if they can be called that (they were more like mini-debates, though more because of the atmosphere of conflict and strife than because of any controversy aired), consisted of a public exhibition of patience by the politicians of the center and the left, and a display of rudeness—when not of jingoistic hysteria—by the politicians on the right. I was left with the impression (possibly illusory) that some (precisely those supported by the majority of the electorate) took the position of recently liberated offenders still subject to the will (more imaginary than real) of their ex-jailers, and the others (those supported by a much smaller portion of the electorate) took a proud stance, the stance of gentlemen wounded to the quick, but also of badly behaved children, of bullies who don't intend to concede a single point to their adversaries, completely forgetting that politics is above all the art of dialogue and tolerance.

And it's here that the word *abject* turns up again. A difficult and cumbersome abjection that at times seems unshakable. It's true that the left committed an infinity of crimes, by commission or omission. To require of the Chilean politicians on the left (who I suspect have committed very few crimes of commission) that they intone a permanent *mea culpa* for the Stalinist concentration camps is from any point of view an excessive demand. It's toward this, however, that political discourse seems to tend. Toward an incessant penitence that takes the place of the exchange or expression of ideas. But this penitence isn't even penitence. Its real purpose is to cover up one of the nation's essential qualities: its ridiculousness and tweeness, the horrific seriousness of Chileans dressed up in the trappings of the twee, of that precious, pretentious vulgarity.

Sometimes, when I'm in the mood to think pointless thoughts, I ask myself whether we were always like this. I don't know. The left committed verbal crimes in Chile (a specialty of the Latin American left), it committed moral crimes, and it probably killed people. But it didn't put live rats in any girl's vagina. It didn't have the time to create its own evil, it didn't have the time to create its own forced labor camps. Is it possible that it would have, if given the time? Of course it's possible. Nothing in our country's history allows us to imagine a more optimistic alternate history. But the truth is that in Chile the concentration camps weren't the work of the left, and neither were the firing squads, torture, the disappeared, repression. All of this was accomplished by the right. All of this was the work of the government that took power after the coup. Nevertheless, as we enter the third millennium the politicians of the left are still asking to be forgiven, which after all isn't so bad, and, upon reflection, is even advisable, on the condition that *all* politicians—those on the left and those on the right and those in the center—ask for forgiveness for all the real crimes that their fathers and grandfathers committed here and in other countries (especially in other countries!), and that they also ask forgiveness for the string of lies that their fathers and grandfathers told and that they themselves are prepared to keep telling, and for the secrets and the back-stabbing, and then wouldn't that be a pretty picture, as Hart Crane says, all the country's politicians asking to be forgiven, and even competing to see who can ask most convincingly or most loudly.

Of course, I would rather that we entered the twenty-first century (which incidentally means nothing) in a more civilized fashion, perhaps engaged in conversation, which also means *listening* and *reflecting,* but if, as everything seems to indicate, that won't be possible, then it wouldn't be a bad thing, or at least not the worst thing, to enter the third millennium asking for forgiveness right and left, and in the meantime, while we're at it, we should raise a statue of Nicanor Parra in Plaza Italia, a statue of Nicanor and another of Neruda, but with their backs turned to each other.

At this point, I foresee that more than one alleged reader will say to himself (and then run to tell his friends and relatives): Bolaño says Parra is the poet of the right and Neruda is the poet of the left.

Some people don't know how to read.

OUT IN THE COLD

Long ago, when I was young, a friend showed me an anthology of contemporary poetry in Spanish, one of the many lackluster volumes that appear each year. This one had been published in Chile, and the contribution of one of the editors, a poet of certain standing, was to insist that at least half of the anthology be devoted to Chilean poetry. In other words, if the anthology was three hundred pages long, thirty pages were devoted to Spanish poetry, twenty to Argentine poetry, twenty to Mexican poetry, five to Uruguayan poetry, five to Nicaraguan poetry, maybe ten to Peruvian poetry (and Martín Adan wasn't included), three to Colombian poetry, one to Ecuadorian poetry, and so on until one hundred and fifty pages were filled. Across the other hundred and fifty pages Chilean poets strolled at their leisure. This anthology, the title and editors of which I prefer not to recall, is a fair reflection of the image that Chilean poetry once had of itself. Poets were poor but they were poets. Poets lived off state patronage but they were poets. Until it all came to an end. Then the Chilean poets descended from the Chilean Olympus—which, incidentally, excepting the five greats (who might only be four, or possibly three), had little significance in other latitudes—in Indian file, reluctantly, bewildered and terrified, and they saw how their former home, the famous House of Handouts, had been taken over by an illustrious group of writers who called themselves novelists, noveltrixes, and even *nouveau* novelists. The recent arrivals, as one might expect, were quick to explain this change of tenancy with the magic word *modernism* or *postmodernism*. Novelists (in the absence of filmmakers) are modern and therefore they are the real mirror in which a modern society should examine itself. The poets, who, with a few exceptions, had until then carefully cultivated an apocalyptic aesthetic mixed with the crudest kind of nationalism, didn't make a peep. They abandoned the field, surrendering to the evidence of sales figures. Chile is no longer a country of poets. To-day there's little chance that a couple of Chilean poets would think to put together an anthology of contemporary poetry in Spanish in which Chileans occupied more than half the pages. That supreme ignorance, that brutish provincialism, is today the exclusive heritage of the Chilean novel. The poets, those poor Chilean poets between the ages of thirty and fifty-five, today bow their heads and wonder what's happened, why it's suddenly started to rain, what are they doing out there in the cold, their minds blank, not sure which way to run. Anywhere else this would be a nightmare, but in Chile it's a good thing. Literary status acquired by trickery and deceit was blown to pieces. Poetry's respectability was reduced to a handful of dust. Now Chilean poets live out in the cold again. And they can go back to reading poetry. And they can even read or reread some Chilean poets. And they can see that what those poets wrote wasn't bad, and that sometimes it was even good. And they can go back to writing poetry.

CHILEAN POETRY UNDER INCLEMENT SKIES

The picture I have of Chilean poetry is like my memory of my first dog, Duke, a mongrel who was part St. Bernard, German shepherd, and Alsatian. He lived with us for many years, and when I was lonely he was like father, mother, teacher, and brother all in one. To me, Duke is Chilean poetry and I have the vague suspicion that Chileans see Chilean poetry as a dog, or as dogs in their various incarnations: sometimes as a savage pack of wolves, sometimes as a solitary howl heard between dreams, and sometimes—especially—as a lap dog at the groomer's. I think of Neruda, Gabriela Mistral, Huidobro, Parra, de Rokha, but I also think of Pezoa Véliz and his poem about the hospital, a poem that deserves a place in the annals of Latin American melancholy, and about the songs of Violeta Parra—straight out of the repertoire of Archaic Greece—that speak unflaggingly of the tragedy of Latin America.

So it is for us Chileans: this seems to be our fate and our

particular splendor. And that's how I think of Lihn, as an undeserved luxury, who throughout his work tried to teach us to avoid melodrama, and that's how I think of Teillier, who retreated to one of Santiago's most miserable neighborhoods to die, accepting his fate as a poet and alcoholic. After Lihn and Teillier, nothingness or mystery offers us its little paw and even wags its tail. Zurita creates a wonderful body of work that marks a point of no return for the poetics of the previous generation and for which he stands out among his generation, but his eschatology and his messianism are also the pillars of a mausoleum or a funeral pyre toward which almost all the poets of Chile marched in the 1980s. That *dolce stil novo* tried to be fresh and epic, and in some ways it was, though its fringes were bitter and pathetic.

The poetry of Gonzalo Millán, as consistent and lucid as anything on the Chilean and even the Latin American scene, has stood for some years as the only secular poetry in the face of an avalanche of sacramental verse: it's a relief to read Millán, who doesn't present himself as the voice of the nation or of the oppressed. Juan Luis Martínez makes a fleeting study of Duchamp (the perfect study, in a way) and disappears. Rodrigo Lira blazes a path and is lost. But one must reread Lira. Instead of trying to be Dante, he tries to be the cartoon bird Condorito. Instead of trying to gain entrance to the House of Handouts (which for so long was the House of Poets), he tries to gain entrance to the House of Destruction. Diego Maquieira writes just two brilliant books, and then opts for silence. What, I ask myself sometimes, was Maquieira trying to tell us? Did he wag his tail, did he growl, did Chilean poetry toss him a little stick to fetch and he never came back? With Maquieira anything is possible, good or bad. And yet the ultimate rebel of my generation is Pedro Lemebel, who writes no poetry but whose life serves as an example for poets. In Lemebel there's tenderness, a sense of the apocalypse, fierce bitterness. With him there are no half measures; to read him requires deep immersion.

Chilean poetry is a dog and now it lives out under inclement skies again. Bertoni, who gathers seaweed on the coast, is the perfect example.

ON BRUNO MONTANÉ

His poems are brushstrokes suspended in the air. Sometimes they're only jottings, other times miniatures, occasionally long existentialist works shrunk to eight or twelve lines. His poems are blood suspended in the air. His intent, or his attitude toward the world and culture, vacillates between irreconcilable poles. From this prolonged struggle he has been able to extract paradoxical verses. He writes like a naturalist who believes in very little and who nevertheless continues to stubbornly do his work, his stubbornness at times confused with indifference. I believe that he's one of Chile's best contemporary poets.

EIGHT SECONDS WITH NICANOR PARRA

There's only one thing I can say for sure about Nicanor Parra's poetry in this new century: it will endure. This means very little, of course, as Parra would be the first to acknowledge. Still, it will endure, along with the poetry of Borges, Vallejo, Cernuda and a few others. But this, it must be said, hardly matters.

Parra's wager, his probe into the future, is too complex to be explained here. And it's too dark. It possesses the darkness of motion. The actor who speaks or gestures, however, is perfectly visible. His features, his trappings, the symbols that accompany him like tumors are familiar: he's the poet who sleeps sitting in a chair, the beau who gets lost in a cemetery, the lecturer who tears at his hair until he pulls it out, the brave man who dares to piss kneeling, the hermit who watches the years go by, the anguished statistician. In order to read Parra, it's worth asking the question that he asks himself and that Wittgenstein asks us: is this hand a hand or isn't it a hand? (The question should be asked as one gazes at one's own hand.)

I wonder who will write the book that Parra planned and never wrote: a history of World War II told or sung battle by battle, concentration camp by concentration camp, exhaustively, a poem that somehow became the instant antithesis of Neruda's *Canto general* and of which Parra retains only one text, the *Manifiesto*, in which he expounds upon his poetic credo, a credo that Parra himself has ignored whenever necessary, among other things because that's exactly what credos are for: to give a vague sense of the unexplored territory into which one is heading, and—infrequently—to single out the real writers. When it comes to concrete risks and dangers, credos aren't worth much.

Let the brave follow Parra. Only the young are brave, only the young are pure of heart among the pure. But Parra doesn't write juvenile verse. Parra doesn't write about purity. He does write about pain and loneliness; about pointless and necessary challenges; about words fated to drift apart just as the tribe is fated to drift apart. Parra writes as if the next day he'll be electrocuted. As far as I know, the Mexican poet Mario Santiago was the only one with a clear understanding of his work. The rest of us have just glimpsed a dark meteor. First requirement of a masterpiece: to pass unnoticed.

There are moments in the journey of a poet when he has no choice but to improvise. He may be able to recite Gonzalo de Berceo from memory and he may have expert knowledge of Garcilaso's heptasyllables and hendecasyllables, but there are moments when all he can do is throw himself into the abyss or stand naked before a clan of ostensibly polite Chileans. Naturally, one has to know how to accept the consequences. First requirement of a masterpiece: to pass unnoticed.

A political note: Parra has managed to survive. It's not

much, but it's something. He has survived the Chilean left, with its deeply right-wing convictions, and the memory-challenged, neo-Nazi Chilean right. He has survived the neo-Stalinist Latin American left and the Latin American right, now globalized and until recently the silent accomplice of repression and genocide. He has survived the mediocre Latin American professors who swarm on American university campuses and the zombies who stagger through the village of Santiago. He has even survived his own followers. And I would go further—probably carried away by enthusiasm—and say that Parra, along with his comrades (Violeta at the head) and his Rabelaisian forefathers, has achieved one of poetry's greatest goals of all time: to wear out the public's patience.

Lines picked at random: "It's a mistake to think the stars can help cure cancer," said Parra. Right he is. "Apropos of nothing, I remind you that the soul is immortal," said Parra. Right again. And we could go on like this until the room was empty. I remind you, nevertheless, that Parra is a sculptor too. Or a visual artist. These explanations are perfectly useless. Parra is also a literary critic. He once summed up the entire history of Chilean literature in three lines: "The four great poets of Chile / are three: / Alonso de Ercilla and Rubén Darío."

The poetry of the first decades of the twenty-first century will be a hybrid creation, as fiction has already become. We may be heading, with terrible slowness, toward new earthquakes of form. In this uncertain future, our children will watch as the poet asleep in an armchair meets up on the operating table with the black desert bird that feeds on the parasites of camels. At some point late in his life, Breton talked about the need for surrealism to go underground, to descend into the sewers of cities and libraries. Then he never spoke on the subject again. It doesn't matter who said it: THE TIME TO SETTLE DOWN WILL NEVER COME.

THE LOST

It's hard to talk about emblematic figures, figures who might serve us as totem or bridge between the twentieth and the twenty-first centuries. Especially in Latin America, where disastrous, tragic, and caricaturish models have abounded, among them the founding fathers of both the right and the left, who have plunged the continent into something like a cross between a swamp and Las Vegas. But it occurs to me now that Rodrigo Lira could be such a figure, and also that if Rodrigo Lira read this he would laugh. He certainly lived a modest life, but modesty, in Rodrigo's case, didn't mean what it does elsewhere on the planet or at least in Latin America, where it's synonymous with silence and also castration. Modesty, in Rodrigo Lira's case, was a dangerous mix of elegance and sadness. An elegance and a sadness that could be extreme, that often were extreme, and that in public (and also in private, I suppose, which here means in the most boundless solitude) appeared clad from head to toe in the most caustic humor, as if Rodrigo were a medieval knight lost in a dream that suddenly became a nightmare. He was a poet, of course. Sometimes it's tempting to think that he was Chile's last poet, one of the last poets of Latin America. He was born in 1949, which means that he was twenty-four at the time of the coup. From what he wrote, the reader sometimes gets the sense that his world, the geography through which he moved, was limited to a few university departments and a few libraries in Santiago, the city of his birth. Many of his poems are commentaries on the work of older Chilean poets whom he frequented and whose patience he tried: at first glance they seem like jokes, frivolous glosses, insults proffered by a younger man who refuses to grow up, who refuses to enter the adult world. Behind the invective, behind the poet's laughing response to the frozen carnival of literature, one can find other things, among them horror and a prophetic gaze that proclaims the end of the dictatorship but not the end of stupidity, the end of the military presence but not the end of the quicksand and silence that came with it and that will presumably last forever or for such a long time that, in human terms, it's an eternity. Prophetic and visionary as he may be, however, it's other things that really interest Lira. He's interested in a few women who invariably leave him or even refuse to talk to him. He's interested in his hair, which he's losing (as his bald spot grows, so do his sideburns, from tiny to big and bushy, the sideburns of an Independence hero). He's interested in flowered shirts. He's interested in a few books that are like black holes, or pretend to be. He's interested in sociability: imagine someone friendly, attentive, cultured, sensitive, a good son and a good friend, a young man always ready to lend a hand, although this young man is really a time bomb, this young man listens in a *different way*, this young man is driven by a *different kind* of loyalty. He's interested in street talk, argot, the Chilean slang that is our poverty but also one of the few riches we have left (argot, sex, automatic excess), though hidden behind his argot, like a cornered terrorist, is the ultimate vision of what those who own the nation call *nation*: a territory that was once snatched away from death and that death is now reconquering with a giant's slow strides. And he writes, and, sometimes— rarely—publishes, but he gives readings, and in this sense Rodrigo Lira is like so many of the Latin American poets of the 1970s and '80s who drift along and give readings, except that Rodrigo Lira, unlike most of his contemporaries, isn't an involuntary inhabitant of an incomprehensible dream, but a voluntary resident, someone with his eyes open in the middle of a nightmare. His modesty, however, the modesty that makes him a rare bird, also causes him to soften as much as possible the otherness that the well-intentioned try to pass off as normality. He likes to walk, he likes to give readings, he tries to dress well or at least look as groomed as possible. In 1981 he decides to kill himself. To play it down, in his suicide note he explains that he's killing himself to protest the recent increase in the price of bread. Or sugar. I can't remember which. I'm writing this without access to reference books. Enrique Lihn is one of the few who's written anything about Rodrigo Lira, after Lira was already dead, and I don't have Lihn's piece at hand. I seem to remember that he got into a hot bath and slit his wrists. That's always struck me as a brave and contemplative way to die. Death comes not suddenly but slowly and there's plenty of time to think: to remember the good moments and the bad, to bid a silent farewell to the beloved and the despised, to recite poetry from memory, to weep. In Rodrigo Lira's case, it wouldn't surprise me if he'd also had time to laugh. The best thing about Latin America are its suicides, voluntary or not. We have the worst politicians in the world, the worst capitalists in the world, the worst writers in the world. In Europe we're known for our complaining and our crocodile tears. Latin America is the closest thing there is to Kafka's penal colony. We do our best to fool a few naive Europeans and a few ignorant Europeans with terrible books, in which we appeal to their good nature, to political correctness, to tales of the noble savage, to exoticism. The only thing our university graduates and intellectuals want is to teach at some college lost in the American Midwest, just as the goal was once to travel and live on neo-Stalinist handouts, which we thought of as an unprecedented achievement. We're experts at winning scholarships, scholarships that are sometimes awarded more out of pity than because we deserve them. Our discourse on weath is the closest thing there is to a cheap self-help book. Our discourse on poverty is an imaginary discourse in which the only voices are those of madmen speaking of bitterness and frustration. We hate the Argentines because the Argentines are the closest thing in these parts to Europeans. The Argentines hate us because we're the mirror in which they see themselves as what they truly are—Americans. We're racists in the purest sense: that is, we're racists because we're scared to death. But our suicides are the best. Take Violeta Parra, who wrote some of our continent's best songs and fought with everyone and everything and shot herself next to the tent where every night she sang and howled. Take Alfonsina Storni, the most talented woman in Argentina, who drowned herself in the Río de la Plata. Take Jorge Cuesta, gay Mexican writer, who—before he put a bag over his head—castrated himself and nailed his testicles to the door of his bedroom, as a final unreciprocated gift. These great suicides and all their brethren, those who refuse to come in out of the storm (not because they like it out there but among other reasons because they have no place to go), give reason to believe that not everything is lost, as preached by the rise of neoliberalism and the resurgence of the church. We're children of the Enlightenment, said Rodrigo Lira as he strolled through a Santiago that more than anything resembled a cemetery on another planet. In other words, we're reasonable human beings (poor, but reasonable), not spirits out of a manual of magic realism, not postcards for foreign consumption and abject national masquerade. In other words: we're beings who have the historic chance of opting for freedom, and also—paradoxically—life. To the countless number of those killed by the repression one must add the suicide victims who killed themselves for the sake of reason, in the name of reason, which is also the abode of humor. Like so many Latin American poets who died without ever publishing a thing, Rodrigo Lira knew that. In 1984, a small publishing house put out a collection of his poems titled *Proyecto de Obras completas* [Plan for a Complete Works]. Now, in 1998, it's impossible to find. And yet no one has taken the trouble to reissue it. In Chile quite a number of books—most of them bad—are published. Rodrigo Lira's elegance, his disdain, make him off limits for any publisher. The cowardly don't publish the brave.

THE TRANSPARENT MYSTERY
OF JOSÉ DONOSO

It's hard for me to write about Donoso. We disagree about almost everything. I heard that when he was dying, he asked to have Huidobro's *Altazor* read to him, and the image of Donoso on his deathbed listening to *Altazor* makes me sick. I don't have anything against Huidobro, I like Huidobro, but how can a dying man ask to be read that poem? I don't understand it. Or maybe I do, and then I understand it even less, as if Donoso were a mirror in which the essence of Chile and the essence of the writing life were reflected, and that double image, throbbing with sickness, superficiality, and indulgence, just makes me sad, because in it one can see, though only darkly, as Donoso would have liked, the ultimate poverty of the writing life and of national pride. The cup that he drank to the dregs.

Donoso wrote three good books. One of them very good and the other two powerful enough to linger in readers' memories. The first is *Hell Has No Limits*, a book about desperation and precision. The others: *The Obscene Bird of the Night*, an ambitious and uneven novel, and *The Garden Next Door*, which presents itself as game and testament, and which, in the end—and this is not the least of the paradoxes of Donoso's work—really was his literary testament. Among other things, *The Garden Next Door* tells the story of a failed Chilean writer who lives in Catalonia and doesn't want to return to Chile. To return is to fail. To return, to accept yourself as you are, to allow others like you to accept you, to acknowledge you, on the sole condition that you accept and acknowledge them, becomes as bitter as a Latin American soccer player's discovery that he isn't wanted or needed in the European leagues anymore and that he must return to his home team. I've forgotten what choice Donoso's character makes, whether he goes back or stays in Europe. Maybe he stays. Donoso never lost his taste for losers, combined with a rare (and unblinking) acceptance of bad luck. In any case, the decision, whatever it was, is irrelevant, because the defeat—and the humor, because this may be Donoso's funniest novel—awaits him either way. For the protagonist of *The Garden Next Door* there is no exit anymore. After this novel, there's no exit for José Donoso, the writer, either.

Donoso's legacy is a dark room. In that dark room the beasts fight. To say that he's the best Chilean novelist of the century is to insult him. I don't think Donoso had such paltry aspirations. To say that he's among the century's best writers in Spanish is an exaggeration, no matter how you look at it. Chile isn't a country of novelists. There are four, maybe five, great Chilean poets, and no novelist can stand the most superficial comparison to them. There are a few prose writers, not many, but no novelists. In a landscape dominated by Augusto D'Halmar and Manuel Rojas, José Donoso's work clearly shines. In the grand theater of Lezama, Bioy, Rulfo, Cortázar, García Márquez, Vargas Llosa, Sábato, Benet, Puig, Arenas, Donoso's work automatically pales and takes second place.

His followers, those who today carry Donoso's torch, the Donositos, try to write like Graham Greene, like Hemingway, like Conrad, like Vonnegut, like Douglas Coupland, with varying degrees of success, with varying degrees of abjection, and through the lens of these bad translations they undertake to read their master, to publicly interpret the great Chilean novelist. From the neo-Stalinists to the Opus Dei, from the thugs of the right to the thugs of the left, from the feminists to the sad little macho men of Santiago, everyone in Chile, secretly or not, claims to be his disciple. A serious mistake. It would be better if they read him. It would be better if they stopped writing and started reading instead. Much better to read.

ON LITERATURE, THE NATIONAL LITERATURE PRIZE, AND THE RARE CONSOLATIONS OF THE WRITING LIFE

First of all, so there can be no mistake about it: Enrique Lihn and Jorge Teillier never received the National Literature Prize. Lihn and Teillier are dead now.

To the matter at hand, then. Asked to choose between the frying pan and the fire, I choose Isabel Allende. The glamour of her life as a South American in California, her imitations of García Márquez, her unquestionable courage, the way her writing ranges from the kitsch to the pathetic and reveals her as a kind of Latin American and politically correct version of the author of *The Valley of the Dolls*: all of this, though it may seem hard to believe, makes her work highly superior to the work of born paper-pushers like Skármeta and Teitelboim.

In other words: Allende's work is bad, but it's alive; it's anemic, like a lot of Latin Americans, but it's alive. It won't live long, like many sick people, but for now it's alive. And there's always the possibility of a miracle. Who knows? The ghost of

Juana Inés de la Cruz could appear to Allende one day and present her with a reading list. Or the ghost of Teresa of Avila. Or all else failing, the ghost of Emilia Pardo Bazán. There's no such hope for the work of Skármeta and Teitelboim. Even God can't save them. Still, to write—I swear I read it in a Chilean newspaper—that we need to hurry up and give Allende the National Prize before she wins the Nobel is no longer just a ridiculous farce, but proof that the author of such a claim is a world-class idiot.

Are there really innocents who think like this? And are the people who think like this actually innocents or simply incarnations of a folly that has swept not just Chile but all of Latin America? Not long ago, Nélida Piñon—celebrated Brazilian novelist and serial killer of readers—said that Paulo Coelho, a kind of soap opera Rio witchdoctor version of Barbusse and Anatole France, should be admitted into the Brazilian Academy because he had made the Brazilian language known all over the globe. As if the "Brazilian language" were a sanctified essence, capable of withstanding any translation, or as if the long-suffering readers on the Tokyo metro spoke Portuguese. Anyway, what is this "Brazilian language"? You might as well talk about the Canadian language, or the Australian language, or the Bolivian language. True, there are Bolivian writers who seem to write in "American," but that's because they don't know how to write very well in Spanish or Castilian, even though— for better or for worse—they ultimately do write in Spanish.

Where were we? That's right, Coelho and the Academy and the vacant seat that he was finally given, thanks among other things to his popularization of the "Brazilian language" around the world. Frankly, reading this one might get the idea that Coelho has a (Brazilian) vocabulary on a par with Joyce's "Irish language." Wrong. Coelho's prose, in terms of lexical richness, in terms of richness of vocabulary, is poor. What are his merits? The same as Isabel Allende's. He sells books. In other words: he's a successful author. And here we come to the heart of the matter. Prizes, seats (in the Academy), tables, beds, even golden chamber pots belong, of course, to those who are successful or to those who play the part of loyal and obedient clerks.

Let's just say that power, any power, whether left-wing or right-wing, would, if left to its own devices, reward only the clerks. In this scenario, Skármeta is the favorite by far. If we were in neo-Stalinist Moscow, or Havana, the prize would go to Teitelboim. It frightens me (and makes me sick) just to imagine it. But success also has its champions: all those mental dwarfs in search of shelter, who are legion. Or all the writers who hope for a favor from Isabelita A. Anyway, forced to choose among these three, I'd take Allende too. But if it were up to me I'd give the prize to Armando Uribe, or Claudio Bertoni, or Diego Maquieira. As far as I'm concerned, any one of them has produced a body of work more than worthy of such an honor. I'll be told that all three are poets and that this year it's the novelists' turn. Who ever heard of such a stupid rule, unwritten or otherwise? For a long time, Nicaragua turned out great poets, from old Salomón de la Selva to Beltrán Morales. Novelists and writers of prose, on the other hand, were in short supply, most of them also completely forgettable. According to this backward logic, a brilliant group of poets should have shared the prize with an inferior group of prose writers and novelists. This is the first thing about the National Literature Prize that should be changed. And it'll probably be the only thing that changes. Young writers with no fortune and only their names to make are still left out in the cold and will continue to be left out in the cold, where the annointed and self-satisfied hunt them down. For the sake of these young writers, and for their sake alone, it may not be entirely pointless to say a bit more. The self-satisfied tend to be quick to anger, but they are also cowards. Their arguments are the arguments of mediocrity and fear and can be dismantled with laughter. Chilean literature, so prestigious in Chile, can boast of only five names worth citing: remember this as a critical and self-critical exercise. Remember, too, that in literature you always lose, but the difference, the enormous difference, lies in losing while standing tall, with eyes open, not kneeling in a corner praying to Jude the Apostle with chattering teeth.

It's probably clear by now that literature has nothing to do with national prizes and everything to do with a strange rain of blood, sweat, semen, and tears. Especially sweat and tears, although I'm sure Bertoni would add semen. I can't say where Chilean literature fits in. Nor, frankly, do I care. That will have to be worked out by the poets, the novelists, the playwrights, the literary critics who labor in the cold, in the darkness; they—who amount to little or nothing just now alongside the strutting peacocks—will face the challenge of making Chilean literature into something more decent, more radical, more free of chicanery. Shoulder to shoulder or all alone, they are the ones called to shape Chilean literature into something reasonable and visionary, an exercise of intelligence, adventure, and tolerance. If literature isn't all of that plus pleasure, what the hell is it?

3.
BETWEEN PARENTHESES

I.
(JANUARY 1999–APRIL 2000)

THE BEST GANG

If I had to hold up the most heavily guarded bank in Europe and I could choose my partners in crime, I'd take a gang of five poets, no question about it. Five real poets, Apollonian or Dionysian, but always real, ready to live and die like poets. No one in the world is as brave as a poet. No one in the world faces disaster with more dignity and understanding. They may seem weak, these readers of Guido Cavalcanti and Arnaut Daniel, these readers of the deserter Archilochus who picked his way across a field of bones. And they work in the void of the word, like astronauts marooned on dead-end planets, in deserts where there are no readers or publishers, just grammatical constructions or stupid songs sung not by men but by ghosts. In the guild of writers they're the greatest and least sought-after jewel. When some deluded kid decides at sixteen or seventeen to be a poet, it's a guaranteed family tragedy. Gay Jew, half black, half Bolshevik: the Siberia of the poet's exile tends to bring shame on his family too. Readers of Baudelaire don't have it easy in high school, or with their schoolmates, much less with their teachers. But their fragility is deceptive. So is their humor and the fickleness of their declarations of love. Behind these shadowy fronts are probably the toughest people in the world, and definitely the bravest. Not for nothing are they descended from Orpheus, who set the stroke for the Argonauts and who descended into hell and came up again, less alive than before his feat, but still alive. If I had to hold up the most heavily fortified bank in America, I'd take a gang of poets. The attempt would probably end in disaster, but it would be beautiful.

THE WOMEN READERS OF WINTER

During the winter they seem to be the only ones brave enough to venture out into the icy cold. I see them at the bars in Blanes or at the station or sitting along the Paseo Marítimo by the water, alone or with their children or a silent friend, and always carrying some book. What do these women read? wondered Enrique Vila-Matas a few years ago. Whatever they can. Not always great literature (though what is great literature?). Sometimes it's magazines, sometimes the worst bestsellers. When I see them walking along, bundled up, buffeted by the wind, I think about the Russian women who fought the revolution and who endured Stalinism, which was worse than winter, and fascism, which was worse than hell, and they always had books with them, when suicide would have been the logical choice. In fact, many of those winter readers ended up killing themselves. But not all of them. A few days ago I read that Nadezhda Yakovlevna Khazina, exceptional reader, author of two memoirs, one of them called *Hope Against Hope*, and wife of the assassinated poet Osip Mandelstam, took part, according to a recent biography, in a threesome with her husband, news that inspired astonishment and disappointment in the ranks of her admirers, who took her for a saint. I, however, was happy to hear it. It told me that in the middle of winter Nadeshda and Osip didn't freeze and it confirmed for me that at least they tried to read *all* the books. The saintly readers of winter are women of flesh and blood, and they couldn't be braver. Some, it's true, committed suicide. Others endured the horrors and returned to their books, the mysterious books that women read when it's cold and it seems as if winter will never end.

PASTRY COOKS

My friend Joan Planells, pastry cook of Blanes, claims he never gets sick and is always in a good mood. He says this half in jest and half seriously, but in fact he's the only person I know who's made it through this terrible winter without catching the flu. It must have to do with my job, says Joan, suddenly a bit gloomy. Maybe. The pastry profession yields characters with iron constitutions. Take the generous and selfless Raguenau, humble patron of Cyrano de Bergerac, and J. V. Foix, poet and pastry cook of Sarrià, whose pastry shop I visit occasionally, when I go to see my editor. At Foix's pastry shop in Sarrià, one can admire a bust of Cyrano, which is the kind of thing few pastry shops in the world give themselves the luxury of displaying. Most uncanny, though, is the behavior of the saleswomen. They all seem to have been reading (for years) the complete works of Foix. All of them, the girls as well as the older women, wait on the customers they don't know—that is, the ones drawn to the pastry shop by the emanations of the poet who claimed to see everything more clearly in his sleep—like professors of Catalan literature or hosts at a strange conference. In fact, that may even be what they are. The point is that every time I go into Foix's pastry shop, I get the sense that they're sizing me up. The youngest salesgirls silently pity me and the less young say "you'll never be a poet, because the secret of poetry is . . ." At this point our telepathic conversation breaks off and I walk out eating a sweet roll and thinking about the iron constitution of pastry cooks. My friend Joan Planells says that the secret is to stay relaxed and read a lot and work constantly. But don't you ever get sad? I ask him. Sometimes I get sad, he says almost in a whisper, but I'm always happy.

THE BOOKSELLER

We all have the bookshops we deserve, except for those of us who have none. Mine is the Sant Jordi, in Blanes, the book-shop of Pilar Pagespetit i Martori, in the town's old riverbed. Once every three days I go there to poke around and some-times I exchange a few words with my bookseller. Pilar Pages-petit, who, as her name suggests, is a small woman, spends the mornings and some afternoons, too, when there aren't many customers, sorting orders and delivery requests and reading her favorite books. At these times of day, Pilar Pagespetit is present and she isn't present. In other words, she's there, but it's as if she's not. At these times of day, the bookstore becomes an explorer's outpost in who knows where. In a wild country, maybe, or barren lands. And everyone who comes in looks like a castaway, even the women who're there to buy *Pronto*.

At these times of day, there's jazz playing at the Sant Jordi (which puts me on edge and relaxes Pilar), although at other times there might be classical music, ethnic music, or Brazilian music, the sounds of which also serve to relax my bookseller. Certainly, any bookseller has more than enough reasons to be nervous, I say to myself when I hear the somber chords of John Coltrane, although my bookseller, surrounded by soothing music, doesn't seem to take things too hard. When I ask her if this was the kind of work she always wanted to do, she says she doesn't know. She began as a librarian in Tordera, and eighteen years ago, when she came to live in Blanes, she opened her bookstore and she seems happy. I'm reasonably happy with my bookseller, too. She gives me credit and she usually finds me the books I want. That's all anyone can ask for.

TOMEO

There's a new novel out by Javier Tomeo and his fans are rubbing their hands in glee. The novel is called *Napoleon VII* and inevitably, of course, it's about a madman who thinks he's Napoleon and who watches from a balcony as his soldiers gradually gather at the door to his house. (In a way, the character is reminiscent of the madman from *El canto de las tortugas* [The Song of the Turtles], who thought he could talk to animals.) Here the madman, Hilario, thinks he can talk to his left big toe, which is sometimes Murat, sometimes Soult, and sometimes Napoleon's ill-starred secretary. Hilario, naturally, is the loneliest man in the world, a man who *listens* to the television so as not to feel alone, and who thinks when he watches it that he's receiving signals beamed exclusively to him. The other character, the other voice lost in this Napoleonic dream, is Hilario's cross-dressing neighbor, who, dressed as Josephine, is preparing for a date that night with Napoleon VII and who recklessly—that is, in a way that leaves room for *hope*—addresses himself directly to the abyss. Two typical Tomean characters, created by an author whose novels can in principle be divided into two categories: those featuring a dialogue between two dissimilar beings, linked only by loneliness (a dialogue that often ends up becoming an anguished monologue that leads, in the blink of an eye, to the edge of reason), and those in which there is only one character, someone who has generally lost his sanity or what the world deems sanity. Tomeo's eye wanders, in a fashion perhaps uncommon in Spanish literature, through the hell of the everyday and also through its unexpected (because familiar) verbal paradises, offering us a starkly real picture of our capacity for endurance.

MEMOIRS

Of all books, memoirs are the most deceitful because the pretense in which they engage often goes undetected and their authors are usually only looking to justify themselves. Self-congratulation and memoirs tend to go together. Lies and memoirs get along swimmingly. No memoirist (though exceptions do exist) has ever been known to speak ill of himself or poke fun at himself or coldly recount an embarrassing episode from his life, as if nothing embarassing had ever happened to him. No memoirist has ever boasted of his cowardice. In fact, memoirists aren't just brave, they usually live in the eye of the storm, or have passed through it. The most flagrant example of this kind of memoirist in recent literary history is Pablo Neruda and his deplorable *Memoirs*. Occupying a somewhat different position is Ernesto Sábato's last book, *Antes del fin* [Before the End] (Seix Barral), published after more than twenty years of silence. For a reader of Sábato, the truth is that the book lacks flavor—or, rather, for a reader who hasn't already resigned himself to the fact that Sábato wrote only three novels and will probably never write anything else. The first thing one notices is its length: it's just 188 pages long, skimpy for a memoir, by any measure. But later, as the reader makes some headway into what is in no way a strident book, he realizes that 188 pages is enough and even too much to say what must be said, in other words that unhappiness still exists and that utopia can also exist, that we breathe and that we stop breathing. And that's all Sábato thinks he has to tell us.

SPRINGTIME IN BLANES

Spring comes to Blanes, the season that makes us all equals, and even the town's most disagreeable residents attempt not a smile but a different kind of gaze, as if spring were a spinster machine, in other words a machine incomprehensible in principle, incontrovertible, that comes to town from who knows where, maybe the sea, maybe the mountains, maybe the fields where black men and white men work hard planting who knows what and they stop in the middle of a row or in the middle of digging in the same way that the most disagreeable townspeople stop at a corner suddenly swarming with flies to watch the arrival of spring, the spinster machine that children, even the most disadvantaged children, understand better than adults, and that's it, there's nothing else to discuss, spring comes to town and Blanes becomes Blanes Ville or Blanes sur Mer, as Joan de Sagarra would say, our imaginary little city, our city in thrall to the whims of the spinster machine that came from somewhere though no one knows where, surely not from the sea, because even the sea seems surprised by its arrival, and in fact, if you think about it (in other words, if you start to think like a spinster machine), spring seems to have come in from the tower of Sant Joan, which is, along with the Gothic fountain, the only structure in town that remains unperturbed, as if the four seasons coexisted in its molecular makeup, and it's this tower that some residents of Blanes feel is the perfect gateway not only for the arrival of spring but for many other things, an eschatological page by Joaquim Ruyra, for example, or the reddest shrimp on the Costa Brava, or the joy of being alive with no need for further discussion.

CHILEAN LITERATURE

Quiet days in Blanes. I'm teaching a course on new Chilean fiction. I'm the teacher of the course and the only student in the course. Which is fine. Although sometimes my laziness as a student horrifies me and sometimes my clumsiness as a lecturer brings on sudden fits of sleep. These fits are called narcolepsy, which is what River Phoenix had in that Gus Van Sant movie. But River Phoenix also had Keanu Reeves, or to put it another way: Phoenix had a place to rest his weary head and I can only rest mine on books. And books, especially if one mistakes them for pillows, can cause nightmares. Despite it all, I sleep and read. Chilean literature, I say to myself in my sleep, is an endless nightmare: for so many writers, for so many critics, for so many, many readers. The presence of the nightmare wakes me all of a sudden and I go out. It's seven in the evening. I go to the bank and a man with a cane cuts in front of me when I open the door. I know who he is. Once he threw a beer mug through the window of a bar. Will you hold the door for me? he asks. Of course, I say. And while I'm getting money from the automatic teller, the man with the cane stands in a corner, poring over his savings book. When I leave, he says goodbye and I decide not to reply. I don't like people who read their savings books like novels. And yet, the man with the cane is a relatively cultured person. Once, at a different bar, he talked to me about Peter Pan. He was drunk and he said that a long time ago he had been rich and he cried. River Phoenix would have made a good Peter Pan, I think as I walk away from the bank, and then I think some more about new Chilean fiction. New, say, from Manuel Rojas onward. Before I realize it, my feet take me to a store that sells games. The owner's name is Santi and he's my friend and I owe him three thousand pesetas. Of course: that was why I went to the bank to get cash. The store is full and only Santi is working. Instead of helping him, I stand in a corner, like the man with the cane, and watch the people. Most are kids buying video games. I feel worse and worse. I close my eyes. Suddenly I hear someone talking with an unmistakably Chilean accent. I open my eyes and discover a trio composed of a horrible adolescent with a neutral accent, his mother, who speaks with a kind of Colombian accent, and a man with very black hair, who was the first to speak and who is Chilean. All three are wearing tight pants and boots. All three are short. The adolescent is smoking. He looks tough and doesn't seem too bright, but he can't hide the fact that he's a child. His mother, the Colombian, must be about forty, maybe younger, and she really does have a hard face, but now she seems at peace. The Chilean is with the Colombian, but it's clear he isn't the kid's father, he must be thirty, if that, and he's as interested or more interested than his stepson in buying games. They seem, the three of them, like recent arrivals from hell. Ready (the Colombian woman) to cook a good meal that night and ready (her two boys) to spend a week playing video games. I think about Guy Debord and the Situationists. I think about virtual reality and the new Chilean novel. Santi shows me a new computer game. I take a look at it, it's called Settlers and must be similar to Age of Empires. I pay him what I owe and leave. On the way home I buy honey and camomile tea. I'm back at my apartment. I'm back in my seminar. I read. I listen to the noises from the street. I fall asleep and dream about a book that is a map of wakefulness and sleep. Then I open my eyes in the dark and on the wall, like Mount Rushmore, I see the faces of the cripple and the diabolical threesome. What writers do the survivors read? I ask aloud. Those hypocrites, my own kin.

FERDYDURKE IN CATALAN

All is not lost, Ferdydurkists. A few months ago, almost on tiptoe, one of the most luminous books of this century of shadows became available for purchase. It's *Ferdydurke* (Quaderns Crema), the first novel by Witold Gombrowicz, originally published in 1937, and whose translation into Spanish, sponsored by the literary circles of Café Rex in Buenos Aires, surely constitutes a landmark of extravagance and generosity, in other words one of our century's landmarks of literary joy. That legendary translation, whose main author was the Cuban writer Virgilio Piñera, is difficult if not impossible to find in the bookstores of Spain, which has deprived readers of the key work in the Gombrowiczian oeuvre, unless one could lay hands on the French or Italian or German version. From now on, however, we'll no longer have to go so far to look for it. Anyone who can read Catalan and who has two thousand pesetas in his pocket will be granted access to one of the key novels of this century, in an excellent translation by Anna Rubió and Jerzy Slawomirski. All of this is made possible thanks to Jaume Vallcorba Plana, a model publisher if ever there was one, in whose catalogues one can find jewels like Lord Byron's *Cain*, Hölderlin's *The Death of Empedocles*, and Novalis's *Fragments*, as well as contemporary Catalan writers like Quim Monzó, Ponç Puigdevall, or Maurici Pla, to name just a few. What was going through Vallcorba's head when he decided to publish *Ferdydurke*? I don't know. Anything, except thoughts of profit. What I do know is that a publisher who sets out to publish Gombrowicz is a publisher to watch and that a language—Catalan—in which it's possible to reproduce the work of the great Polish writer is certainly a living language, a language in which Filidor can live on and continue to scheme. All is not lost, Ferdydurkists.

BERLIN

A little while ago I was in Berlin to read from my novel *Nazi Literature in the Americas*. All fine and good. The hospitality of the Berliners, beginning with my translator and friend Heinrich von Berenberg, was commendable; the food wasn't bad; I walked all over the city, day and night, and met lots of interesting people. All unexceptional. Except for two things. First: the organization put me up in a mansion on the Wannsee, the lake on the edge of the city where, in 1811, von Kleist killed himself along with the unfortunate Henriette Vogel, who did in fact resemble a bird, but a drab and ugly bird, one of those birds that doesn't have to spread its wings to resemble a gateway to darkness, to the unknown. But I read von Kleist when I was twenty, and I thought I had left him behind. I remembered the *Prince of Homburg*, which dramatizes the struggle between the writer and his father, between the individual and the State; I remembered *Michael Kohlhaas*, published as part of the old Austral series, a story about bravery and its twin, stupidity, and also a story called *The Earthquake in Chile*, published in 1806, from which there are still moral and aesthetic lessons to be learned. But the fact is that I'd left von Kleist behind. I'd been told that other writers stayed at the mansion and that the scene there was lively, especially after sundown, which was when the residents, Eastern Europeans, a Greek or two, the odd African, came out to drink and discuss literature in one of the castle's countless halls. The first night I got in very late. They left me the key in a kind of mailbox made to look like a drainpipe, with a note informing me of my room number. Oddly, the key opened one of the outside doors to the castle, a side door once used by the service, as well as the door to my room. Surprise. There wasn't a soul anywhere. The place was huge. In one hall I saw fallen flags (Heinrich said that during the day they were shooting a period film). In another hall there was a long table. In another there was nothing but an ancient iron lamp that didn't work. And there were corridors everywhere, shadows that stretched high up the walls, and stairs that led nowhere. When I found my room at last, the window was open and the walls were covered with mosquitos, the mosquitos of Wannsee, a plague the likes of which I hadn't seen in years, ever since I was in Panama, which in itself was an odd thing, because one can accept mosquitos in Panama or the Amazon as a normal if annoying phenomenon, whereas in Berlin it's certainly not what one expects. Upset, I went to ask someone for insect repellant and only then did I realize that I was alone in that enormous mansion on the lake. There were no writers, no staff, no one. I was the only overnight guest there that week. On tiptoe, trying not to make a sound, I went back to my room and spent all night killing bugs. After my fortieth victim I stopped counting. In between I pressed my nose to the window, which I didn't dare to open now, and I thought I could see, on the shores of the Wannsee, the ghost of von Kleist dancing in a cloud of phosphorescent mosquitoes. But one can get used to anything and at last I fell asleep.

The second strange thing I saw in Berlin was much more disturbing. I was with a friend, in her car, driving along the Bismarckstrasse, when all of a sudden a stretch of boulevard no more than fifteen yards long became a street in Lloret de Mar. The very same street.

CIVILIZATION

For the Robert Duvall character in *Apocalypse Now*, there was no better breakfast than the smell of napalm. According to him, it smelled like victory. Perhaps. The smell of burning (with that tinge of acid said to be left hanging in the air) is sometimes like victory, and other times like fear.

I've never smelled napalm. I've smelled gunpowder, and gunpowder definitely doesn't smell like victory. Sometimes it smells like verbena and other times it smells like fear. In contrast, the smell of tear gas (which tends to precede the smell of gunpowder in some countries) is reminiscent of sporting events and rotting guts. Triumphal marches always smell like dust, a hyaline and solar dust that clings like leprosy to the skin and arms. Crowds in closed spaces smell like dust and death, which may be the same thing. Crowds in big open spaces, like stadiums or esplanades, smell like fear. I hate soccer matches, concerts, and rallies: the fear that clings to them is unbearable.

Instead, I like to walk with the dirty old men along the Paseo Marítimo in Blanes in the summer. I like to watch the beach. There, from that triumphal throng of half-naked bodies, beautiful and ugly, fat and thin, perfect and imperfect, a magnificent smell wafts up to us, the smell of suntan lotion. I like the smell that rises from that mass of bodies in all shapes and sizes. It isn't strong, but it's bracing. Though it isn't perfect. Sometimes it's even a sad smell. And possibly metaphysical. The thousand lotions, the sunscreens. They smell of democracy, of civilization.

THE POET OLVIDO GARCÍA VALDÉS

A while ago I was in Toledo with Carolina and our son Lautaro and we visited the poet Olvido García Valdés and her partner, the poet Miguel Casado. I had come to know Miguel through a kind of epistolary and telephonic friendship, and through my admiration for his poetry, in my judgment some of the liveliest being written in Spain today. Actually, my friendship with Miguel began in an unusual way. One day I received a letter from him. My ignorance of the wasps' nest of contemporary Spanish poetry meant that his name didn't ring any bells, but I suspected that he might be a poet and in response I asked him to send me some of his poems. Miguel sent me a journal, *El signo del gorrión* [The Sign of the Swallow], and— much later, as befits a Castilian poet, by nature modest and retiring—one of his books. From that moment on I became a faithful reader of his work. The poets of his generation that I had read struck me as terrible, and for years I had chosen to ignore what was being written in Spanish poetry by those born after 1950, contenting myself with reading and rereading Pere Gimferrer, Leopoldo Panero, and a few others of the previous generation. But discovering Miguel Casado reconciled me to a certain extent with the poetry of my own generation, though it would be more accurate to say that it reconciled me with *one* poet of my generation; in any case a friendship grew up between us, and Miguel's collections of poems became daily fare, the kind of books that once read are left somewhere around the house near at hand and that one takes to the movies or the bathroom, rereading one or two poems at random, and whose ability to inspire discomfort, reflection, and aesthetic pleasure doesn't wane as time goes by. The three books of his that I own (*Inventario* [Inventory], published by Hiperión, and *Falso movimiento* [False Move] and *La mujer automática* [The Automatic Woman], both Cátedra), were dedicated succinctly to Olvido. I didn't know back then that Olvido was Olvido García Valdés, considered by many to be the best Spanish woman poet of the twentieth century, which sounds extreme, but isn't so much if one considers the scarcity of female voices in twentieth-century Spanish poetry. Anyway, that was my baggage before traveling to Toledo to spend a few days there. I had read Miguel in a conscientious way and each reading had brought him closer to me. I hadn't read Olvido (although I did know her by name long before I met Miguel) and what people told me about her was wild and even terrifying. There were those who compared her to Santa Teresa, others who said that she was too serious, even gruff, and those who claimed that even her friends were stunned by her arrogance. I looked for a picture of her. I found one in which she appeared with a group of writers, but it was blurry. In another, published in a poetry journal, she was surrounded by old men, poets of Madrid, like in the Poussin painting *Susanna and the Elders*. Finally I went to a bookstore in Barcelona and looked for one of her books, but they told me that the most recent ones had sold out and there was no picture of her in the only one they had. So we left for Toledo with no face for Olvido García Valdés. What we finally discovered exceeded all our expectations. In a single day, hand in hand with Miguel, but especially hand in hand with Olvido, we saw *all* the synagogues, mosques, and cathedrals of Toledo. We lunched and dined opulently. At the first toy store we passed, Olvido bought my son three toys.

My son, naturally, fell in love with her. And continuing on in the same Rabelaisian vein, that night, after showering, I read straight through *Ella, los pájaros* [*She, the Birds*], a collection of poems by Olvido that dazzled me as only true poetry can dazzle. Much later, when I was back in Blanes and far from Toledo, I read *Caza nocturna* [Night Hunt], her most recent book (Ave del Paraíso, 1997), and my admiration for her grew even more, if possible. We have almost nothing in common. The poets she likes I don't like, and vice versa.

ROBERTO BRODSKY

New Chilean fiction, which is hardly new and sometimes hardly fiction, has just gained a new practitioner: Roberto Brodsky, a Chilean born in 1957, who in this first novel delves confidently into horror's forgotten corners. The novel is called *El peor de los héroes* [The Worst of Heroes] (Alfaguara, 1999) and its subject, or one of its subjects, is sadness in the face of the irrevocable, though it can also be read as an existential adventure story. The protagonist, lawyer Bruno Marconi, recalls Chile's recent history as he tries to piece together a contemporary picture in his memory and the reader's mind: that of bodies piled in a refrigerator like a shipment of frozen chicken, which Marconi discovers by chance. Roberto Brodsky, in addition to being from the same country as me and sharing the same name, is my friend, and sometimes I ask myself how often he's been on the verge of death, in what strange way he isn't also the "worst of heroes." When he was a boy, fishing on a deserted beach, he got his hand caught in the rocks. Then the tide began to rise and no matter how hard he pulled he couldn't get it loose. When he told me this story I imagined he was making it up, but deep down I knew it was true. I also imagined that Brodsky the boy had died and I was talking to a ghost. At the last minute, of course, a fisherman appeared who dove down and freed his hand from the rocks. A few months ago Brodsky was at my house in Blanes with Paula, his wife, and his incorrigible son, Pascual. *El peor de los heroes* hadn't come out yet. We talked about sadness and bravery, two constants in his novel, and I think sadness won. We talked about laughter, which follows Brodsky the way other people are followed by dogs. We talked about likely and unlikely adventures and we agreed that the two were one and the same.

JULY STORIES

July has been a strange month. The other day I went to the beach and I saw a woman of about thirty, pretty, wearing a black bikini, who was reading standing up. At first I thought she was about to lie down on her towel, but when I looked again she was still standing, and after that I didn't take my eyes off her. For two hours, more or less, she read standing up, walked over to the water, didn't go in, let the waves lap her shins, went back to her spot, kept reading, occasionally put the book down while still standing, leaned over a few times and took a big bottle of Pepsi out of a bag and drank, then picked up the book again, and, finally, without ever bending a knee, put her things away and left. Earlier the same day, I saw three girls, all in thongs, gorgeous, one of them had a tattoo on one buttock, they were having a lively conversation, and every once in a while they got in the water and swam and then they would lie down again on their mats, basically a completely normal scene, until all of a sudden a cell phone rang, I heard it and thought it was mine until I realized it had been a while since I had a cell phone, and then I knew the phone belonged to one of them. I heard them talking. All I can say is that they weren't speaking Catalan or Spanish. But they sounded deadly serious. Then I watched two of them get up, like zombies, and walk toward some rocks. I got up too and pretended to brush the sand off my trunks. On the rocks, I watched them talk to a huge, hideously ugly man covered in hair, in fact one of the hairiest men I've ever seen in my life. They knelt before him and listened attentively without saying a word, and then they went back to where their friend was waiting for them and everything went on as before, as if nothing had happened. Who are these women? I asked myself once it was dark and I had showered and dressed. One drank Pepsi. The others bowed down to a bear. I know who they are. But I don't really know.

A.G. PORTA

There's a new novel out (*Braudel por Braudel [Braudel by Braudel]*, El Acantilado) by my friend A.G. Porta, whom I've known since his son was practically an infant and now the kid is twenty-one or twenty-two, a film student, and is taller than his father and taller than me, too. I remember that I met A. G. Porta in 1978, at the offices of a fringe Barcelona publishing house that only published poetry and that resignedly called itself La Cloaca, or The Sewer. It wasn't a great start, but for us—poets at the time and the foosball champions of Barcelona's fifth district—it was at least a promising start. I'll never forget that when I didn't have a cent my friend would show up at my apartment on Calle Tallers with yogurt and cigarettes, sensible gifts. Then the years went by. I left for Girona and later Blanes, and A. G. Porta stayed in Barcelona. But my first novel is also his first novel, for the simple reason that we co-wrote it. Its title: *Consejos de un discipulo de Morrison a un fanático de Joyce* [Advice from a Morrison Disciple to a Joyce Fanatic]. Many times I've been asked which of us was the Morrison disciple and which of us was the Joyce fanatic. A. G. Porta, clearly, was the Joyce fanatic. He'd read everything by Joyce and in fact his subsequent long silence is in some way a product of his reading. I remember that for many years he wrote or collected random sentences from *Ulysses* with which he assembled poems that he called readymades, à la Duchamp. Some were very good. Now, at last, he's written another novel. *Braudel por Braudel* is about life, about the flow of life, about appearances, about deceit, and about happiness. His writing is as clear as a Hockney painting. Whoever picks up the novel won't be able to put it down until the last page.

FRIENDS ARE STRANGE

One is prepared for friendship, not for friends. And sometimes not even for friendship, but at least we try: usually we flail in the darkness, a darkness that's not foreign to us, a darkness that comes from inside us and meshes with a purely external reality, with the darkness of certain gestures, certain shadows that we once thought were familiar and that in fact are as strange as a dinosaur.

Sometimes that's what a friend is: the distant shape of a dinosaur crossing a swamp, a dinosaur that we can't grab or call or warn of anything. Friends are strange: they disappear. They're very strange: sometimes, after many years, they turn up again and although most have nothing to say to us anymore, some do, and they say it.

Recently I had the rare privilege of seeing an old friend again. I met him in Chile, in 1973, and I saw him again last year. After the usual niceties, my friend launched into his story, telling it to my wife and me. It was a story full of danger, adventure, prisons, bloodshed. At a certain moment he recalled a night on which two kids dodged the bullets of a night patrol, leaping through the yards of a suburban neighborhood. My wife was listening carefully. I started to listen carefully too. It didn't sound real. One of those kids was my friend. When I asked him who the other one was, he said: Don't you remember? No, I didn't remember. The other one was you, he said. At first I didn't believe him. That night had been erased from my memory. But later I remembered and it was then that I saw the dinosaur or the shadow of the dinosaur slipping across the swamp with every gun in the world pointed at its head.

PLANES

The other day I was on my way back from America and it was night and the plane was over Brazil, I guess, and everyone or almost everyone was asleep; the plane was flying with the cabin lights dimmed and there was a movie on the TV, a comedy, I think, that played silently except for the insomniacs, except for the fanatic omnivores of film, when suddenly a voice came over the speakers and told us to fasten our seatbelts and then a stewardess who only spoke English hurried down the aisle waking us and telling us to put on our seatbelts, and the seatbelt lights came on, ordering us to fasten our seatbelts and not to unfasten them until further notice. And we did as we were told, and the plane entered a patch of turbulence that didn't wake us up although in our dreams we felt the creaking of the plane, the vibrating, as if another dream had invaded our dream or as if we were sick in the middle of the dream (inside the dream) and that was all there was to it. But then the plane shuddered all along its length and we began to drop.

My wife, one of the insomniacs, clutched our son and me. I woke up just when all the plane's lights (already dim) went off, including the TV and its movie. I woke up and it was dark and there were screams in the dark. The plane was dropping at an impressive speed, although the word impressive is meaningless here. The sense I had, huddled with my wife and son, was of *reality.* A dense, heavy, irrevocable reality. There was nothing fake. No lights, no movies, no stewardesses telling us what to do. Cries and whimpers, yes. An old sense of reality familiar to all human beings. Then, ten seconds later, the plane leveled out. Some people went back to sleep. Others asked for whiskey. One of the passengers claimed to have seen a stewardess praying on her knees in the kitchen.

DIMAS LUNA, PRINCE

Just now I was talking to a prince. His name is Dimas Luna, but his friends sometimes call him Dimas Moon. I think he's descended from popes, although his lineage can be traced not to Valencian lands but to the dry plains of Toledo. It hardly matters: he carries in his blood the benignity of a certain long-lost Vatican and it shows in the way he treats others, whether friends, customers, or employees. Meanwhile, his curiosity is boundless: as far as I know he never went to college, and during the radiant summers of Blanes he speaks more than four languages. Now, with the arrival of Russian tourism, he even attempts a few words in the language of Pushkin, who would doubtless roll over in his grave if he heard him. His guardian angel is the Mediterranean. His great love, the movies. For a while he invented the strangest cocktails. I think he even won first prize at a competition in Lloret de Mar with a combination that included vodka, milk, and some sweet liqueur, plus other purely decorative things that I can't remember. With Dimas Luna in Blanes I know that no one will ever be completely alone. The spirit of the Spanish tavernkeeper lives on in him unchanged: he came to the world to have fun, to do good, and not to give anybody a hard time.

ANA MARÍA NAVALES

I knew a few things about Ana María Navales. I knew she was a poet, I'd read a few of her poems somewhere, and I knew that she enthusiastically and successfully edited the Aragón literary journal *Turia*. A while ago two books of hers came into my hands: *El laberinto del quetzal* [The Labyrinth of the Quetzal], published by Calima Ediciones in 1997, and *Cuentos de Bloomsbury* [Bloomsbury Stories] (Calambur, 1999, though there is a previous edition). *El laberinto del quetzal* is a novel and I haven't read it yet. The *Cuentos de Bloomsbury* are stories that revolve around the eponymous English group, and appearing in them are, of course, Virginia and Leonard Woolf, Lytton Strachey, Dora Carrington, Lady Ottoline Morrell, Virginia's sister Vanessa Bell, the extraordinary Katherine Mansfield, the disturbing and lovely Vita Sackville-West, but also other figures, lesser known or—at least to me—scarcely known at all, like Ethel Smyth, suffragette, or Mark Gertler, painter, or Richard Kennedy, apprentice printer. Clearly, Ana María Navales knows everything there is to know about her subject or subjects. At no point do her stories seem ventriloquized or threaten to become funeral rites. They are elegant and perceptive. She's bold enough to write in the first person, even when that first person is the voice of Virginia Woolf, and the result is first-rate and often unsettling. These are, as might be expected, stories in which literature and art have an important place. But they are also texts that radiate a deep love of life and freedom. Special mention must be made of the story "Mi corazón está contigo" [My Heart Is With You], a cruel and unflinching tale in the innocent guise of a letter written by Virgina Woolf to the now aging suffragette and feminist Ethel Smyth.

HELL'S ANGELS

A long time ago, in 1966, the American journalist Hunter S. Thompson wrote a book about the Hell's Angels, the West Coast motorcycle gang, in which perplexed readers learned about some of the peculiarities of that most violent of urban tribes. The Hell's Angels traveled the country on Harleys, drinking huge quantities of beer and getting into fights that today seem more picturesque than bloody, although some of their skirmishes were probably bloody too, the enactment of an aesthetic born out of the mythology of Westerns, out of the legend of desperadoes who, in unison, chose freedom and excess, white proletarian kids, macho and racist, uneducated and underemployed, perhaps the future members of the Aryan brotherhoods that sprang up in the prisons of the United States when the dream of the Angels, the endless highway, perished of its own inanity. Thompson lived with them for a few schizophrenic and exhausting months, and the result is this wild book (wild like all his books, since Thompson was, incidentally, always wilder than the Angels). Eminently readable even thirty years later, it lets us relive the Dionysian gang's parties in the California of the beatniks and the first hippies, the orgies and the crude sexual commerce in which the Angels were experts, the police raids, and the vain and naïve attempts of Allen Ginsberg to ideologically redirect the cold-blooded gang. What became of the Hell's Angels? There are still some on the West Coast but they don't scare anybody. Their fame is just another Hollywood souvenir. Any gang of Chicanos or black kids (once so despised by the swastika-blazoned motor-cyclists) could wipe them out in a single night.

THE GHOST OF ÀNGEL PLANELLS

Some winter afternoons in the center of Blanes one can glimpse the ghost of Àngel Planells. He appears to be on his way from the house of his nonagenarian sisters to the house of his nephew, the pastry cook Joan Planells, who today owns perhaps the largest collection of his works. Sometimes I stop by Joan's pastry shop, and we talk about his uncle. A while ago he showed me a photograph of the first surrealist exhibi-tion in London in 1936, at the New Burlington Galleries: in it you can see a small painting by Àngel Planells. The surrealist exhibition of London—Picasso, Domínguez, Dalí, and Miró were among the Spaniards shown—was a landmark in the revolutionary activities of a group that tried to export subver-sion on a worldwide scale. Later, for Planells, would come the Civil War and long years of obscurity during which, in order to survive, he had to paint horrible still lifes and give painting classes in a Barcelona where compassion was just an empty word in the mouths of priests and church ladies—hell's caul-dron. What did Planells learn in those years? We'll never know. Maybe he perfected the art of humility. Maybe he learned the vanity of all striving. During the summers, however, he came up to Blanes and spent his time writing and painting at his sisters' house. Little by little, at a time when surrealism had gone back underground, he turned to his old subject matter. This melancholy return is evidenced by the canvas *Mariner esperant l'arribada de no sap què* [Sailor Awaiting the Arrival of Something Unknown], dated 1974. It's possible that at some point I crossed paths with him on the streets of downtown Blanes and didn't see him. Now I do. Now sometimes I see him walking along our Paseo Marítimo. A slip of a ghost, lost in thought. The painter Àngel Planells, 1901 - 1989.

BLANES CHRISTMAS STORY

In the winter, some of the towns on the Costa Brava are like ghost towns. The tourist areas, especially, lapse into a lethargy that makes them resemble the cities of dreams or nightmares: cities of tall buildings and small apartments where we make the kinds of mistakes we regret forever, not knowing exactly why, just vaguely sensing that we could have done better, or simply not done anything at all, not made the effort, like the battles that Sun-Tzu or Clausewitz advised should never be fought. In fact, S-T or C advised that the only battles we should fight were battles that could definitely be won. The other day, strolling through one of those clusters of empty apartment blocks, I thought I saw a friend. He was coming out of a ghost building built in the sixties and probably afflicted with aluminosis, and he was dressed up as one of the Three Kings. Despite the Magi costume and the fast-approaching darkness, I recognized him and waved. He, however, was slow to recognize me. It had been a long time since we saw each other. He was accompanied, as might be expected, by the other two Kings. With some surprise, I discovered that both were black. My friend introduced them to me. They were two Gambians who usually worked in the fields outside of Blanes and who were for the moment unemployed. I only needed one black guy, he said, but I couldn't find anyone white to be

Caspar. We were the only people on that completely deserted street. So what are you doing here? I asked. I live in one of these apartments, said my friend. This is where I keep the robes, where we change. I gave them a ride. What will happen if a kid tells you there's one black guy too many and one white guy too few? I asked before they got out of the car. My friend laughed and said that times change. And the kids are the first to know it.

II.
(MAY 1999–JULY 2001)

AN AFTERNOON WITH HUIDOBRO AND PARRA

Soon it will be two years since my friend Marcial Cortés-Monroy brought me to Las Cruces, where we had lunch and spent the afternoon with Nicanor Parra. The author of *Poems and Antipoems*, originally published in 1954, has a house there on a steep hillside from which one can gaze out at the vast sea and also at the grave of Vicente Huidobro, on the other side of the bay. Actually, to see Huidobro's grave from Parra's wooden terrace, it helps to have binoculars, but even without them the grave of the author of *Altazor* is fully visible or at least as visible as Huidobro would have wanted.

Do you see that forest? asks Parra. Yes, I do. Which one? asks Parra, who not for nothing used to be a teacher. The one up above or down below? The one on the left or on the right? I see them all, I say, as I stare out at a vaguely lunar landscape. All right, look at the forest on the left, says Parra. Beneath it there's a kind of road. Like a line, but it's not a line, it's a road. See it? Now look up and you'll see the forest. He's right: I see a scratch that must be the highway or a country road, and I also see the forest. In the upper part of the forest there's a white spot, says Parra. It's true: the forest, seen from his terrace, is a dark green color, almost black, its uniformity broken by a white spot near the top edge. I see the spot, I say. That's Huidobro's grave, says Parra, and he turns and goes back into the living room. Marcial follows him and for an instant I'm left there alone as a gust of wind blows up from the beach, staring at the tiny white spot where the bones of Vicente Huidobro lie rotting.

Then I feel something tug at my pants leg. Huidobro's ghost? No, it's Parra's cats, six or seven stray cats that come every afternoon to the yard of the greatest living poet in the Spanish language to be fed. Like me, basically.

LICHTENBERG IN THE FACE OF DEATH

Lichtenberg is our philosopher. Sometimes it's tempting to say that he's our only philosopher, but there's also Pascal, who died of pancreatitis, and Diogenes, who was a first-class joker. And yet we (and frankly, when I say "we," I don't know what I'm talking about) find consolation in Lichtenberg, in his mirrors, in his mood swings, in his doubts and in his tastes, which sometimes amount to the same thing.

A little more than two hundred years ago the sage of the venerable city of Göttingen wrote the following: "On the night of February 9, 1799, I dreamed that while on a journey I was eating at an inn, or rather a roadside shack, where they were playing dice. Sitting across from me was a fresh-faced young man who seemed a bit dissipated and who, without paying any attention to the people around him, whether seated or standing, was eating his soup; nonetheless, he tossed every second or third spoonful into the air, caught it again in his spoon, and swallowed it calmly. What I find so singular about this dream is that it inspired my *habitual* remark: that such things cannot be invented, only seen (by which I mean that no novelist would ever have come up with the idea); and yet I had just invented it myself. At the table where they were playing dice, a tall, thin woman sat knitting. I asked her what could be won at this game, and she answered: *Nothing!* When I asked her whether anything could be lost, she said: *No!* The game struck me as very important."

This passage—must it be said?—foreshadows Kafka and much of twentieth-century literature. It also sums up the Enlightenment, and upon it a culture could be founded. It anticipates the philosopher's own death, on February 24 or fourteen days after the dream, as if death had paid Lichtenberg a visit two weeks before their final encounter. And how does our philosopher respond when visited by the withered old crone? He responds with humor and curiosity, the two most important components of intelligence.

SERGIO PITOL

For a few months now, *Tríptico del Carnaval* [Carnival Triptych] (Anagrama), a three-volume set by the enigmatic and often unclassifiable Mexican writer Sergio Pitol, has been in bookstores. Why enigmatic? Because Pitol—unlike Carlos Fuentes and others writers of his generation who enjoyed the fruits of the Boom—always held himself a little apart, whether in terms of his work, unsurpassed in Mexico and on a par with that of a select few in the Spanish language, or his reading habits: one mustn't forget that we owe Pitol the translation of a memorable novel by Jerzy Andrzejewski, *The Gates of Paradise*, and his always astute readings of Witold Gombrowicz.

His remoteness, punctuated by multiple trips and global wanderings, or his presence, suddenly revealed to us as absence, has yielded a figure that, while admired by the few of us fortunate enough to boast of a close acquaintance with his work, is at the same time unfamiliar to most, a giant shadow acknowledged to possess certain merits but avoided like a hedgehog in the middle of the road. And yet, in my opinion Pito is superior to Salvador Elizondo or García Ponce, for example, two Mexican novelists who also scarcely register on most people's lists.

Tríptico del Carnaval comprises *El desfile del amor* [The Parade of Love] (awarded the Premio Herralde in 1984), a vast Mexican labyrinth that continually reconstructs itself as a crime novel and as historic impossibility; *Domar a la divina garza [Taming the Sacred Heron]*, a glimpse of hell and a display of the Pitolian sense of humor; and *La vida conyugal* [Conjugal Life], a reflection on reality and writing that's also not lacking in humor—like all of Pitol's work, incidentally.

It goes without saying but it must be said: Pitol, who is now sixty-six, continues to be a rebel and a brave man.

THE INCREDIBLE CÉSAR AIRA

If there's currently a writer who defies all classification that writer is César Aira, from Coronel Pringles, Argentina, a city in the province of Buenos Aires that I have no choice but to accept as real, though it sounds invented by Aira, its most illustrious son, an exceptionally perceptive chronicler of mothers (a verbal mystery) and fathers (a geometric certainty), and a man whose position in contemporary literature in Spanish is as complicated as the position of Macedonio Fernández was at the turn of the century.

To begin with, it must be said that Aira has written one of the five best stories I can remember. It's called "Cecil Taylor" and it's collected in an anthology of Argentine literature edited by Juan Forn. Aira is also the author of four memorable novels: *How I Became A Nun*, which tells the story of his childhood; *Ema, la cautiva* [Emma the Captive], which describes the luxury of the Indians of the pampa; *The Literary Conference*, which recounts an attempt to clone Carlos Fuentes; and *El llanto* [The Weeping], which retails a kind of epiphany or insomnia.

Of course, these aren't his only novels. I'm told that Aira writes no fewer than two books a year, books that are sometimes published by the small Argentine publishing house Beatriz Viterbo, named after the Borges character in "The Aleph." The few books that I've been able to find were published by Mondadori and Tusquets Argentina. It's too bad, because once you've read Aira, you don't want to stop. His novels are like stagings of Gombrowicz's theories, with one fundamental difference: the Pole was the abbot of some plush imaginary monastery, whereas Aira is a nun or novice of the Discalced Sisters of the Word. Sometimes he's reminiscent of Roussel (a Roussel on his knees in the red tub), but the only contemporary writer to whom he can be compared is the Barcelonan Enrique Vila-Matas.

Aira is an eccentric, but he's also one of the three or four best Spanish-language writers alive today.

A new story collection by the Mexican writer Juan Villoro, *La casa pierde* [The House Loses] (Alfaguara), has just hit the shelves of bookstores in Spain, ten excellent stories invested with Villoro's rare power not to look into the abyss but to teeter for a long time on its brink, to teeter and thereby make us, his readers, teeter, in a kind of half-sleep or perhaps a state of heightened clarity.

The first time I met Villoro was at the Universidad Autonoma of Mexico, at an awards ceremony. He had received second prize for a short story and I had received third prize for poetry. Villoro was sixteen or seventeen and I was three years older. My memories of that day are mostly hazy. I remember a tall, eager adolescent. I don't know whether back then he had a beard yet or not, maybe not, although in my mind I see him with a beard, talking to me for a few minutes, neither of us paying much attention to the other, neither of us contemplating the future, a future that was beginning to open up before us, though not like a curtain parting or like a sudden vision but like a metal garage door that rises with a clatter, neither cleanly nor harmoniously. This is it. This is what you've been allotted. But we didn't know that and we talked about the kinds of things young writers talk about. Then more than twenty years went by and not long ago I saw him again. He's a little taller than he was then, I think, and maybe a little thinner. His stories are much better than they were then; in fact his stories are some of the best written in Spanish today, comparable only to those of the Guatemalan Rodrigo Rey Rosa.

But that isn't the important thing, I realize, as I watch Villoro gaze at the Mediterranean. Is the important thing that we're still alive? No, though that counts for something. The important thing is that we have our memories. The important thing is that we can still laugh and not splatter anyone with blood. The important thing is that we're still standing and we haven't become cowards or cannibals.

HANNIBAL, BY THOMAS HARRIS

Strange, this novel. It's a bestseller, intended for a mass audience, but I wish most contemporary novelists wrote this well. Thomas Harris has read the classics of English literature. Dickens, Stevenson, Jane Austen, the Brontë sisters. And he knows how to pace a story. He isn't a great novelist. He's a craftsman, but every once in a while it's nice to read someone who can tackle something long without boring us to death before we get to page fifty. And Hannibal Lecter is a great character. With lapses, purple passages, even soft spots, but ultimately a great character. His views on crime are chaotic. There's no rhyme or reason to them. But his views on pain and the brevity of life can be magnificent, and they make him a virtuous hero. The secondary characters are at once believable and implausible: in other words, they're literature. Like ambitious Inspector Pazzi of the Florence Questura, whose fate is anticipated in a Renaissance fresco; or like Carlo, the Sardinian kidnapper who's always chewing on a deer tooth and who smells like a pigsty; or like Deputy Mogli, gray-haired and corrupt and also brave in his own way; or like Barney, the black nurse and autodidact, a brilliant character who gives us a fuller sense if not of the literature that Harris has stored in his head then of the books from which he has profited and his capacity for observation: the relationship between Barney and Mason Verger's lesbian sister is sketched with the delicacy and clarity of Vermeer—whose paintings, scattered in museums around the world, Barney wants to see in person at least once in his life. Not to mention Agent Starling, who will always look like Jodie Foster to us, but who in Harris's dreams is probably prettier than Jodie Foster; or like Mason Verger, millionaire, pederast, martyr, and arch-villain, the only one of Lecter's victims who survives. At once Lecter's nemesis and the flip side of the same coin.

MIGUEL CASADO: POET

Miguel Casado, born in 1954, a high school teacher in Toledo, Spain, is one of my favorite poets. A while ago he sent me a poem and a letter. With some trepidation, I've finally decided to send you this, he wrote. Then he told me that it was his first poem in a long time. As if he'd forgotten how to write poetry, which isn't true, though it is a difficult art, and some poets do forget or repeat themselves, or, even worse, repeat other poets. Not Casado. His untitled poem is about a trip from Toledo to Madrid to Málaga, first by bus, then by train, the parched landscape, the Madrid metro where the poet is passed by a black father and son speaking Spanish, the long line of old men who enter a public toilet one by one. All of this takes place as the traveler recalls a conversation he'd had the night before with a friend who'd flown across the Atlantic, and the plane, according to the poet's friend, went down and the passengers started to scream in the dark, and reality thickened and thus became more real or maybe more true. At some point, the poem mentions a child crying. Elsewhere, the poet gazes out the window of the train on the outskirts of Córdoba, where it's not sunny either. He says: The trip languishes as if all around it a void had been created. Toward the end, Norman O. Brown is quoted: "Democracy has no monuments. It strikes no medallions. It does not bear the head of a man on its coins. Its true essence is iconoclasm." The dream, Casado tells us, is collective, even when it's impossible to say who's dreaming. Then the train halts to switch tracks, and just there, before it reaches its geographic terminus but having long since reached its creative destination, the poem stops.

THE RAPIER-SHARP PEN OF RODRIGO REY ROSA

I'm an assiduous reader of Rey Rosa, a Guatemalan writer born in 1958 and a tireless traveler through the deserts of Africa and the villages of India when he's not visiting liquid apartments, at once strange and familiar. A while ago I reread his last collection, *Ningún lugar sagrado* [No Sacred Place] (Seix Barral, 1998), set mostly in New York City, where Rey Rosa has lived at different times in his life. It's a book of short stories, of which Rey Rosa is the consummate master, the best of my generation, which happens to include many excellent short-story writers.

Rey Rosa's prose is methodical and judicious. He doesn't scorn an occasional flick of the whip—or rather, the distant crack of a whip we never see—or the use of camouflage. Rather than a master of endurance, he's a shadow, a ray of lightning shooting across the space of normality. His elegance never detracts from his precision. To read him is to learn how to write and also an invitation to the pure delight of letting oneself be carried away by uncanny or fantastic stories. Until recently he lived in Guatemala and he didn't have his own house: one day he would stay with his mother, another day with his sister, the rest of the time at friends' houses. One night we talked on the phone for almost two hours: he'd just gotten back from Mali. Now he's in India, writing a book that he doesn't know whether he'll finish or not. That's how I like to imagine him:

with no fixed address, fearless, checking in to cheap hotels, sitting at bus stations in the tropics or in chaotic airports with his laptop or a blue notebook into which his curiosity—his entomologist's boldness—calmly unspools.

To some, this prose—especially that of the stories of *Ningún lugar sagrado*—seems cold, and it probably is: a giant freezer room where words pop, alive, reborn. And then one can't help but think about the terror unleashed in Guatemala, the depravity and the bloodshed. And one thinks about Miguel Ángel Asturias, Augusto Monterroso, and now Rodrigo Rey Rosa, three giant writers from a small, unhappy country. And the vision that lingers in the mirror is terrible, and it's alive.

OSVALDO LAMBORGHINI: MARTYR

There are books that inspire fear. Real fear. More than books they seem like time bombs or like taxidermied animals that'll go for your throat when you're not looking. This is a fear I've known only twice. The first time was long ago, in 1977 or 1978; I was reading a novella in which, on a certain page, the reader is warned that he could die at any moment. That is, he could die literally, fall to the floor and not get up. The novella was *La asesina ilustrada* [The Enlightened Assassin] by Enrique Vila-Matas, and as far as I know none of its readers died on the spot although many of us emerged transformed from our reading of it, conscious that something had changed forever in our relationship with literature. Along with *Los dominios del lobo* [The Wolf's Haunts], Javier Marías's first novel, *La asesina ilustrada,* marks the departure point for our generation.

The second novel that's truly frightened me (and this time the fear is much stronger, because it involves pain and humiliation instead of death) is *Tadeys*, the posthumous novel by

Osvaldo Lamborghini. There is no crueller book. I started to read it with enthusiasm—an enthusiasm heightened by Lamborghini's original prose (with its sentences like something out of Flemish painting and a kind of improbable Argentine or Central European pop art) and guided as well by my admiration for César Aira, Lamborghini's disciple and literary executor as well as the author of the prologue to this unclassifiable novel—and my enthusiasm or innocence as a reader was throttled by the picture of terror that awaited me. There's no question that it's the most brutal book (that's the best adjective I can come up with) that I've read in Spanish in this waning century. It's incredible, a writer's dream, but it's impossible to read more than twenty pages at a time, unless one wants to contract an incurable illness. Naturally, I haven't finished *Tadeys*, and I'll probably die without finishing it. But I'm not giving up. Every once in a while I feel brave and I read a page. On exceptional nights I can read two.

SARA AND STEVA

I've just read a book, *Art i conjuntura* [Art and Conjuncture] (Di7 edició), whose subtitle, "La jove plàstica a Mallorca 1970-1978," [Young Mallorcan Artists 1970-1978] immediately establishes the ground that its author, Jaume Reus Morro, will cover. What ground is this? At first glance, it's the terrain of nostalgia or the history of art, a discipline that often bears a strong resemblance to entomology, but as the reader turns the pages he finds there's more to it than that: youth's long march, its discontents, the fluctuations of taste, the wagers on radicalism that are almost always lost, among other reasons because the odds are winner-take-all and because the young makers of such wagers don't rig them.

In 1977, when I was new to Barcelona, I met one of those young Mallorcans at a café on the Gran Vía. His name was Steva Terrades and he was a brilliant and radical painter. Also, it goes without saying, he was generous and curious in a way that people could only be generous and curious in those days, in a Barcelona that was the incarnation of utopian spirit. Through him I met Sara Gibert, the only Barcelonan painter of the Mallorcan group Neón de Suro. Sara, tall and thin, unpredictable and capable, with her exacting sense of humor, was the perfect archetype of the woman-mirror or the woman-razor, ungraspable and somewhat lofty.

The two of them, Sara and Steva, introduced me to a world of painters: works by Miquel Barceló, Andreu Terrades (Steva's twin brother), Cabot, and Mariscal shone, among those by others whose names I've forgotten but who are scrupulously memorialized in this book. For me, the happiness of Barcelona, the energy and unhappiness of youth, are linked to them: to their works, their words, cold mornings in District 5, the figure of Lola Paniagua vanishing into the night, the clouds of Baudelaire.

MOSLEY

A little while ago I read the latest novel by Walter Mosley (*Gone Fishin'*, Anagrama), Bill Clinton's favorite thriller writer and the creator of the detective Easy Rawlins, a black man who isn't really a detective but simply a black American, or an African-American, as the politically correct would have it, who always has the losing hand and whose story Mosley has told over the course of six novels—two of them great or very close to great—which have so far covered a long stretch of twentieth-century American history, from 1939 to the 1960s, with Easy growing older from novel to novel, and if in the first he's a World War II veteran, a young black man from Texas who learns to kill whites in Europe, in the latest he's a man who works hard and has only one real concern, his children. Because Easy Rawlins isn't really a detective, he's a smart guy who occasionally solves problems, searches for people who've disappeared, tries to clean up small-time messes that inevitably, a few pages in, become matters of life or death, problems that grow until they become unbearable, when the machinery of reality starts up and everything leads the reader to believe that this time Easy won't make it out alive, among other things because he's black and poor and there's no political or religious power behind him, because he's a man who can only rely on a certain amount of physical strength, decent intelligence, and nothing more. But Easy always finds his way out of the dead ends into which Mosley steers him. Bruised, battered, older and more cynical each time, he still escapes, like the protagonists of Chandler, Hammett, Jim Thompson, or Chester Himes. And his character's ability to survive is one of the main gifts that Mosley has given us. He's created the modern stoic. Or in other words, the classic stoic. With Easy Rawlins's desperate and unflinching vision, he's revitalized two genres, the hard-boiled novel and the American behaviorist novel.

BORGES AND THE RAVENS

I'm in Geneva and I'm looking for the cemetery where Borges is buried. It's a cold autumn morning, although to the east there's a glimpse of sun, a few rays that cheer the citizens of Geneva, a stubborn people of great democratic tradition. The

Plainpalais, the cemetery where Borges is buried, is the perfect cemetery: the kind of place to come every afternoon to read a book, sitting across from the grave of some government minister. It's really more like a park than a cemetery, an extremely manicured park, every inch well-tended. When I ask the keeper about Borges's grave, he looks down at the ground, nods, and tells me how to find it, not a word wasted. There's no way to get lost. From what he says it's clear that visitors are always coming and going. But this morning the cemetery is literally empty. And when I finally reach Borges's grave there's no one nearby. I think about Calderón, I think about the English and German Romantics, I think how strange life is, or, rather: I don't think anything at all. I just look at the grave, the stone inscribed with the name Jorge Luis Borges, the date of his birth, the date of his death, and a line of Old English verse. And then I sit on a bench facing the grave and a raven says something in a croak, a few steps from me. A raven! As if instead of being in Geneva I were in a poem by Poe. Only then do I realize that the cemetery is full of ravens, enormous black ravens that hop up on the gravestones or the branches of the old trees or run through the clipped grass of the Plainpalais. And then I feel like walking, looking at more graves, maybe if I'm lucky I'll find Calvin's, and that's what I do, growing more and more uneasy, with the ravens following me, always keeping within the bounds of the cemetery, although I suppose that one occasionally flies off and goes to stand on the banks of the Rhone or the shores of the lake to watch the swans and ducks, somewhat disdainfully, of course.

The other day I was at the beach and I thought I saw a dead body. I was sitting on one of the benches along Blanes's Paseo Marítimo, brushing the sand off my feet, waiting for my son to brush the sand off his feet so we could go home, when I thought I saw a body. I got up and looked again: an old woman was sitting under a beach umbrella reading a book and next to her was a man, the same age or maybe a few years older, in a tiny bathing suit, lying in the sun. This man's head was like a skull. I saw him and said to myself that he would soon be dead. And I realized that his old wife, reading peacefully, knew it too. She was sitting in a beach chair with a blue canvas back. A small but comfortable chair. He was stretched out on the sand, only his head in the shade. On his face I thought I glimpsed a frown of contentment, or maybe he was just sleeping while his wife read. He was very tan. Skeletal but tan. They were tourists from up north. Possibly German or English. Maybe Dutch or Belgian. It doesn't really matter. As the seconds went by, his face looked more and more skull-like. And only then did I realize how eagerly, how recklessly, he was exposing himself to the sun. He wasn't using sunscreen. And he knew he was dying and he was lying in the sun on purpose like a person saying goodbye to someone very dear. The old tourist was bidding farewell to the sun and to his own body and to his old wife sitting beside him. It was a sight to see, something to admire. It wasn't a dead body lying there on the sand, but a man. And what courage, what gallantry.

Barry Gifford, creator of Perdita Durango and Romeo Dolorosa, is known for his habit of giving his fictional characters catchy and colorful names, but in this book, *The Sinaloa Story* (Destino), the most recent of his novels to fall into my hands, he probably goes too far. The main character is called Ava Varazo, a name that instead of a palindrome hides a dark riddle. Her friend is DelRay Mudo. It's possible to find weird last names like these among the Mexicans living in the north of Mexico and the southern United States. Unlikely but possible. DelRay's father, however, is Duro Mudo, and here we head straight into the realm of madness. Ava Varazo's boss, a thug from the Texas-Mexico border, is Indio Desacato, Mr. Desacato to outsiders, Indio to his friends. The whorehouse madam is Santa Niña de las Putas and her saint day is celebrated "when there is a second full moon in the month on the final day of February in a leap year." A young messenger and flyweight amateur boxer is Framboyán Lanzar. There's another boxer called Danny Molasses, whom Lanzar calls Melaza, and another one called Chuy Chancho. Indio Desacato's bodyguard and factotum is a six-foot-seven, 380-pound former football player called Thankful Priest. The only goodhearted old man in town is called Arkadelphia Quantrill Smith, but his friends—in other words everybody—call him Arky. And so on, through more than fifty names.

What lies behind Gifford's taste for colorful last names? Many things: the loneliness of the border, that mythical territory between the United States and Mexico, and the loneliness of all men. The madness of parents who try to perpetuate themselves or to perpetuate something they don't understand but can sense. The desperate pride of possessing at least one thing that's unique and showing it off. Humorous portraits sketched of dust and wind.

For some of those of my generation, William Burroughs was the affectless man, the shard of ice that never melts, the eye that never closes. They say he possessed every vice there was, but I think he was a saint who attracted all the sinners in the world because he was gracious and unwise enough never to shut his door. Literature, his livelihood for the last thirty years, interested him, but not too much, and in that regard he was like other classic American figures who focused their efforts on observing life or on experience. When he talked about what he read one got the impression that he was remembering vague stretches of time in prison.

He was certainly familiar with prison, and his writing on the prison system in the United States might be some of the sharpest ever penned. He traveled all over the world: his vision of the planet is perhaps one of this century's bleakest. And he experimented with all kinds of drugs and escaped unscathed from fifteen years of heroin addiction.

His observations on certain hard drugs give him a kinship to the great chroniclers of hell, except that in Burroughs there's no moral or ethical motive, only the description of a frozen abyss, the description of an endless process of corruption. Language, he said, is a virus from outer space, in other words, a disease, and he spent his whole life trying to fight that disease.

He loved guns. He killed his wife while they were practicing their William Tell act in Mexico. He was a follower of Wilhelm Reich and he built orgone boxes in the shabby backyards of lost cities, to which (the cities and the boxes) he retreated like an Andromedan Dracula.

He had no liking at all for life on earth, or human life, and he would rather have been born on any other planet. A planet of spiders or giant insects. In the cover photograph of *My Education* (Península), he appears with a shotgun, and from the way he looks at us it's clear he's not afraid to use it. In his later years he played small roles in a number of films: *Drugstore Cowboy* was perhaps the most memorable.

NEUMAN, TOUCHED BY GRACE

Among young writers who've already published a first book, Neuman may be the youngest of all, and his precocity, which comes studded with lightning bolts and proclamations, isn't his greatest virtue. Born in Argentina in 1977, but raised in Andalusia, Andrés Neuman is the author of a book of poems, *Métodos de la noche* [Night Methods], published by Hiperión in 1998, and *Bariloche*, an excellent first novel that was a finalist for the most recent Herralde Prize.

The novel is about a trash collector in Buenos Aires who works jigsaw puzzles in his spare time. I happened to be on the prize committee and Neuman's novel at once enthralled—to use an early twentieth-century term—and hypnotized me. In it, good readers will find something that can be found only in great literature, the kind written by real poets, a literature that dares to venture into the dark with open eyes and that keeps its eyes open no matter what. In principle, this is the most difficult test (also the most difficult exercise and stretch) and on no few occasions Neuman pulls it off with frightening ease. Nothing in this novel sounds contrived: everything is real, everything is an illusion. The dream in which Demetrio Rota, the Buenos Aires trash collector, moves like a sleepwalker, is the dream of great literature, and its author serves it up in precise words and scenes. When I come across these young writers it makes me want to cry. I don't know what the future holds for them. I don't know whether a drunk driver will run them down some night or whether all of a sudden they'll stop writing. If nothing like that happens, the literature of the twenty-first century will belong to Neuman and a few of his blood brothers.

COURAGE

Everything there is to say about courage has already been said by the poet Archilochus, who lived in the seventh century BC. Of his tumultuous life little is known with certainty. He was born on the island of Paros and he was a mercenary and his inclinations may have been more Dionysian than Apollonian. "My ash spear is my barley bread, / My ash spear is my Ismarian wine. / I lean on my spear and drink,"* he wrote. There's little doubt that he took part in small battles, in countless skirmishes where glory shone by its absence, under the command of different lords. During one of these encounters, Archilochus himself tells us, he abandoned his shield and ran, which in that age was synonymous with shame and dishonor. And yet Archilochus tells or sings of his cowardice without the slightest blush: "Some Saian mountaineer / Struts today with my shield. / I threw it down by a bush and ran / When the fighting got hot. / Life seemed somehow more precious. / It was a beautiful shield. / I know where I can buy another / Exactly like it, just as round."

Far from Greece, and in a different age, another poet, Snorri Sturluson (1179-1241), who loved the valiant, also came face to face in a single night with fear and the true picture of valor: a field of bones that we all must cross. Courage takes

*All translations from Archilochus are by Guy Davenport, from *Archilochus, Sappho, Alkman: Three Lyric Poets of the Late Greek Bronze Age*, Univ. of California Press, 1980. —tr.

many forms. Sometimes it's a ghost that hovers over our heads. Sometimes it's a gleam to which we're irrationally faithful. For my generation the picture of courage is Billy the Kid, who gambled his life for money, and Che Guevara, who gambled it for generosity; Rimbaud, who walked alone at night, and Violeta Parra, who opened windows in the night. Courage is useless, we were told happily, carelessly, by the poet and Spanish soldier Alonso de Ercilla, the most generous of brave men and perhaps one of the most swiftly forgotten, but we can't live without it.

WILCOCK

Many years ago, when I lived in Gerona and was poor, or at least poorer than I am now, a friend loaned me the book *The Temple of Iconoclasts*, by J. Rodolfo Wilcock, published by Anagrama, Number 7 in the Panorama de Narrativas collection, which was just getting underway.

In those days I didn't have the money to buy books and everything I read was borrowed from the library (it was there that I discovered Tomeo, there that I read Liddell Hart and all the books I could find on the Napoleonic wars), although every once in a while some friend (always the same one, now that I think about it) would loan me a new novel, something that had just come out. This friend's name was Carles and he was a sportswriter, but he was sent books from Anagrama, why I don't remember, since of course he never reviewed a single one. Nor can I say that Carles was a fan of literature, which he in fact viewed with some distrust and perplexity, being on much surer ground, this friend of mine, in matters of local sports and even the crime beat, which he sometimes worked.

But he was a good person, and when I went to see him I always left with a book, which fifteen days later I religiously returned.

Thus it was that *The Temple of Iconoclasts* came into my hands, during a cold, wet winter, and I still remember the enormous pleasure it brought me, and the consolation, too, at a time when almost everything was full of sadness. Wilcock's book restored happiness to me, as is only the case with those masterpieces of literature that are also masterpieces of black humor, like Lichtenberg's *Aphorisms* or Sterne's *Tristram Shandy*. Of course, Wilcock's book tiptoed out of bookstores. Today, seventeen years later, it has just been reprinted. If you want to have a good time, if you want to cure what ails you, buy it, steal it, borrow it, but most importantly, read it.

PUIGDEVALL THE STRANGE

Among my friends, the strangest is Ponç Puigdevall. Sometimes I see him walking the winding streets of Gerona, completely oblivious of everything around him, and then I know he's mulling over the framework of a story, the secret mechanisms of structure, that jungle full of predatory beasts from which most writers flee and through which he strolls like Stewart Granger through the ruins of King Solomon's mines or like Edgar Allan Poe through the icy landscapes of Antarctica, or in other words in the calmest and most inscrutable fashion, and it's only because of this that Ponç sometimes fails to recognize or greet anyone while he's wandering the streets of Gerona, or if he does greet you it's in a mechanical way, as if he were seeing you in a dream or after many sleepless nights.

Cult writer, difficult writer, strange writer: Ponç's work is hard to classify. Sometimes I see him walking with his dog, who's called Book, and besides not being able to tell who's walking whom, I get the sense that both of them, the dog-book and the man-reader, are heading straight for the abyss or toward a similar accident with an indifference and elegance that I haven't encountered in any other Catalan writer or any other dog. This must be a consequence of the esteem I feel for Ponç, which, by the way, doesn't extend to the dog, who once growled at me in my own house and who, as his name suggests, is a somewhat overwrought animal. And yet I haven't known Ponç for long: three years, if that. Then why do I feel so close to him? It may be his fragility and his radicalism. Because Ponç, who writes like one possessed, hasn't received grants or assistance or anything: his books are the product of a vast storm-tossed library and of his intelligence and scrupulousness, not of a comfortable situation or prior agreements made with anyone. His devotion to literature might frighten some. Do I need to say that in my opinion he's one of the three or four best living Catalan writers, and that I feel honored to be his friend?

JAVIER CERCAS COMES HOME

I met Javier Cercas when he was seventeen. I was living in Gerona at the time, and he lived in Gerona too, and he was a kid who wanted to be a writer. He was a friend of Xavi Coromines, who introduced him to me. I don't know what happened to Coromines, whom I liked, but I do know, at least by hearsay, what happened to Cercas. After he graduated from college he spent a long time teaching in the United States, in the Midwest. He wrote a short novel, *El inquilino* [The Tenant], and a long one, *El vientre de la ballena* [The

Belly of the Whale]—the first published by Sirmio and the second by Tusquets—that got the attention of readers and especially of writers because of the glimpse the novels gave of an uncommonly talented writer; he also wrote a story collection and a collection of literary essays in which he expresses his irrational enthusiasm for John Irving, an enthusiasm that I don't share. One day he decided to return to Catalonia and he got a job teaching at the University of Gerona. But although he worked in Gerona, Cercas lived in Barcelona and made his life in Barcelona. When I saw him again he was married and had a son, Raulito, a fan of the Teletubbies. His life in those days was extreme, mostly because Cercas is essentially extreme, capable of uniting in himself the understated and the outlandish, rationalism and eccentricity. Now, at last, Cercas is back in Gerona. He's here to take it easy. Or at least that's the official explanation. Or so his wife and son can have a yard. Or to be closer to his job, so he isn't killed in a car accident. The truth is, I doubt all of these explanations. Cercas has come home to write the big books that are up there in his head. He's back home to become one of the best writers in the Spanish language. Only great challenges make it worthwhile to pack up and move all one's books.

NERUDA

I've just read, or reread, or randomly flipped through, the way you might skim your grandfather's business correspondence and love letters, the first volume of Pablo Neruda's *Obras completas* [Complete Works], (from *Crepusculario* to *Las uvas y el viento* [The Grapes and the Wind], 1923–1954), published by Galaxia Gutenberg–Círculo de Lectores in an excellent edition compiled by Hernán Loyola, a Chilean and top Neruda scholar, with the assistance of the Argentine poet Saúl Yurkievich.

The book, more than twelve hundred pages long, contains the main body of Neruda's work and includes the three volumes that, for different reasons, brought the poet worldwide fame: *Twenty Love Poems and a Song of Despair* (1923–1924), *Residence on Earth* (1925–1935), probably the greatest Neruda, and *Canto general* (1938–1949), an endless, repetitive Neruda, the place where Whitman's influence takes a crucial turn in Latin American poetry, a book in which extraordinary poems sit side by side with others that are clearly unsalvageable.

But in this first volume of the *Obras completas* readers will also find other, lesser known books, like *The Captain's Verses,* the love poems of a mature Neruda who embarks on a new love affair with characteristic abandon; or the poems of *Las uvas y el viento*, postcards from a man naively or stubbornly blind as he travels the length and breadth of the Soviet Union and notices nothing, absolutely nothing, belying the vaunted notion of a poet's instinct, because poets may sometimes be beggars or adventurers in their hearts, but most of the time they are courtesans; or *Tentativa del hombre infinito* [Venture of the Infinite Man], a young Neruda full of discoveries; or one of his least known books, *El habitante y su esperanza* [The Inhabitant and His Hope] from 1926, which Neruda calls a "novel," and which may very well be one, an interesting book, of poetic prose with one foot in modernism and the other in the avant-garde, a book of formal inventiveness and mannerisms, of weaknesses and taut gestures.

Pezoa Véliz is without a doubt the quintessential minor poet of the Chilean Parnassus and also one of the most mysterious, to begin with because of his last name, which some spell with a *z* and others with an *s*. Armando Donoso, one of the first experts on his work, although here the word *expert* is clearly an overstatement, introduces him by saying that he wasn't much of a poet, author of only three decent poems. Then he calls him a layabout, a more or less conscious plagiarist, a social climber, and an opportunist, although at the same time he spends more than two pages challenging the claim that he was a bastard or born out of wedlock, a charge that weighed heavily on the poet and that Armando Donoso relies on letters to clear up with more vigor than objectivity.

In the Chile of 1927, date of the publication of *Poesías y prosas completas* [Complete Poems and Prose] by Carlos Pezoa Vélis (Nascimiento, compiled and with an introduction by Armando Donoso, who, one gathers, was a somebody back then and today is a nobody) and nineteen years after the poet's death at the age of twenty-eight, whether he was or was not a bastard wasn't a trivial matter. And Donoso tackles the affair with an energy that today looks neurotic. Given historians of this caliber, it's almost better to be forgotten.

Nevertheless—and here Donoso doesn't err—certain facts are inescapable. Pezoa was poor all his life. He had a mother who was less a mother than a gypsy curse. His education was lacking. His poetry suffers from almost all the tics of modernism and possesses few of its virtues. His relationships with women were complicated. His relationship with society was impossible: in the end, Pezoa, like so many writers, simply wanted to get ahead, although to reach this point he had to go through stages as contradictory as anarchism, which seduced him, and bureaucracy, where he found peace of mind, a salary, basic sustenance, and some time to write. The stories that survive him are the kind that bring a person to tears: a Chile in black and white, as if the country had never existed. But he wrote more than three good poems (maybe six or seven), and one really good one, "Tarde en el hospital" [Afternoon in the Hospital], perhaps shortly before he died. And there he remains, in his hospital bed, melancholy Pezoa Véliz.

UNA CASA PARA SIEMPRE

When Enrique Vila-Matas's *Una casa para siempre* [A Home Forever] (Anagrama, 1988) was published, two critics blasted it. The first said it was a terrible novel. The second said it was the kind of book that should never have been written. By all indications, readers took the critics at their word, and the fate of the novel was sealed. Some years later, however, it was translated into French and was chosen, along with a novel by Javier Marías, as one of France's books of the year.

Today, when so much water has passed under the bridges of Spain and France, and when Vila-Matas's excellence is an undisputed fact, the fate of *Una casa para siempre* remains unchanged, though it's a book praised by writers like Rodrigo Fresán and Juan Villoro. The first edition, which has yet to sell out, is still on the shelves of some bookstores; the book, which is about ventriloquists and daily acts of subversion, still lives in the proud limbo of books marked by a fate not theirs, though they, the books, accept it with a courage some national heroes might envy.

What is Una casa para siempre? A tragedy and a comedy. An epiphany and a call to the guillotine. A Vila-Matas novel in its purest and most gracious state. The drama of a ventriloquist with a voice of his own, for some writers a virtue to be constantly yearned for and sought, but for the ventriloquist a curse, for obvious reasons. Style is a fraud, said De Kooning, and Vila-Matas agrees. To have a voice of one's own is a blessing, whether one is a writer, painter, or ventriloquist, but it can lead or perhaps in fact inevitably leads to conformism, flatness, monotony. Every work, Vila-Matas tells us, peering out at us from the pages of this book, should be a fresh leap into the void. Whether anyone is watching or not.

GRASS'S CENTURY

From a writer like Günter Grass, one expects a masterpiece even on his deathbed, though by all indications *My Century* (Alfaguara) will be only the second-to-last of his great books. It's a collection of short stories, one for each year of the century now behind us, in which the great German writer examines the frequently tortured fate of his country. From the first soccer teams to World War I, from the economic crisis of the twenties to the rise of Nazism, from World War II and the concentration camps to the German Miracle, from the post-war period to the fall of the Berlin Wall, everything has a place in this book, which manages to seem short though it's more than four hundred pages long, perhaps because the succession of horrors, the succession of disasters, and the human instinct for survival despite everything make it feel that way: the century has exhaled.

The Grass of this book, of course, isn't the Grass of *The Tin Drum* or of *Dog Years* or *The Flounder*, to mention just three of his great and all-encompassing works. Here we have before us a crepuscular and fragmentary Grass, as merited by the occasion, and also a seemingly (though only seemingly) weary Grass, who embarks on the review of his German century, which is also the European century, with the conviction of having traversed an enduring piece of hell and also with the certainty, the old and maligned and magnificent certainty of the Enlightenment, that human beings deserve to be saved, even though often they aren't saved. We're exiting the twentieth century marked by fire. That's what Grass tells us. And he tells it in some wonderful stories, alive with humor and pain, written as if by a young man of thirty, full of energy and with a long life ahead of him.

THE RHAPSODE OF BLANES

Don Josep Ponsdomènech is eighty-eight and sometimes I see him sunning himself in the square next to the Joaquim Ruyra School, at noon, when I come to pick up my son. It's just a wayside stop for him, because Don Josep Ponsdomènech is tall and lean and he's always on the move, from the Plaza de Cataluña to the port, from the Avinguda de Dintre to the narrow streets of the town center, where the sun rarely shines. By trade he's a poet, a rhapsode, he says, and he's comfortable in the role, at peace with it. His pockets are full of paper on which he writes his daily poems in elegant copperplate. Some he writes just because, inspired by the muses; other times he writes to alleviate suffering or to quiet memories. But always he writes in a spirit of hope, convinced that poetry possesses healing powers. If a woman has lost her husband, for example, Don Josep Ponsdomènech writes her a poem that lauds the deceased while at the same time reminding the widow of the need to keep living. Even those who die utterly alone have their poems.

The rhapsode remembers everyone. No one pays him. His art is free. At some point Don Josep Ponsdomènech told me the story of his life: full of pleasures of every sort, he stresses, as well as misfortunes, intrinsic to existence, he sighs, and from all of it he's emerged unscathed and cooler than a cucumber. His favorite authors are definitely the modernists, Rubén Darío first among them, but I've also heard him express his admiration for Salvat-Papasseit, that brave young man, and so modern. Don Josep Ponsdomènech is brave too, of course, and, in his own way he was once modern, but his principal virtue, among the many with which he's graced, is the most human of all: happiness.

It's nice to live in Blanes and to know that on sunny days our rhapsode, well bundled up, is strolling the Paseo Marítimo and the heart of the town.

A SOUL SOLD TO THE DEVIL

Norberto Fuentes, the author of *Condenados de Condado* [The Condemned of Condado], in a number of ways a memorable book, has sold his soul to the devil. Norberto Fuentes is Cuban. He lives in the United States now, but not so long ago he lived in Havana, where one can imagine he walked the streets with a lordly air. His most recent book, *Dulces guerreros cubanos* [Sweet Cuban Warriors], is just out from Seix Barral, and in it he appears to tell the story of his friendship with General Ochoa and the De la Guardia brothers, that is, the men who were shot or locked up by the Cuban regime in 1989. Ochoa and the De la Guardias were men of the Cuban revolution, and Norberto Fuentes, in syncopated style, describes some of their adventures, as well as the adventures of many other characters with roles in the regime's military and political apparatus: from Fidel Castro to the countless bureaucrats who taped conversations.

Norberto Fuentes—and this is one of the oddities of the book—doesn't hide that he was a favored son of the revolution. He struts the streets of Havana wearing a Rolex, and tells us about the curious penchant of the top commanders for owning duplicates of everything: two Rolexes, two houses, two wives. He also discusses the prisons and wars of the regime, a regime that he defended with bellicose ardor until things turned ugly. It's as if Raúl Castro were to go into exile in Miami today and write a book lamenting the injustices committed by his brother during forty years of dictatorship. But Norberto Fuentes was once a writer of some talent, and his talent persists, barely a shadow of what it was or could have been, but it's still there. And it can be felt. He doesn't ask for forgiveness. He tries to justify himself. He adopts a cynical and nihilistic stance, but he doesn't ask for forgiveness. The Cuban revolution appears in his book as what it is: a gangster movie shot in the tropics. And in that movie Norberto Fuentes thinks he played an important role, when really he was just one of the big man's jesters, nothing more. In his American exile, Cuba's official Hemingway expert tries to write like Hemingway, but he doesn't manage it. The book is about indignity and shame and Fuentes's writing oozes indignity and shame. Parties and power are a distant memory. The drives around Havana in his tricked-out Lada are a distant memory.

Norberto Fuentes is no longer a writer, he's a lost soul.

THE ANCESTOR

We all have some idiot ancestor. All of us, at some point in our lives, discover the trace, the flickering vestige of our dimmest ancestor, and upon gazing at the elusive visage we realize, with astonishment, incredulity, horror, that we're staring at our own face winking and grinning at us from the bottom of a pit. This exercise tends to be depressing and wounding to our self-esteem, but it can also be extremely salutary. My idiot ancestor was called Bolano (Bolanus) and he appears in the first book of Horace's *Satires*, IX, in which Bolano accosts the poet as he walks along the Via Sacra. Says Horace: "Suddenly a fellow whom I knew only by name dashed up and seized me by the hand. 'My dear chap,' he said 'how are things?' 'Quite nicely at the moment thanks,' I said. 'Well, all the best!' He remained in pursuit, so I nipped in quickly: 'Was there something else?' 'Yes,' he said. 'You should get to know me. I'm an intellectual.' 'Good for you!' I said." What follows is a tiresome stroll for Horace, since he can't shake Bolano, who ceaselessly offers advice, praising his own work and even his talent for singing. When Horace asks if he has a mother or family to care for him, Bolano answers that he's buried them all and he's alone in the world. Lucky for them, thinks Horace. And he says: "That leaves me. So finish me off! A sinister doom is approaching which an old Sabine fortune-teller foresaw when I was a boy." The walk, nevertheless, continues. Bolano then confesses that's he's out on bail and must appear in court, and he asks Horace to lend him a hand. Horace, of course, refuses. Then a third person appears and Horace tries in vain to slip away. It must be added, in Bolano's defense, that this new character, Aristius Fuscus, a dandy of the era, is just as much an idiot as Bolano and actually is Horace's friend. In the end, it's Aristius Fuscus who accompanies Bolano to his appointment with the law.

There's no moral to this story. We all have an idiot ancestor. He's a specter, but he's also our brother, and he lives deep inside each of us under different names that express our degree of implication in the crime: fear, ridicule, indifference, blindness, cruelty.

For Antoine Bello, French author born in Boston in 1970, every novel is, among other things, a puzzle. I've just read his first novel, *The Missing Piece* (Anagrama), which really is a puzzle: that is, it's a crime novel complete with a serial killer, professional puzzle players, even puzzle championships, and it's structured like a puzzle whose pieces the reader must put together to find the killer—for one thing—but also and above all for the sake of pleasure, since pleasure, pure and simple, is the ultimate goal of any novel. By this, of course, I mean pleasure or enjoyment that isn't at odds with horror or with the greatest rigor or with the writer's responsibility to his story (which, incidentally, is often his own story).

In the tradition of Georges Perec, Bello's outstanding novel is conceived as a machine, structured in three parts. The first part is called "The Enigma," and in it summaries are given not just of the murders but of some of the most important aspects of the world of puzzles and its most competitive and public manifestation, the professional puzzle championship circuit. The third part is called "The Solution." In it, obviously, we're told the name of the killer and the reason for his abominable deeds. In between is the second part, consisting of 48 chapters, each of which represents a piece of a 48-part puzzle, with the added detail that the 48th piece, in other words the last, is blank. It's on this "missing piece" that the novel turns, and as we follow its trail we're told the curious tale of the Bantamolians, the Central African tribe whose existence is closely bound to the puzzle, functioning as construction and also as deconstruction, or as a device that parses and dictates fate; and also the tale of a craftsman who makes crime-scene puzzles, many of which are missing a piece, an absence that contains presences or that is the key to interpreting and deciphering an enigma.

Then, too, Antoine Bello's novel is narrated from different points of view and through the lens of various genres, among them the epistolary novel, the detective novel, the satire, the adventure novel, the ethnographic novel, the populist novel, the symbolist novel, and the naturalist novel, not to exclude chapters in which the storytelling is based on mathematics, logic, or religion. In sum, we have before us a great novel, and above all a great novelist, scarcely thirty years old, whose future work undoubtedly has great surprises in store for us.

A PERFECT STORY

A while ago, at a lunch with Nicanor Parra, the poet made mention of the stories of Saki, especially one of them, "The Open Window," which is part of the book *Beasts and Super-Beasts*. The great Saki's real name was Hector Hugh Munro and he was born in 1870 in Burma, which in those days was a British colony. His stories, heavily seasoned with black humor, generally belong to the genre of horror and supernatural fiction, so popular among the British. When World War I broke out, Saki enlisted as a volunteer, a fate he could surely have avoided by virtue of his age (he was over forty), and he died fighting at Beaumont-Hamel in 1916.

During that long postprandial conversation, which lasted until nightfall, I thought about a writer of the same generation as Munro, though stylistically he was very different: the great Max Beerbohm, who was born in London in 1872 and died in Rapallo, Italy, in 1956, and who, in addition to stories, wrote novels, newspaper pieces, and essays, without ever giving up two of his first loves: drawing and caricature. Max Beerbohm may be the paradigm of the minor writer and the happy man. In other words: Max Beerbohm was a good and gracious soul.

When we finally took our leave of Nicanor Parra and the Caleuche and returned to Santiago, I thought about the story that I believe is Beerbohm's best, "Enoch Soames," which was included by Silvina Ocampo, Borges, and Adolfo Bioy Casares in the magnificent and often hard to find *Antologia de la literatura fantastica* [Anthology of Fantastic Literature]. Months later I reread it. The story is about a mediocre and pedantic poet whom Beerbohm meets in his youth. The poet, who has written only two books, one worse than the next, befriends the young Beerbohm, who in turn becomes an involuntary witness to his misfortunes. The story thus becomes not just a testament to the life of all poor fools who in a moment of madness choose literature, but to late nineteenth-century London. Thus far, of course, it's a comic tale, vacillating between naturalism and reportage (Beerbohm appears under his real name, as does Aubrey Beardsley), between satire and the broad brushstrokes of *costumbrismo*. But suddenly everything changes, absolutely changes. The critical moment comes when Enoch Soames, lost in thought, glimpses his mediocrity. He's seized by despair and apathy. One afternoon Beerbohm runs into him at a restaurant. They talk, and the young narrator tries to cheer up the poet. He points out that Soames's financial situation is all right, he can live on his income for the rest of his life, maybe he just needs a holiday. The bad poet confesses that all he wants to do is kill himself and that he would give anything to know whether his name will live on. Then someone at the next table, a man with the look of a scoundrel or miscreant, asks permission to join them. He introduces himself as the Devil and he promises that if Soames sells him his soul he'll send him into the future, say one hundred years, to 1997, to the British Library Reading Room where Soames often goes to work, so he can see for himself, *in situ*, whether his name has stood the test of time. Despite Beerbohm's pleas, Soames accepts. Before he leaves he agrees to meet Beerbohm again at the same restaurant. The next few hours are described like something out of a dream—a nightmare—in a Borges story. When at last they meet again, Soames is as pale as death. He really has traveled to the future. He couldn't find his name in any encyclopedia, any index of English literature. But he did find the Beerbohm story called "Enoch Soames," in which, among other things, he's mocked. Then the Devil comes and takes him away to hell, despite Beerbohm's efforts to stop him.

In the last lines there's still a final surprise, having to do with the people Soames claims to have seen in the future. And there's yet another surprise, this one much smaller, concerning paradoxes. But these two final surprises I'll leave to the reader who buys the *Antología de la literatura fantástica* or who rifles through libraries in search of it. Personally, if I had to choose the fifteen best stories I've read in my life, "Enoch Soames" would be among them, and not in last place.

ALPHONSE DAUDET

Time passes at dizzying speed. When I was an adolescent and I lived in the south of Chile, I discovered Daudet, Alfonso Daudet, as he was called then, his name Hispanicized to make it more familiar, though I've never heard of Charles Baudelaire or Paul Verlaine being called Carlos Baudelaire or Pablo Verlaine.

Reading Daudet back then was (and still is) a pleasure and a luxury that only an adolescent lost at the end of the world could fully appreciate, with the happy sense of license that comes after a perfect theft and the feeling of freedom derived from smoking one's first cigarettes, outside under a tree on a rainy afternoon. His books have accompanied me ever since, especially *Tartarin of Tarascon*, a treatise on the joy of living which can be ridiculous at times, though it isn't unusual to come upon the truth, hidden beneath the ridiculous, a brave, relative truth containing great doses of epicureanism; and also *Letters from my Mill*, a collection of cameos and miscellaneous prose to which the early work of Arreola is much indebted; or the *Memoirs*, a melancholy book in which Daudet, so well sketched by Jules Renard in his *Journal*, doesn't lecture on the human and the divine but rather glides, like a sleepwalker, from the human to the divine, from Cartesian clarity to pure song, from the useful to the useless, and even from the useless to the useless, this last a feat worthy of real writers; or *The Nabob*, a reflection on the figure of a politician; or *L'Arlesienne*, which Bizet set to music; not to forget the sequels to the unforgettable *Tartarin*: *Tartarin on the Alps* and *Port Tarascon*.

Daudet was a friend of Victor Hugo, whose work he admired, and yet he didn't allow Hugo's titanic force to negatively influence his own work, which is much lighter, more delicate, approaching at moments the naturalism of Zola and Maupassant. Despite his prestige and success, he always saw himself as a lesser writer, easy to like. In other words, he never took himself too seriously. He was generous and, according to his contemporaries, lacking in envy, a sentiment all too common in the backbiting world of letters (which pretends to be so civilized). He loved his children. One of them, León Daudet, born in 1867, when his father was twenty-seven, became a writer, and his works rank among the worst of French literature, though it would've hurt his father more to know that in 1907, his crooked offspring would found, with Maurras, the Action Française, organ of the far right and seed of French fascism. But Alfonso Daudet didn't live to see it. He died in 1897, after suffering from a nervous complaint for many years. Today, in the south of Chile, almost no one reads Daudet. Not even writers, to whom Daudet sounds vaguely like the name of a pop singer or balladeer.

JONATHAN SWIFT

Why does an author become a classic? Certainly not because he writes well; if that were the case, the world of literature would be overpopulated with classics.

A classic, as it's most commonly defined, is a writer or work that not only permits multiple readings but ventures into new territory and in some way enriches (that is, illuminates) the tree of literature and smooths the path for those who follow. A classic is the writer or work able to decode and reorder the canon (usually not a book that's considered required reading, at least from a small-minded perspective). And then there are those classics whose main virtue, whose elegance and validity, is symbolized by the time bomb: a bomb that not only hurtles perilously through its age but is capable of flinging itself into the future. It's to this latter category—though the two categories aren't mutually exclusive—that Jonathan Swift belongs, and it's from the very rich and varied Swiftean oeuvre that the publishing house Península has recently culled a selection of fragments, published under the title *Ideas para sobrevivir a la conjura de los necios* [Ideas for Surviving the Confederacy of Dunces].

Here we can find gems like this: "When a true genius appears in the world, you may know him by this sign, that the dunces are all in confederacy against him" (from *Thoughts on Various Subjects*). Or "men are never so serious, thoughtful, and intent, as when they are at stool" (from *Gulliver's Travels*).

Or "Silenus, the foster-father of Bacchus, is always carried by an ass and has horns on his head. The moral is that drunkards are led by fools and have a great chance to be cuckolds" (from *Miscellanies*). Or "every man desires to live long; but no man would be old (from *Thoughts on Various Subjects*). Or "I have got materials toward a treatise proving the falsity of that definition, *animale rationale*, and to show it should only be *rationis capax*. Upon this great foundation of misanthropy the whole building of my *Travels* is erected" (from the *Letters*).

If our parents and grandparents had really read Swift, they wouldn't have taken us to see the animated movie version of *Gulliver's Travels* that I believe came out in the 1960s. Actually, if the authorities or those benighted souls called teachers had really read Swift, they would've found a way to ban the movie in Chile. Because one of the great Irishman's qualities is that no matter how sugarcoated the adaptation of his masterpiece, it's still a time bomb.

Of course, making a film of *A Tale of a Tub* would seem to be an impossible undertaking. And if anyone tried to make a film of *A Modest Proposal for Preventing the Children of Poor People in Ireland from Being a Burden to Their Parents or Country and for Making Them Beneficial to the Public* it would surely elicit heated protests from some Association for the Protection of Minors that has failed to come to the obvious conclusion that neither in our day nor in Swift's are children commonly served up as appetizers to cannibals.

"I have never expected sincerity of anyone, and I'm no more angered by the lack of it in a man than by the color of his hair," says a Swift weary of imbeciles. And he also says: "I have ever hated all nations, professions, and communities; and all my love is toward individuals." And: "My main purpose in everything I do is rather to enrage than to amuse."

This Swift is dangerous. He wallops his readers and keeps them up at night. And yet, if we don't want to be slaves, if we don't want our children to be slaves, we must read him and read him again. The task is urgent.

ERNESTO CARDENAL

In 1973, any twenty-year-old who wanted to be a poet read Ernesto Cardenal, author of *Epigramas* [Epigrams], *Oración por Marilyn Monroe* [Prayer for Marilyn Monroe], *Psalms*, *Homage to the American Indians*, this last a new, if flawed, response to Whitman and superior in many ways to Neruda's *Canto general*.

Out now is a book of memoirs with the lapidary title *Vida perdida [Lost Life]* (Seix Barral), and reading it one can't help but remember a time when reading Cardenal, a Catholic priest, was fascinating to us—precisely *us,* lustful sinners who never went to Mass, partly because the priests were such a drag but mostly because we didn't believe in God. And we had no plans to mend our ways, instead becoming bigger and bigger sinners, and in this endeavor we were helped along, not to say spurred on, by the poetry of Ernesto Cardenal. Now this book appears, uneven like almost all memoirs (and like life), and Ernesto Cardenal's voice hasn't changed but everything else has changed, and what was once hope, an invitation to the unknown (or so it seemed to us), now seems more like silence and stillness, a silence and stillness emanating from a lost province where Cardenal still lives and goes about his business, despite all the battles he's lost, recounting in stately prose the vicissitudes of his family, because that's what *Vida perdida* is about, the fate of a family and the fate of a man who's one of the great poets of Latin America, plus sketches of some friends who live on after death, like the great American writer Thomas Merton, also a priest, and what we're left with in the end is a life that's more triumph than failure: a final image of Cardenal as a man who lives in limbo, which isn't a bad way to live, next door to heaven.

A NOVEL BY TURGENEV

When I was eighteen I read a book by Ivan Turgenev that dogged me for the next eighteen years. By that I don't mean to say I thought about the novel and its protagonist's tragicomic fate every day, but from time to time the story seemed to loom over me like a serial killer or a question mark. I don't even remember the title. It isn't among the books by Turgenev that I own. I can't be sure, but I think it was *Rudin*. Without a doubt it's one of the saddest novels I've read in my life.

The plot is as follows: a young man arrives at a country house, owned by one of the richest men in the region. I don't remember what brings him there. Probably he's been hired as a tutor to the landowner's children. He's from Moscow or St. Petersburg, of course, and he's versed in the latest city fashions as well as its most advanced ideas. In a word: he's an intellectual and also as handsome as the young Werther, and in time he infects the children with the virus of adventure and revolution, in a manner calling to mind the first chapters of *Explosion in a Cathedral,* by the Cuban writer Alejo Carpentier, except that in Carpentier's book the children are on their own, orphans in a sense, and orphans, as we know, are a blink away from adventure or just about anything, and in Turgenev, Carpentier's precursor, the young students aren't orphans and the revolution is thousands of versts away. Of course, this distance matters little to the young Russians, and it matters even less to the older of the two siblings, a beautiful, headstrong girl who begins to dream of a bohemian life in Paris, in the company of her tutor, naturally. At first, the young Moscow intellectual (let's say he's from Moscow) is flattered by the love his student professes for him, but later, as he glimpses the future that awaits him, he begins to have his doubts. First, he doubts that the student's love will survive the daily privations of a life lived hand to mouth, even a life lived between Paris and Venice or Paris and Geneva. Then he doubts himself, because it's one thing to preach change, political or personal, and quite another to actually strive for it. He begins to consider the likely reaction of the girl's father, who respects him as a tutor and an intellectual and who, when the moment comes, won't hesitate to call on influential friends in Moscow (or St. Petersburg) to help the young man find a better job and begin to build a secure and possibly even brilliant future for himself, but who would in no way tolerate the young man's marriage to his daughter. Finally, he thinks about himself, about what he wanted when he left the city (the help of the rich landowner, etc.), and what he'll have if he listens to his heart and runs away with the disinherited heiress.

Along very broad lines, that's the whole novel, similar in some ways to Stendhal's *The Red and the Black*, though definitely a lesser work. Of course, the handsome young intellectual chooses security (his security) and eloquently rejects the love of the girl, who, I seem to recall, soon marries her former suitor, an utter peabrain, which goes to show that either she isn't very smart after all or she's a confirmed masochist. But then comes the best part of the novel, just when it seems as if everything's settled and the end is near. The young intellectual suddenly realizes that he is in love with the heiress. And he also realizes that his behavior has been shameful and despicable. I'm not sure, but I think he writes the girl a letter and then tries to kill himself on the grounds of the country house. He can't do it, discovering in a single night his love and his cowardice. The next day he leaves the house empty-handed, with no letters of recommendation. In Moscow, back in the outside world, he disappears. He isn't heard from again. Thirty years go by. In the novel's last chapter or final paragraphs, the reader is shown a barricade in Paris, described with great sympathy, a barricade manned by the poor, by the disinherited, but also by adventurers and bohemians from the most far-flung corners of Europe. The army charges. From the top of the barricade a white-haired old man whose appearance betrays the vestiges of a lost grace urges on the defenders. He's felled by a bullet. Some strangers or possibly friends carry him to his poor foreigner's room. As he lies dying, the old man speaks in Russian, and Turgenev suggests to us that not only has he found courage but also the burning bridge that links words and acts. When I was eighteen, I waited until the very last sentence for his former beloved to suddenly appear at his bedside. But she never came.

HORACIO CASTELLANOS MOYA

The first person who talked to me about Castellanos Moya was Rodrigo Rey Rosa, after paella in Blanes with Ignacio Echevarría. The second person was Juan Villoro. This was some time ago now. Of course I tried, without much hope, to find his books at two bookstores in Barcelona, and, as I expected, I couldn't find them. A little while later I received a letter from Castellanos Moya himself and after that we kept up an irregular and melancholy correspondence, tinged on my end by an admiration for his work, which little by little has come to populate my bookshelves.

So far I've read four of his books. The first was *El asco* [Nausea], maybe the best of all, or at least the darkest, a long tirade against El Salvador that caused Castellanos Moya to receive death threats obliging him to go into exile yet again. *El asco*, of course, isn't just a settling of scores or a writer's response to a moral and political situation that he finds profoundly discouraging, it's also a stylistic exercise, a parody of certain works by Bernhard, and the kind of book that makes you laugh out loud. Sadly, very few people in El Salvador have read Bernhard, and fewer still have a sense of humor. One's country is no laughing matter. That's the word, and not just in El Salvador, but also in Chile and Cuba, Peru and Mexico, and even Austria and more than a few other European countries or regions. If Castellanos Moya were Bosnian or Kosovar and he had written and published this book in Bosnia or Kosovo, chances are he wouldn't have had time to catch a plane out. Herein lies one of the book's many virtues: nationalists can't abide it. Its acid humor, like a Buster Keaton movie or a time bomb, threatens the hormonal stability of the idiots who, upon reading it, feel an irresistible urge to string the author up in the town square. Truly, I know of no greater honor for a real writer.

The second book I read was *The She-Devil in the Mirror*, a grim novel, in fact an extremely grim novel, though it's narrated by a daddy's girl or pampered princess or rich bitch from San Salvador, after the end of the civil war, when the country has moved fully into a no-holds-barred capitalism. The victim is a friend of the narrator, the wife of a businessman. The narrator's voice—a voice full of tics, a voice brilliantly realized, a voice that leads us from a darkish room to a darker room and so on gradually to a room plunged in total darkness—is only one of its achievements. This book, I believe, is the first by Castellanos Moya to be issued in Spain, by the small publishing house Linteo.

The third book that I read is also out in Spain, from Casiopea, another small publishing house. It's a reissue of *El asco*, preceded by two long stories: "Variaciones sobre el asesinato de Francisco Olmedo" [Variations on the Killing of Francisco Olmedo], a text that surely deserves a place in any anthology of contemporary Latin American short fiction, and "Con la congoja de la pasada tormenta" [With the Sorrow of the Spent Storm]. Both stories delve into the garbage pit of history, and, like crime novels, their premises are speculative, though they tumble (from the very beginning) toward a vaguely familiar horror, one that we know or have heard about.

The last book by Castellanos Moya to fall into my hands was the novel *El arma en el hombre* [The Human Weapon], published by Tusquets Mexico, which in a certain way expands upon matters dealt with in *The She-Devil in the Mirror*, the stories of some characters who were marginal or barely sketched and who here take center stage, like Robocop, a former soldier from an assault troop who, at the end of the war, is left without work and who decides (or maybe it's decided for him) to become a killer for hire. One of his victims is Olga Trabanino, the close friend of the narrator of *The She-Devil in the Mirror*, and the crime is one also featured in *El asco*, so prominently that it could be said that the killer of that poor bourgeois housewife constitutes one of the focal points of Castellanos Moya's fiction. The other focal points are horror, corruption, and a sense of the quotidian that trembles on every page and makes his readers tremble.

Horacio Castellanos Moya was born in 1957. He's a melancholic and he writes as if from the bottom of one of his country's many volcanoes. This sounds like magic realism. But there's nothing magic about his books, except possibly the boldness of his style. He's a survivor, but he doesn't write like a survivor.

BORGES AND PARACELSUS

Like all men, like all living things on earth, Borges is inexhaustible. In one of his lesser-known books, *Shakespeare's Memory* (1983), a slender collection of four stories, three of them previously published elsewhere plus one new one that lends the volume its title, the reader can find and read or reread "The Rose of Paracelsus," a very simple text, diaphanous in execution, that describes how Paracelsus is visited by a man who wants to be his disciple. That's all there is to it. The story is told with a kind of languor suited to the time of day, which is dusk. Paracelsus is tired and a small fire burns in the hearth. Then night falls and Paracelsus, who has dozed off, hears someone knocking. The stranger at the door wants to be his disciple.

The story begins like this: "Down in his laboratory, to which the two rooms of the cellar had been given over, Paracelsus prayed to his God, his indeterminate God—any God— to send him a disciple." And the disciple, when the skies have long been dark, has come at last, and he hands Paracelsus a pouch full of gold coins and a rose. At first Paracelsus thinks that the disciple wants to become an alchemist, but the disciple soon clears up the misunderstanding. "Gold is of no interest to me," he says. What does he want, then? The path to the Stone. To which Paracelsus replies: "The path *is* the Stone. The point of departure is the Stone. If these words are unclear to you, you have not yet begun to understand. Every step you take is the goal you seek."

The stranger says that he's ready to endure every necessary

hardship alongside Paracelsus, but before he takes the final step he needs some proof. Paracelsus, troubled, doesn't ask what proof he demands, but *when* he wants to see this proof. Immediately, the stranger answers. "They had begun their discourse in Latin; they now were speaking German," writes Borges. "You are famed," says the stranger, "for being able to burn a rose to ashes and make it emerge again, by the magic of your art. Let me witness that prodigy. I ask that of you, and in return I will offer up my entire life."

From this point on, the conversation turns philosophical. Paracelsus asks if he believes anyone is capable of destroying a rose. No one is incapable, says the aspiring disciple. Paracelsus argues that nothing that exists can be destroyed. Everything is mortal, answers the stranger. "If you cast this rose into the embers," says Paracelsus, "you would believe that it has been consumed, and that its ashes are real. I tell you that the rose is eternal, and that only its appearances may change. At a word from me, you would see it again." The stranger is puzzled by this response. He insists that Paracelsus burn the rose and make it rise from the ashes, whether with alembics or with the Word. Paracelsus resists: he talks about semblances that sooner or later lead to disenchantment, he talks about faith and credulity, he talks about the search. The stranger takes the rose and throws it on the fire. It burns to ashes. The stranger, says Borges "for one infinite moment awaited the words and the miracle." But Paracelsus doesn't do anything, he just sits there sadly and is reminded of the physicians and pharmacists of Basilea who believe he's a fraud. The stranger thinks he understands and tries not to humiliate him any further. He ceases his demands, takes back his gold coins, and politely leaves. Despite the love and admiration he feels for Paracelsus, vilified by all, he understands that under the mask there is nothing. And he asks himself: who am I to judge and expose Paracelsus?

A little while later they bid each other farewell. Paracelsus accompanies the stranger to the door, telling him he'll always be welcome in his house. The stranger promises to return. They both know they'll never see each other again. Alone now, and before he puts out the lamp, Paracelsus scoops up the ashes and utters a single word in a low voice. And in his hands the rose springs back to life.

JAVIER CERCAS'S NEW NOVEL

It's called *Soldiers of Salamis* (Tusquets, 2001) and the narrator is someone by the name of Javier Cercas, who clearly isn't the Javier Cercas I know and with whom I often have long conversations on the most unusual subjects. The man I know is married, has a child, his father is still living. Meanwhile, the narrator of *Soldiers of Salamis* introduces himself like this, at the very start of the novel: "Three things had just happened: first my father had died; then my wife had left me; finally, I'd given up my literary career." These three statements are false, or rather, in this combination of possibilities that we call reality, they're false, although in some other configuration of reality, or of nightmare logic, they're probably true. The hypothetical Cercas is preparing a piece on the writer Sánchez Mazas, an entirely real character who was one of the founding fathers of Spanish fascism.

Everything we're told about Sánchez Mazas in the novel cleaves strictly (although with Cercas nothing is strict) to historical fact: Sánchez Mazas's early years, his books, his friends, his political activities, his misfortunes. Then comes the Civil War and the writer is imprisoned in the Republican zone. The incident that sparks the novel comes at the end of the war and today it may strike us as an unusual story (or not), but in those days it was a common and brutal practice: Sánchez Mazas and a group of nationalist prisoners are taken to a small Catalan town and shot. They're all killed, except for Sánchez Mazas, who escapes and is pursued without much enthusiasm. At some point, one of the soldiers who's giving chase finds him hidden in the bushes. The leader of the group asks whether the soldier sees anything. The Republican soldier looks at Sánchez Mazas, looks him in the eye, and says there's no one here. Then he turns around and goes.

The second part of the novel tells the story of Sánchez Mazas (whose only positive quality, in my view, is that he fathered Sánchez Ferlosio, one of the best Spanish prose writers of the twentieth-century) and the endless intellectual disillusionment of the Spanish Falangists, which never translated into productive discontent.

The third part centers on the unknown Republican soldier who saved Sánchez Mazas's life, and here there appears a new character, someone by the name of Bolaño, who is a writer and Chilean and lives in Blanes, but who isn't me, in the same way that the narrator Cercas isn't Cercas, although both characters are possible and even probable. Through this Bolaño the reader learns the story of Miralles, a soldier, who, as he retreated, passed the place where the Falangists were killed and Sánchez Mira was nearly killed, and who later crossed the border into France and spent a while in a concentration camp on the outskirts of Argèles, and who, to escape the camp, enlisted in the French Foreign Legion, and who, after the fall of France in 1940, followed General Leclerc on his great march from the Maghreb to Chad, and who took part in several battles against the Italians and the Afrika Korps, and who then, assigned to the French 2nd Armored Division, fought in the battle of Normandy and entered Paris and then fought near Strasbourg until a mine, in German territory, put an end to his war, if not his life. The search for this Miralles, whom Bolaño got to know over the course of three summers at a campground near Barcelona, becomes the key to the novel. Of course, Cercas doesn't know (nor does his friend) whether Miralles is alive or not. All he knows is that he lived in Dijon, that he had acquired French citizenship, and that now he must be past eighty or dead. The third part of the novel is the search for Miralles. If he really is the soldier who chose not to kill Sánchez Mazas, Cercas has just one question for him: Why not?

With this novel, published to critical acclaim and appearing in French and Italian translations a few days before it even landed in Spanish bookstores, Javier Cercas joins the small group at the leading edge of Spanish fiction. His novel flirts with hybridization, with the "relato real," or "true fiction" (which Cercas himself invented), with historical fiction, and with hyper-objective fiction, though whenever he feels so inclined he has no qualms about betraying these generic categories to slip toward poetry, toward the epic without the slightest blush: in any direction, so long as it's forward.

BRAQUE: ILLUSTRATED NOTEBOOKS

Braque was seventy years old in 1952, when *Illustrated Notebooks* was published by Gallimard, a book scarcely one hundred pages long that is now being issued in Spanish by the publishing house El Acantilado. The least that can be said of it is that it's a precious book, in the literal sense of the word, composed of notes, reflections, and aphorisms that the painter tossed off between 1917 and 1952—obviously they are anything but his principal occupation, which is precisely what makes them so interesting, what gives the book the aura of a secret project, never exclusionary but always exacting.

Braque, along with Juan Gris and Picasso, made up the holy trinity of cubism, in which the role of God the Father belonged wholly to Picasso and the role of the Son to the surprising and still misunderstood Juan Gris—who in a different production could easily have played a Cyclops—whereas fate reserved for Braque, the only Frenchman of the trio, the role of the Holy Spirit, which as we know is the most difficult of all and the one that gets the least applause from the audience. The *Illustrated Notebooks* seem to testify to this, with notes like the following: "In art no effect can be achieved without straining the truth." "The artist is not misunderstood; he's unrecognized. People exploit him without knowing it." "We will never have repose. The present is perpetual."

Some of his aperçus, like Duchamp's or Satie's, are infinitely superior to those of many writers of his day, even some writers whose main occupation was to think and reflect: "Every age limits its own aspirations. This is what gives rise, not without complicity, to the illusion of progress." "When all is said and done, I prefer those who exploit me to those who follow me. The former have something to teach me." "Action is a series of desperate acts that allow one to maintain hope." "It's a mistake to wall off the unconscious on the fringes of reason." "You must choose: a thing cannot be true and likely at the same time."

At once a humorist and a pessimist (in the same way that he's simultaneously a man of faith and a materialist, or that he seems to move too fast when he's really as motionless as a mountain or a turtle), Braque offers us these gems: "Memory of 1914: Joffre's only concern was to recreate Vernet's battle paintings." "Whatever is not taken from us remains with us. It is the best part of ourselves." "As you grow older, art and life become one and the same." "Only the one who knows what he wants is wrong."

The book closes with an appendix of no little interest, the near-manifesto "Thoughts and Reflections on Painting," published in *Nord-Sud* Number 10, in 1917. But I'd rather bid farewell to this magnificent book with one of its many triumphs: "Be wary: talent is prestigious."

IL SODOMA

Giovanni Antonio Bazzi, called Il Sodoma, was born in 1477 and died in 1549. I first heard of him from Pere Gimferrer, who not only is a great poet but has read practically everything. We were talking about a story called "Sodoma" and Gimferrer asked me whether it was about the Biblical city or the painter. The city, of course, I answered. I had never heard of a painter called Sodoma. For a moment I thought Gimferrer was joking, but no, Il Sodoma really existed, and even Giorgio Vasari devoted a few pages to him in his canonical tome, *Lives of the Most Excellent Painters, Sculptors, and Architects*. His name, Il Sodoma, alludes clearly to his sexual preferences.

It's said that children chased him, shouting "Sodoma," when Il Sodoma was on his way back to his studio, and then it was the women, the laundresses of Siena, who took up the name-calling, amid laughter—Sodoma, Sodoma—and soon everybody knew him by that name: a violent, brutal name that in some way matched Il Sodoma's painting, to the point that one day Bazzi began to sign his canvases with the nickname, which he assumed with pride and in the carnivalesque spirit that would never abandon him.

His house, which was also his studio, looked more like a zoo than like the house or studio of a Renaissance painter.

Through the door there was a dark passageway, wide enough to fit a horse cart, and then there was a talking raven that announced the visitors who crossed the house's threshhold. The raven called "Sodoma, Sodoma, Sodoma," and also "Someone's here, someone's here, someone's here." Sometimes it was shut up in a cage and other times it flew free. There was also a monkey, which roamed the inner courtyard and climbed in and out of the windows, and which Il Sodoma had surely bought from some African traveler. And there was a donkey (a theological donkey, said its owner) and a horse and a multitude of cats and dogs, and birds of many species hanging in cages on the walls inside and outside of the house. It was said that he had a tiger or *a tigrillo*, but this is doubtful. Most extraordinary, however, was the raven, which every visitor wanted to hear talk. For days on end it might lapse into an obstinate silence, but at other times it was capable of reciting the verse of Cavalcanti. Never, so far as anyone knows, did it relinquish its duties as gatekeeper, and this was how the neighbors were informed of Sodoma's late night visitors, by the shrieks of the raven that startled them awake in the early morning hours, croaking in ironic and anguished tones the word *Sodoma*.

Il Sodoma was a humorist and his work, scattered through the galleries of Siena, London, Paris, New York, has the bold colors of the start of a carnival, before they're faded by drunkenness, excess, and exhaustion. I've only seen one of his paintings. It was in Florence, at the Uffizi. Vasari was right, there's something brutal about him, but there's also something noble-hearted that we've lost. At the Villa Farnesina in Rome there are frescoes of his that I've never seen but that the critics say are excellent.

A few days ago, Juan Villoro and I were remembering the writers who were important to us in our youth and who today have fallen into a kind of oblivion, the writers who at the peak of their fame had many readers and who today suffer the ingratitude of those same readers and who—to make matters worse—haven't managed to spark the interest of a new generation of readers.

We thought, of course, of Henry Miller, who in his day was read all over Spain, and whose name was on everyone's lips, but whose fame was perhaps due to a misunderstanding: probably more than half the people who bought his books did so expecting to find a pornographer, which in some sense was justified, and also understandable in the Spain that emerged after almost forty years of censure under Franco and the church.

At the other extreme we remembered Artaud, the very spirit of asceticism, who in his day also sold well and had not a few Spanish and Mexican admirers, and if today one makes the mistake of mentioning his name to someone under the age of thirty, the response will surely be devastating. These days, even film buffs have never heard of Antonin Artaud.

The same is true of Macedonio Fernández: his books—except in Argentina, I imagine—are impossible to find in bookstores. And it's true of Felisberto Hernández, who had a small resurgence in the 1970s, but whose stories today can only be found after much searching in second-hand bookstores. Felisberto's fate, I presume, is different in Uruguay and Argentina, which brings us to a problem even worse than being forgotten: the provincialism of the book market, which corrals and locks away Spanish-language literature, which, simply put, means that Chilean authors are only of interest in Chile, Mexican authors in Mexico, and Colombians in Colombia, as if each

Latin American country spoke a different language or as if the aesthetic taste of each Latin American reader were determined first and foremost by national—that is, provincial—imperatives, which wasn't the case in the 1960s, for example, when the Boom exploded, or in the 1950s or 1940s, despite poor distribution.

But anyway, that's not what Villoro and I talked about. We talked about other writers, like Henry Miller or Artaud or B. Traven or Tristan Tzara, writers who contributed to our sentimental education and who are now impossible to find in the depths of bookstores for the simple reason that they have hardly any new readers. And also about the youngest ones, writers of our generation, like Sophie Podolski or Mathieu Messagier, who were simply incredible and highly talented and who not only can no longer be found in bookstores but can't even be found on the Internet, which is saying a lot, as if they'd never existed or as if we'd imagined them. The explanation for this ebb of writers, however, is very simple. Just as love moves according to a mechanism like the sea's, as the Nicaraguan poet Martínez Rivas puts it, so too do writers move, and one day they appear and then they disappear and then maybe they appear again. And if they don't, it doesn't really matter so much, because in some secret way, they're us now.

PHILIP K. DICK

In my long conversations with Rodrigo Fresán about Philip K. Dick in bars and restaurants around Barcelona or at each other's houses we've never run out of things to say.

These are some of the conclusions we've reached: Dick was a schizophrenic. Dick was a paranoiac. Dick is one of the ten best American writers of the twentieth century, which is saying a lot. Dick was a kind of Kafka steeped in LSD and rage. Dick talks to us, in *The Man in the High Castle*, in what would become his trademark way, about how mutable reality can be and therefore how mutable history can be. Dick is Thoreau plus the death of the American dream. Dick writes, at times, like a prisoner, because ethically and aesthetically he really is a prisoner. Dick is the one who, in *Ubik*, comes closest to capturing the human consciousness or fragments of consciousness in the context of their setting; the correspondence between the story he tells and its structure is more brilliant than similar experiments conducted by Pynchon or DeLillo. Dick is the first, literarily speaking, to write eloquently about virtual consciousness. Dick is the first, or if not the first then the best, to write about the perception of speed, the perception of entropy, the perception of the clamor of the universe in *Martian Time-Slip*, in which an autistic boy, like a silent Jesus Christ of the future, devotes himself to feeling and suffering the paradox of time and space, the death toward which we're all heading. Dick, despite everything, never loses his sense of humor, which means that he owes more to Twain than to Melville, although Fresán, who knows more about Dick than me, raises some objections. For Dick all art is political. Don't forget that. Dick is possibly one of the most plagiarized authors of the twentieth century. In Fresán's opinion, *Time's Arrow*, by Martin Amis, is a shameless ripoff of *Counter-Clock World*. I prefer to believe that Amis is paying tribute to Dick or to some precursor of Dick (let's not forget that Amis's father, the poet Kingsley Amis, also championed science fiction and was a great reader of it). Dick is the American writer who in recent years has most influenced non-American poets, novelists, and essayists. Dick is good even when he's bad and I ask myself, though I already know the answer, whether the same could be said of any Latin American writer. Dick portrays suffering as forcefully as Carson McCullers. And *VALIS* is more disturbing than any novel by McCullers. Dick seems, at moments, like the king of beggars, and at others like a mysterious millionaire in hiding, and by this he may have meant to explain that the two roles are really one. Dick wrote *Dr. Bloodmoney*, which is a masterpiece, and he revolutionized the contemporary American novel in 1962, with *The Man in the High Castle*, but he also wrote novels that have nothing to do with science fiction, like *Confessions of a Crap Artist*, written in 1959 and published in 1975, which shows how well-loved he was by the American publishing industry.

There are three images of the real Dick that I'll carry with me always, along with my memories of his countless books. First: Dick and all his wives—the incessant expense of California divorces. Second: Dick receiving a visit from the Black Panthers, an FBI car parked outside his house. Third: Dick and his sick son, and the voices Dick hears in his head advising him to go back to the doctor again to inquire about a different illness, very rare, very serious, which Dick does, and the doctors realize their mistake and they perform emergency surgery and save the boy's life.

THE BOOK THAT SURVIVES

Although it may seem like a memory exercise, it isn't. The first book I was given by the first girl I fell in love with and lived with was a book by Mircea Eliade. I still don't know what she was trying to tell me. Somebody else, somebody less foolish, would have realized immediately that the relationship wouldn't last and would've taken the proper steps to protect himself from suffering. I can't remember the first book my mother gave me. I do vaguely recall a fat illustrated history, almost a comic book, though closer to Prince Valiant than Superman, about the War of the Pacific, that is, the war between Chile and the Peruvian-Bolivian alliance. If I remember right, the hero of the book—a kind of *War and Peace* of underdevelopment—was a volunteer who had enlisted in the Séptimo de la Línea, a famous infantry regiment. I'll always be grateful to my mother for giving me that book instead of the children's classic *Papelucho*. As for my father, I don't remember him ever giving me a book, although occasionally we would pass a bookstore and at my request he would buy me a magazine with a long article in it on the French electric poets. All those books, including the magazine, along with many other books, were lost during my travels and moves, or else I let people borrow them and never saw them again, or I sold them or gave them away.

But there's one book I'll never forget. Not only do I remember when and where I was when I bought it, but also the time of day, the person waiting for me outside the bookstore, what I did that night, and the happiness (completely irrational) that I felt when I had it in my hands. It was the first book I bought in Europe and I still have it. It's Borges's *Obra poetica*, published by Alianza/Emecé in 1972 and long out of print. I bought it in Madrid in 1977 and, although Borges's poetry wasn't unfamiliar to me, I started to read it that night and didn't stop until eight the next morning, as if there was nothing in the world worth reading except those poems, nothing else that could change the course of the wild life that I'd lived up until then, nothing else that could lead me to reflect (because Borges's poetry possesses a natural intelligence and also bravery and despair—in other words, the only things that inspire reflection and that keep poetry alive).

Bloom maintains that it's Pablo Neruda, more than any other poet, who carries on Whitman's legacy. In Bloom's opinion, however, Neruda's effort to keep the Whitmanian tree growing and thriving ends in failure. I think that Bloom is wrong, as he so often is, even as on many other subjects he's probably our continent's best literary critic. It's true that all American poets must—for better or for worse, sooner or later—face up to Whitman. Unfailingly, Neruda does so as the obedient son. Vallejo does so as the disobedient or prodigal son. Borges—and this is the source of his originality and his cool head—does so as a nephew, and not even a very close one, a nephew whose curiosity vacillates between the chilly interest of the entomologist and the stoical ardor of the lover. Nothing more alien to him than the quest to shock or to stir admiration. No one more indifferent to the vast masses of America on the march, although somewhere he wrote that what happens to one man happens to all men.

And yet Borges's poetry is the most Whitmanian of all: Whitman's themes are always present in his verse, as are their counterarguments and rebuttals, the reverse and the obverse of history, the heads and tails of the amalgam that is America and whose success or failure is yet to be decided. But that isn't all he is, which is no small feat.

I began with my first love and with Mircea Eliade. She still lives in my memory; the Romanian has long since been banished to the purgatory of unsolved crimes. I end with Borges and with my gratitude and astonishment, though careful not to forget the lines of "Almost Final Judgment," a poem that Borges hated: "I have said astonishment where others say only habit."

Blood Meridian is a Western, a cowboy novel by a writer who seems to specialize in the genre. Many enterprising types thought that Cormac McCarthy would never be translated into Spanish and they ransacked him shamelessly, abetted by ignorance and a rather curious understanding of intertextuality. And yet *Blood Meridian,* set in the mid-nineteenth century, isn't just a Western but also a fevered, ultra-violent novel about life and death, with all kinds of underlying themes (nature as man's great enemy, the absolute impossibility of redemption, life as inertia); a novel that, in part, tells the story of a group of Americans who launch a murderous raid into the state of Chihuahua and then, after crossing the Sierra Madres, into the neighboring state of Sonora, and whose mission, for which they're well compensated by the governments of both states, is to hunt down and scalp Indians, which isn't just difficult but also costly in time and lives, and so they end up massacring whole Mexican towns, where the scalps are ultimately similar enough that it makes no difference.

Blood Meridian is also a novel about place, about the landscape of Texas and Chihuahua and Sonora; a kind of anti-pastoral novel in which the landscape looms in its leading role, imposingly—truly the new world, silent and paradigmatic and hideous, with room for everything except human beings. It could be said that the landscape of *Blood Meridian* is a landscape out of de Sade, a thirsty and indifferent landscape ruled by strange laws involving pain and anesthesia, the laws by which time often manifests itself.

The other two characters in the novel, Judge Holden and a boy known only as the kid, are antagonists, though they belong to the same gang: the judge is a learned man and a child killer, a musician and a pederast, a naturalist and a gunslinger, a man who yearns to know everything and destroy everything. The kid, by contrast, is a survivor; he's wild but he's a human being or, in other words, a victim. According to the distinguished Harold Bloom, *Blood Meridian* is one of the best American novels of the twentieth century.

Cormac McCarthy was born in 1933 and his life has been rich in adventure and risk. *Blood Meridian* was first published in 1985. The edition reviewed here was published by Debate in 2001, in a translation by Luis Murillo Fort.

TROUBADOURS

What do the troubadours have to say to us today? What's the source of their appeal, their excellence? I don't know. I remember that I was inspired to read them by Pound, and especially by Martín de Riquer's dazzling studies. From then on, little by little I began amassing books and anthologies in which there appeared the names of Arnaut Daniel, Marcabrú, Bertrán de Born, Peire Vidal, Giraut de Bornelh. By the nature of their trade, most were travelers and globetrotters. Some only traveled one or two provinces, but there were others who crossed Europe, fought as soldiers, sailed the Mediterranean, visited Muslim lands.

Carlos Alvar makes a distinction between troubadours, trouvères, and minnesingers. The real difference is geographic. The troubadours were mostly from southern France, Provençal, although some were Catalan too. The trouvères were from the north of France. The minnesingers were German. Time, which has yet to erase their names and some of their works, will finally erase these national differences.

When I was young, in Mexico City, we played a game in which we divided ourselves into champions of the *trobar leu* and the *trobar clus*. The *trobar leu* was, of course, the light song, simple and intelligible to everyone. The *trobar clus*, by contrast, was dark and opaque, formally complex. Despite its conceptual richness, however, the *trobar clus* could often be more violent and brutal than the *trobar leu* (which was generally delicate), like Góngora written by a convict, or more precisely, like foreshadowings of Villon's black star.

Because we were young and ignorant, we didn't know that the *trobar clus* could in turn be divided into two categories, the *trobar clus* properly speaking, and the *trobar ric*, which as its name indicates is sumptuous verse, full of flourishes, and generally empty. In other words: the *trobar clus* trapped in the halls of academe or the court, the *trobar clus* stripped of the vertigo of words and life. We knew that without the troubadours the Italian *dolce stil novo* would never have existed, and accordingly that without the *dolce stil novo* there would be no Dante, but what we liked best were the misspent lives of some of the troubadours. For example: Jaufre Rudel, who fell in love literally by hearsay with a countess who lived in Tripoli, crossed the Mediterranean on what amounted to a crusade in search of her, got sick, and finally ended his days in a Tripoli boarding house, where the countess, aware that here was a man who had celebrated her in many songs and poems, came and permitted Rudel—who now awaited only death—to rest his head in her lap.

I don't know what they have to say to us today, the troubadours. So far away in their twelfth century, they seem naïve. But I wouldn't be too sure about that. I know they invented love, and they also invented or reinvented the pride of being a writer, of gazing fearlessly into the depths.

Editors tend to be bad people. Not to mention critics and the readers at publishing houses and the thousands of lackeys who travel the dim or brightly lit corridors of publishing houses. But writers are often worse, among other things because they believe in lasting glory or in a world ruled by Darwinian laws or maybe because lurking in their innermost souls is a slavishness even more base.

I've had the misfortune of meeting a number of editors who were a burden to their own mothers and I've also been lucky enough to meet several, maybe seven or eight, who were and are responsible people, rather gloomy (melancholy is a mark of the trade), intelligent, with guts to spare and a sense of humor, editors who're determined, for example, to publish authors and books that they know from the start will sell very few copies.

A little while ago the second Targa d'Argento Prize was awarded to the best European publisher, and the recipient was my editor, Jorge Herralde, who beat out many other editors, some about to be wreathed or already wreathed in an aura of legend. Now Herralde has written this book, *Opiniones mohicanas* [Mohican Opinions] (2001), published by El Acantilado, the house of another remarkable editor and writer, Jaume Vallcorba. To read this book, a collection of assorted pieces and jottings scarcely twenty lines long, is to plunge into the recent history of the Barcelona publishing industry and the European and Latin American publishing world, as well as to step into the circle of Herralde's friends, his editorial battles, and the political changes undergone in Spain since the end of the dictatorship.

All kinds of writers parade across its pages. Bukowski, whom Herralde and Lali Gubern visit in California. Patricia

Highsmith, with whom they dine in Madrid, along with the mayor Tierno Galván. Carlos Monsiváis, the great Sergio Pitol, Carlos Barral, whose ghost is still bowed by the shame of having rejected *One Hundred Years of Solitude*. Soledad Puértolas, Carmen Martín Gaite, Esther Tusquets, Belén Gopegui—probably the best four women prose writers in Spain. Not to mention a host of British, French, Italian, and American writers, as well as some Latin Americans and Catalans.

What can I say about Herralde that no one, not even Herralde, can later hold against me? I could say that his prose is elegant and ironic, like Herralde himself. But that's not saying much. What I should really say is that once, during a trip that I made in the grips of the most extreme paranoia, when I reached my destination I discovered several faxes from Herralde at my hotel, in which he told me not to worry and offered all the means at his disposal to get me out of the country at a moment's notice in case my paranoia should grow more acute.

I also remember another time, at his office, when—after I told him I didn't plan to attend a party to which I had been invited because I didn't know the order in which to use the five forks, six spoons, and four knives sure to be standing guard next to my plate—Herralde very patiently explained to me the specific use of each piece of cutlery and the pace of usage or non-usage of the objects in question. It goes without saying that as Herralde explained all this I stared at him in a mixture of confusion, awe, and rage. In this sense Herralde is a proud son of the Catalan bourgeoisie, that cultivated and in no way cowardly bourgeoisie which is vanishing by leaps and bounds.

And what else can I say about him? That literature in the Spanish language wouldn't be the same if Anagrama had never existed, and that if I ever leave the publishing house (home to seven of my books), I'll probably especially miss Lali

Gubern, Teresa, Ana Jornet, Noemí, Emma, Marta, Izaskun, and sweet María Cortés, now retired, among all the other pretty (and smart) girls who work there, but I'll also miss Herralde, the interminable afternoons spent arguing about advances, his brief and always pithy remarks, his devastating opinions, lunches at El Tragaluz and dinners at Il Giardinetto, more devastating opinions, more clashing memories from different perspectives—and his independence as chief of the unvanquishable Mohicans.

SPECULATIONS ON A REMARK BY BRETON

A while ago, in an interview I can't find now, André Breton said that the time might have come for surrealism to go underground. Only there, thought Breton, could it survive and prepare itself for future challenges. He said this toward the end of his life, in the early '60s.

The suggestion, attractive and ambiguous, was never repeated, either by Breton in the many interviews he later gave or by his surrealist disciples, busy directing terrible films or editing literary magazines that by this point had little or nothing to contribute to literature or to the revolution that Breton and his early comrades saw as something convulsive and vague, that familiar amorphous thing.

It always seemed strange to me that a veil should have been drawn over this strategic possibility, if we can call it that. It raises a number of questions, in my opinion. Did surrealism really go into hiding, and did it die there, in the sewers? Did just a part of it—the least visible part, the young people, for example—go underground while the old guard covered the retreat with exquisite corpses and found objects, thereby making it seem as if all had fallen silent when in fact a retrenchment was taking place? What did this underground branch of surrealism become after 1965, a year before Breton's death? How involved was it, along with the situationists, in May 1968? Was there an operational underground movement during the last thirty years of the twentieth century? And if there was, how did it evolve, what did it achieve in the fields of fine arts, literature, architecture, film? What was its relationship with official surrealism, in other words the surrealism of the widows, the cinephiles, and Alain Jouffroy? Did any of these subgroups maintain contact with the surrealists in hiding? Was the area of operations of this underground surrealism limited to Europe and the United States or were there also Asian, African, Latin American branches? Could the underground surrealists have split, in time, into subgroups, first at odds with one another and then lost like wandering tribes in the desert? Might they have forgotten, in a relatively short time, that they were actually underground surrealists? And how are the new underground surrealists recruited? Who calls them at midnight and informs them that from now on they can consider themselves part of the group? And what do the people who get the calls think? That they've fallen prey to a joke, that the voice with the French accent is really the voice of some practical joker of a friend, that they're hearing things? And what orders do the new underground surrealists receive? To hurry up and learn to read and speak French? To report to a place in Paris where someone will be waiting for them? Not to be afraid? Above all: Not to be afraid? And what if that place is a cemetery, one of the many legendary cemeteries of Paris, or a church or a bourgeois house on a bourgeois street? And what if it's a basement located in the darkest corner of the Arab quarter? Should the new underground surrealist—who on top of everything isn't entirely sure he's not the victim of a prank that's gone on too long—report for duty?

It may be that no one ever will receive this call. It may be that the underground surrealists never existed or that by now they're just a handful of old tricksters. It may be that those who receive the call never keep the appointment, because they think it's a joke or because they can't make it. "After centuries of philosophy, we're still living off the poetic ideas of the first men," wrote Breton. This sentence isn't a reproach, as one might think, but a statement of fact on the threshhold of mystery.

AN ATTEMPT AT AN EXHAUSTIVE CATALOG OF PATRONS

I never had a patron. No one ever hooked me up with anyone so I could get a grant. No government or institution ever offered me money, no elegant gentleman ever pulled out his checkbook for me, no tremulous lady (quivering with a passion for literature) ever invited me to tea and committed herself to providing me with a meal a day. But over the years I've come across many patrons, in person or in books.

Most common of all is the fortyish homosexual who suddenly realizes that his life is empty and who devotes himself, belatedly, to filling it with meaning. Deep down, this kind of patron wants to be an artist with a patron of his own, a fortyish and violent patron, who in turn also has a patron, who in turn is taken up by other patrons, and so on ad infinitum. Generally the works that excite this kind of patron are faux self-portraits.

There's also the patron with blood ties. It's usually the brother or sister of the artist or poet in question and the relationship between the two of them is like the bond between a bird and a crag. In these circumstances desperation goes by the name of love. Defeat on all fronts is assured.

Then comes the invisible patron. His protegé will never be on first-name terms with him. In fact, in some cases he'll never see him. The invisible patron is capable of raping a writer without the writer even noticing. The invisible patron isn't a meek and prudent soul, as one might imagine. On the contrary: he's usually a clever brute.

Then we have the melancholy grandma. Who isn't the grandmother of her protegés, of course, or even a great aunt, and who to a certain degree resembles those elderly Russian ladies, lovers of literature, who for a time filled the streets of Paris, Venice, and Geneva. The grandmas dress impeccably. They talk about Proust as if they'd known him. Sometimes they reminisce about candlelit evenings in palaces one has never heard of. They possess (out of ignorance) a high regard for authors who've been translated into more than three languages, and their collections of dictionaries and encyclopedias are often impressive. They're in danger of extinction.

In no danger of extinction, meanwhile, are the cultural attachés who on nights when the moon is full imagine themselves patrons. It goes without saying, since everybody takes it for granted, that cultural attachés are more attaché than cultural. During their brief reigns their friends take what they can get, which may not be much, but which for them is a lot, everything.

Also in no danger of extinction are those Latin American professors at American universities. Their idea of the patron is based on brute force and boundless cowardice. Most are on the left, politically speaking. To attend a dinner with them and their favorites is like gazing into a creepy diorama in which the chief of a clan of cavemen gnaws a leg while his acolytes nod and laugh. The patron-professor in Illinois or Iowa or South Carolina resembles Stalin and that's the strangest and most original thing about him.

Then comes an amorphous mass of patrons of different stripes and assorted misfortunes. There are the neurotic virgins, the good Samaritans, the sourpusses, the frustrated housewives, the suicidal bureaucrats, the poet who suddenly discovers he has no talent, the person who thinks no one understands him, the drunk who recites Sallustius, the fat man who wishes he were thin, the bitter man who wants to create a new canon, the neostructuralist who doesn't understand half of what he says, the priest who yearns for hell, the lady who insists on good manners, the businessman who writes sonnets.

Behind this crowd, however, hides the one true patron. If you have patience enough to search, maybe you'll catch a glimpse of what you're looking for. And when you find it, you'll probably be disappointed. It isn't the devil. It isn't the State. It isn't a magical child. It's the void.

III.
(SEPTEMBER 2002–JANUARY 2003)

JIM

Like everybody else, I once had a friend called Jim. I never saw a sadder American. Once he left for Peru on a trip that should have lasted six months at least, but two months later there he was again. What is poetry, Jim? the Mexican street kids would ask. Jim would listen to them and then he'd vomit. Lexicon, eloquence, quest for the truth. In Central America he was mugged several times. Which was odd for someone who'd been a marine and was a Vietnam vet. His wife was a Chicana poet who every so often threatened to leave him.

Once I saw him watching the fire-swallowers on the streets of Mexico City. I saw him from behind and I didn't say hello, but it was clearly Jim. The ragged hair, the dirty white shirt, the back hunched as if it still felt the weight of a rucksack and of fear. The red neck, a neck that somehow suggested a lynching in the countryside, a black and white countryside without billboards or the lights of gas stations, a countryside as the countryside is and should be: endless vacant lots without remedy, bricked- or boarded-up rooms from which we've escaped and that await our return.

Jim had his hands in his pockets. The fire-swallower shook his torch and laughed fiercely. With his blackened face, he might have been thirty-five or fifteen. He wasn't wearing a shirt, and a vertical scar rose from his navel to his breastbone. Every so often he filled his mouth with flammable liquid and spat out a long snake of fire. People stopped to watch and then went on their way, except for Jim, who stood motionless on the edge of the sidewalk, as if he expected something more from the fire-swallower, a tenth signal after having deciphered the usual nine, or as if in the fire-swallower's sooty face he had spotted the face of an old friend or someone he had killed. For a long time I stood watching him. At the time I was eighteen or nineteen and I thought I was immortal. If I had known that I wasn't, I would have turned around and gotten out of there. Maybe I got tired of staring at Jim's back and the faces of the fire-swallowers. The fact is that I went up to him and called his name. Jim didn't seem to hear me. When he turned around at last I saw that his face was sweaty. He seemed feverish and was slow to recognize me: he nodded at me and then turned back toward the fire-swallower. When I reached him I realized that he was crying. He was probably feverish too. At the same time, I discovered—with less astonishment than with which I write it now—that the fire-swallower was working exclusively for him. Occasionally the flames flickered out just a few feet from where we were standing.

Are you trying to get barbecued? I asked. A stupid, thoughtless thing to say, but suddenly I realized that that was exactly what Jim wanted. "Screw me, voodoo me / screw me, voodoo me," was the chorus, I seem to remember, of a song that was popular that year in some dive bars. Screwed and under some voodoo curse is what Jim looked like he was. Let's get out of here, I said. I also asked whether he was high, whether he was sick. He shook his head. The fire-swallower glanced at us. Then, with his cheeks puffed out like Eolus, the god of the wind, he came toward us. I knew in an instant that it wasn't exactly wind that he was going to spew. Let's go, I said, and I pulled Jim away from the terrible edge of the sidewalk.

We went off down the street, toward Reforma, and a few blocks away we parted. Jim didn't open his mouth the whole time. I never saw him again.

THE SUICIDE OF GABRIEL FERRATER

Countless writers have committed suicide and some of their deaths still retain the original glow, the aura of legend, the blast force or the impact of implosion that so frightened their contemporaries, those who experienced the suicide from up close, because the victim was a friend or a teacher or a colleague, someone they only really noticed at the moment of death. There are suicides that are masterpieces of black humor, like that of the surrealist Jacques Rigaut, or of Jacques Vaché, a forerunner of surrealism. There are suicides that threaten our notion of culture, like that of Walter Benjamin; and others, like that of Hemingway, that seem more like a customs procedure, a long-postponed encounter in an airport.

The suicide of Gabriel Ferrater, one of the best Catalan poets of the second half of the twentieth century, fits the category of cerebral or consciously premeditated suicide, though this in no way means that Ferrater spent his life stroking his own suicide, as other poets stroke their overdeveloped egos.

On the contrary, it seems that sometime in his twenties, closer to thirty than twenty, Ferrater decided to kill himself, and he chose the year 1972, a year as ordinary as any other except that it was the year he would turn fifty, a round number and a landmark age. To live past fifty, he decided, was not simply a waste of time but a surrender to the indignities of age.

After that he gave it no further thought, though it's likely he mentioned it from time to time while out drinking with a few of the younger poets who loved him so much, like Barral and Gil de Biedma. As the fateful date approached but was still very far off, he devoted himself body and soul to reading, translating (Kafka, Chomsky), fucking, drinking, traveling, visiting museums, riding around Barcelona on his motorcycle with quarts of whiskey in his system, making friends, falling in love with very strange women. The photographs we have of him show a generally handsome man, sometimes with the look of a screen actor, white hair, black-framed glasses, turtle-neck sweater, hard and intelligent features, lips with a slight (and more than sufficient) sardonic tilt—lips that must have been feared in his day.

He only wrote a few books of poems. Three, if I remember correctly. All incomparable. In any case, Ferrater lived his life—and wrote his poems—like a Roman. When at last the year 1972 came and he turned fifty, he stepped forth to meet his fate and killed himself, in Sant Cugat del Vallès, a little town near Barcelona. No one found it strange.

RODRIGO REY ROSA IN MALI (I THINK)

It might be a good idea to discuss Rey Rosa's latest books, the book about India and his most recent novel, a little gem that takes a new angle on the noir, a genre in which many try to make their mark and few succeed. To say that Rodrigo Rey Rosa is the most rigorous writer of my generation and at the same time the most transparent, the best crafter of stories and the brightest star, is to say nothing new.

Today I would rather remember a story that he told me. The story is about a trip to an African country—Mali, I think, though I can't be sure. In any case, Rey Rosa flies into the capital, a chaotic city near the coast. After spending a few days there he travels by bus to a town in the interior. There the road ends, or perhaps it instead becomes uncertain, like a desert track that a gust of wind could erase.

The town is near a river and Rey Rosa takes a boat that sails interminably upstream. Finally he reaches a village, and after walking around and talking to people, he comes to a house, a one-room brick house, which is where he was heading. The house—which belongs to a Mallorcan painter, probably one of the best contemporary painters—is empty. In it there's a chest and in that chest, safe from termites, are the painter's books. That night Rey Rosa reads until late, by candlelight, because of course there's no electricity. Then he covers himself with a blanket and goes to sleep.

For a few days he stays at the village, which hardly has enough huts to deserve the name. He buys food from the locals, drinks tea by the river, takes long walks to the edge of the desert. One day he finishes the book he's borrowed from the by now legendary chest and then he puts it back, locks up the house, and leaves. Anyone else would have started back immediately. Rey Rosa, however, leaves the village by the back door, as you might say, and heads for the mountains instead of the river. I've forgotten what they're called. All I know is that at dusk they take on a bluish tinge that gradually shades from pale to metallic blue. Darkness falls, of course, as he walks in the desert and that night he sleeps among the wild things.

The next day he sets out again. And so it goes, until he reaches the mountains, which cradle small barren valleys, where the sea of sand is wearing away the rocks. He spends yet another night there. Then he returns to the village, the river, the town, the bus, the capital, and the plane that carries him back to Paris, where he was living at the time.

When he told me the story, I said that a trip like that would kill me. Rodrigo Rey Rosa—who believes in life as only children and those who've felt the presence of death can—replied that it was nothing.

A FEW WORDS FOR ENRIQUE LIHN

He was without a doubt the best poet of his generation, the so-called Generación del '50, and one of the three or four best Latin American poets born between 1925 and 1935. Or maybe one of the two best. Or maybe he was the best. But at the beginning of the twenty-first century, that doesn't mean much.

In my adolescence, to talk about Lihn and Teillier as opposing choices was commonplace. The sensitive kids, those who didn't want to grow up (or those who wanted to grow up as fast as possible), preferred Teillier. Those who were prepared to argue the point preferred Lihn. This wasn't the least of his virtues. To read much of his poetry is to encounter a voice that questions everything. But it isn't the voice of hell, or of millenarian prophecies, or even a prophetic ego, but the voice of the enlightened citizen, a citizen who awaits the arrival of modernism or who is resignedly modern. A citizen who has learned at the feet of Parra, Lihn's teacher and fellow prankster, and whose Latin American vision is often dazzling and original. But all the dazzle in Lihn is modulated by a constant exercise of intelligence. In the 1970s, that clarity would cause him to be stigmatized and declared anathema by the dogmatic and neo-Stalinist left, which would even go so far as to accuse him of connivance with Pinochetism. The same people who back then didn't speak up to defend Reinaldo Arenas and who today adapt themselves like Putins* to the new situation, tried to wipe him from the map, to delegitimize a voice that had always considered itself a bastard voice, a child at the mercy of fate and necessity, a lone rider.

Are we Chileans deserving of Lihn? This is a pointless question, something he would never have asked himself. I think we are. Not really, not entirely, but we are deserving of him, even if only because of the pure souls, the idiot princes, and the cheerful illiterates who the country once produced with such strange generosity and who are still being produced today, or so one hears from those who've been there recently, though in more limited quantities. In a certain light, Lihn himself could pass for an idiot prince and a cheerful illiterate.

As a writer of poetry, to which he was always faithful, there's only one poet in the Spanish language to whom he can be compared, Jaime Gil de Biedma, though Lihn's range of tone is much wider. As a writer of essays, reviews, manifestos, and even libel, no Chilean writer was ever more free or unerring. In fiction he never reached the heights of Donoso or Edwards, though the suspicion will always linger that deep down, like all of Chile's great poets, he judged the art of fiction as something unnecessary, something short of life-saving.

And yet his stories are still alive, as is *La orquesta de cristal* [The Glass Orchestra], a book so hard to find that it's become a mythical object, and that I don't dare to call a novel, though I know that if it has to be called something, *novel* comes closest

*[Yes, my little hypocrite, that's Putins as in Vladimir, not some Mexican slang version of *putas* (or *putos*).] [*hookers* (or *pimps)*—tr.]

to fitting. There are two prose writers of the Generación del '50 who have yet to be discovered: Lihn and Giaconi.

These days it's strange to think of Lihn, Giaconi, Parra, Teillier, Rodrigo Lira, or Gonzalo Rojas, of poets like Maquieira and Bertoni, of young writers like Contreras and Collyer; it's strange to think of them, and of so many others. One is left with the strange feeling that for once literature has measured up to reality. The famous *re*, the *re*, the *re*, the *re-al-it-y*.

ALL SUBJECTS WITH FRESÁN

My friendship with Rodrigo Fresán is based not only on mutual esteem (and affection, on my side) but also on our endless conversations on the most random topics, which often turn into arguments, though this doesn't always happen in Barcelona, because I live on the Costa Brava and not even on the Costa Brava but more concretely in the living room of my house in Blanes, and he lives in Barcelona, and despite the fact that both of us travel quite a bit (he more than I), neither of us has a car or knows how to drive, and with time we're becoming sedentary.

In general, it could be said that we talk about many things. I'll try to list them in no particular order. 1) The Latin American hell that, especially on weekends, is concentrated around some Kentucky Fried Chickens and McDonald's. 2) The doings of the Buenos Aires photographer Alfredo Garófano, childhood friend of Rodrigo and now a friend of mine and of anyone with the least bit of discernment. 3) Bad translations. 4) Serial killers and mass murderers. 5) Prospective leisure as the antidote to prospective poetry. 6) The vast number of writers who should retire after writing their first book or their second or their third or their fourth or their fifth. 7) The superiority of the work of Basquiat to that of Haring, or vice versa. 8) The works of Borges and the works of Bioy. 9) The advisablity of retiring to a ranch in Mexico near a volcano to finish writing *The Turkey Buzzard Trilogy*. 10) Wrinkles in the space-time continuum. 11) The kind of majestic women you've never met who come up to you in a bar and whisper in your ear that they have AIDS (or that they don't). 12) Gombrowicz and his conception of immaturity. 13) Philip K. Dick, whom we both unreservedly admire. 14) The likelihood of a war between Chile and Argentina and its possible and impossible consequences. 15) The life of Proust and the life of Stendhal. 16) The activities of some professors in the United States. 17) The sexual practices of titi monkeys and ants and great cetaceans. 18) Colleagues who must be avoided like limpet mines. 19) Ignacio Echevarría, whom both of us love and admire. 20) Some Mexican writers liked by me and not by him, and some Argentine writers liked by me and not by him. 21) Barcelonan manners. 22) David Lynch and the prolixity of David Foster Wallace. 23) Chabon and Palahniuk, whom he likes and I don't. 24) Wittgenstein and his plumbing and carpentry skills. 25) Some twilit dinners, which actually, to the surprise of the diner, become theater pieces in five acts. 26) Trashy TV game shows. 27) The end of the world. 28) Kubrick's films, which Fresán loves so much that I'm beginning to hate them. 29) The incredible war between the planet of the novel-creatures and the planet of the story-beings. 30) The possibility that when the novel awakes from its iron dreams, the story will still be there.

Of course, these thirty items come nowhere near to exhausting our topics of conversation. Let me add just a couple of things. I laugh a lot when I talk to Fresán. We almost never talk about death.

A few months ago I was flying from Madrid to Barcelona and I ended up sitting next to a young guy, a Chilean. He turned out to be from Los Ángeles, Bío-Bío, the place I lived longest in Chile. He was on his way to Cairo, on a business trip, god knows what he was selling, and our conversation was brief and not particularly illuminating. He said that Los Ángeles had grown a lot but was still a town, he mentioned two or three factories, he talked about a ranch that produced I don't know what. He was an ordinary and profoundly ignorant kid, but he knew how to travel first class.

After the plane took off I traded seats with a woman who wanted to be next to her children and I went to sit next to a photographer who was sweating profusely. He looked like a Pakistani, so I thought that maybe after a while he would pull out a nail file and hijack the plane. If I have to die, I said to myself, I'd rather die gnawing on the ankle of a Pakistani than sitting next to a Chilean from Los Ángeles. Then I began to think about my childhood and the part of my adolescence that I spent in Bío-Bío.

To my surprise, I realized that I remembered lots of things. For example, I remembered the wooden walls of the house where we lived. And how the walls (and the floorboards) were soaked during the endless southern rains. I also remembered a dwarf lady who lived five houses away. A dwarf lady from Germany, teacher of something at some school, who was the living image of exile, or anyway the nineteenth-century image, the Pontian image. For a while I thought this woman was actually an extraterrestrial.

And more memories: a girl called Loreto, another called Veronica, and the Saldivia sisters, one whose name I've forgotten but whom I kissed on my last day in Los Ángeles. The foosball championships. The face of my friend Fernando Fernández. My mother's asthma attacks. One afternoon when I thought I was going crazy. Another afternoon when I drank lamb's blood.

In Los Ángeles I realized that playing any sport was an aberration, that if I had to choose between O'Higgins and Guiraut de Bornelh I would choose Guiraut, and that without leaving my house I could get to know the whole world.

Of course, I did other things that I still remember: I broke my own record masturbating, broke my own record of pages read in a day, broke my own record of schooldays skipped, broke my own record of happy hours squandered doing absolutely nothing.

I was happy there, but thank goodness my parents decided to leave.

AUTOBIOGRAPHIES: AMIS & ELLROY

I've always thought autobiographies were odious. What a waste of time trying to pass a cat off as a rabbit, when what a real writer should do is snare dragons and dress them up as rabbits. I take it for granted that in literature a cat is never a cat, as Lewis Carroll made clear once and for all.

There are few really memorable autobiographies. In Latin America, there are probably none. The first volume of García Márquez's memoirs is just out now. I haven't read it, but it makes my hair stand on end just to imagine what our Nobel Laureate might have written. And it's even worse when I think of him struggling, in ill health, mustering the little strength he has left simply to undertake a melancholic exercise in navel-gazing.

A while ago I read a couple of memoirs by two of the best

living writers in the English language. *Experience*, by Martin Amis, and *My Dark Places*, by James Ellroy. The one thing the two books have in common is that they're both by young writers—that is, by writers whom one wouldn't imagine ready to take stock of their lives, since those lives, barring the unexpected, are nowhere near the final stretch. That's the extent of the resemblance; after that, the books permanently part company. Amis writes a brilliant, pedantic, bland autobiography, the life of a writer who's the son of a writer. Ellroy, whom many look down upon for stupid reasons like the fact that he's a genre writer, writes a twisted memoir, a book that springs straight from the verge of hell. What Ellroy actually does is to exhaustively investigate and recreate the life of his mother, the last days of the life of his mother, who was raped and killed in 1958 and whose killer was never found.

Since crime seems to be the symbol of the twentieth century, in Amis's memoirs there's also a serial killer, the infamous Fred West, in whose yard the remains of eight women were found, among them a cousin of Amis's who disappeared years ago. But when Amis approaches the abyss he closes his eyes because he knows, like a good college student who has read his Nietzsche, that the abyss can look back. Ellroy knows it too, whether or not he's read his Nietzsche, and that's the main difference between them: he keeps his eyes open. In fact, he doesn't just keep his eyes open. Ellroy is capable of dancing the conga with the abyss staring back at him.

Amis's book isn't bad. But almost all his previous books are better. Those who seek in *Experience* the author of *Money* or *London Fields* or *The Information* or *Night Train* will be disappointed. Ellroy's book, in contrast, is a model book. The second and third parts, which describe Ellroy's childhood and adolescence after his mother's death, are the best things written in the literature of any language in the last thirty years.

Amis's book ends with children. It ends with peace and love. Ellroy's book ends with tears and shit. It ends with a man alone, standing tall. It ends with blood. In other words, it never ends.

THE CURIOUS MR. ALAN PAULS

The first thing I read by Pauls was an utterly original short story, "El caso Berciani" [The Berciani Case], published in *Buenos Aires*, an anthology edited by Juan Forn (Anagrama, 1992). In this collection, alongside texts by writers as relevant as Piglia, Aira, Saccomanno, or Fresán, the story by Mr. Pauls stood out for a number of reasons, the most notable of which was an anomaly: there was something in "El caso Berciani" that suggested a wrinkle in the space-time continuum, not just in the plot (which didn't actually have anything to do with that, by which I mean that it wasn't science fiction or anything of the kind) but in the links between the events described, in the story's fierce, scarcely visible entropy; in the arrangement of paragraphs and sentences.

For a long time I was a fervent reader of Pauls, having read just a single story. I didn't know much about him: he was born in Buenos Aires in 1959, he had published two novels that I could never find, *El pudor del pornógrafo* [The Modesty of the Pornographer] and *El coloquio* [The Colloquium], and an essay on Manuel Puig. So for a long time I had to be satisfied— and this was more than enough—with reading and rereading "El caso Berciani," which by this point, it's clear, seemed to me a perfect story, if there's such a thing as perfect monsters, which isn't exactly a reasonable assumption to make.

Until one day I came into contact with the fabulous Mr. Pauls. I don't know whether I wrote to him or he wrote to me. I think it was he. A letter so deadpan that it left me in awe. Trembling, even. In it he told me about a car trip he'd taken with his daughter, a girl about the age of my son, maybe a little younger. The trip, as far as I could tell after reading the letter ten times (a vice acquired with "El caso Berciani"), had begun in the center of Buenos Aires and ended in the suburbs. The younger Pauls seemed to be a very intelligent child. Her father, an expert driver. The world, inhospitable. I answered the letter by sending greetings to the girl, from me and also from my son. Maybe that wasn't the proper thing to do, because Pauls took his time getting back to me, claiming some mysterious problem with his computer. His daughter ignored the greetings from my son.

A little while later I read two stories or two fragments of a hypochondriacal or medical saga by Mr. Pauls, which as far as I know are still unpublished. Both stories or fragments or whatever they are seemed perfect to me, perfect monsters. By now, as any reader will understand, all I wanted was to read more. So I asked Rodrigo Fresán (who not only is a friend of Mr. Pauls but for a while was his neighbor) to make off with everything by the author on his next trip to Argentina. So I read *Wasabi*, his third and as-of-now latest novel, in which he describes the growth of a boil and the ultimate impossibility of controlling it, and his book of essays on Borges, *The Borges Factor*, a great book, like *Wasabi*, but one that from the beginning presents a series of Borgesian dilemmas: on the title page it says that the book is by Alan Pauls and Nicolás Helft, but on the copyright page it's explained that the text is by Alan Pauls and the images were generously provided by the Archives of the San Telmo Foundation. So why is Nicolás Helft credited on the cover as one of the authors? And who is Nicolás Helft?

According to Fresán, Nicolás Helft is the owner of some of the illustrations or reproductions that appear in the book. I don't believe it. Nor do I believe that it's a pseudonym created by Mr. Pauls, who's little given to such elaborate games, but rather the shadow of a shadow, the shadow of a Polish count, for example, or the shadow of a certain disheartening clarity.

I remember a letter that Mr. Pauls wrote to me a long time ago now. In it he told me that he had gone with his wife—and presumably his daughter—to a Uruguayan hippie commune. Not to live, he explained, but to spend a few days. During those few days all he did was read a long novel, or so I understood after reading his letter ten times, and he watched a kind of dune that the wind kept shifting from place to place in the most obvious way. The strange thing was that no one noticed it. But so it is always, my dear Mr. Pauls, I thought after the tenth reading. You're one of the best living Latin American writers and there are very few of us who know it and can appreciate it.

JAVIER ASPURÚA AT HIS OWN FUNERAL

Not long ago, I learned of the death of Javier Aspurúa from a friend on his way through Barcelona and from a message that arrived by email. The particulars of this death, as is often true in such cases, were not entirely clear. Aspurúa, I calculate, must have been over seventy. He was sick, according to one of my informants; he only had a cold, according to the other. The point is that one afternoon, as he was convalescing in the town where he lived—Quilpué or maybe Villa Alemana, I've forgotten which—a car hit him and he stopped breathing or, in other words, he died.

Some friends and acquaintances say that he made his first appearance in the literary world—the professional literary world, such as it is—when he was fifty-five, others when he was past sixty, after an obscure early retirement from some government job. Like an apparition, he sluiced along courses (or irrigation channels, since we're using hydrographic metaphors) of the strictest propriety. As far as anyone knows, he wrote only book reviews. As far as anyone knows, his complete works appeared in the newspaper *Las Últimas Noticias*, and, though I may be wrong, a one-hundred page volume might suffice to contain them.

I met him in 1999, in Santiago. It was the first and last time I saw him. He was at the offices of *Las Últimas Noticias* to turn in a review; I was there with Andrés Braithwaite and Rodrigo Pinto. I thanked him for a positive review he'd written of one of my books. He blushed and gazed up at the ceiling. Then we went to a bar and at some point during the night there were more than eight people at our table and we were all talking and pontificating, except for Javier Aspurúa, who sat in silence. Next to him was a plastic bag full of books. At one point, the general conversation didn't interest me, and I leaned over and asked him what books he'd bought. He handed me the bag so I could take a look: English novels. We talked about some of the authors. Later on Mr. Aspurúa consulted his watch and said that he had to go because otherwise he would miss the last bus to Quilpué or Villa Alemana.

I walked him outside. When he was out of sight I thought of the invisible man, but a few seconds later, as I turned and went back into the bar, it hit me that Aspurúa wasn't the type, and that in fact all his mannerisms, all his shyness, even his reserve, indicated a man who was fully conscious, maybe painfully conscious, of his visibility and the visibility of others. In this sense, I thought, though I thought this much later, maybe on the plane back to Spain, books—the books that he always read with such enthusiasm, an enthusiasm in which one could glimpse the adolescence that never abandons some old people—were like aspirin for a headache or like the opaque sunglasses that some madmen wear to block out everything and find peace, because the truth, experienced day by day as visibility, is exhausting and draining and sometimes brings on madness. Maybe that was his relationship to books. Or maybe not. Maybe what he expected from books, as I'd like to believe now that he's dead, was messages in a bottle or hard drugs or windows through which, on rare occasions, one sees Alice's white rabbit skim past like a lightning bolt.

According to Braithwaite, who was at his funeral, at some point a rabbit really did run between the gravestones. Not a white rabbit but a gray or brown one, maybe a hare, though from the same family in the end.

THE REAL WAY TO GET TO MADRID

Of the many ways to get to Madrid, my favorite is hitchhiking, like when I was Poil de Carotte, in the melancholy words of Renard in his *Journal*, the time he wet his bed just a little because he was sick and nothing could ever be right again, if it's possible to wet one's bed just a little in a world (and in a bed, which is the flip side of the coin on which the metaphor of the world is etched) where the density of voluntary and involuntary acts is anything but sleep or desire, but instead a tangible and in some way irremediable reality: a yellow liquid that runs down your leg, a liquid that the French author, Schwob's great friend, observes with curiosity and indifference, reminded of himself as a boy, and also of himself as written by himself but so long ago now.

Of the many hotels in Madrid, I prefer the ones between the Plaza de Santa Ana and the Plaza de Lavapiés. Just like when I used to hitchhike and I could go for days without eating or sleeping. Although I'm acquainted with better hotels, like the Wellington, for example, which is the hotel where one day I saw the Baroness von Thyssen sitting alone in the lobby, wrapped in a white fur coat as if it were a shield or the kind of rough quilt that bums and the homeless use to protect themselves from the elements in winter, her look rapidly morphing from baroness to commoner.

When you think about it, living in Madrid or being there isn't much different from living or being in Tacuarembó. The air, maybe, is different. It's so clear that sometimes it blinds the soul, allowing us to see more clearly: the notional streets and the Castilian Spanish, the kind of slang they speak so well in the old capital of the mother country.

And the women, the native daughters of Madrid, the blondes and the brunettes, add mystery to a place already rich in mystery, although it's well known that the Spanish, like Latin Americans, aren't just poorly educated but also no good in bed. That's the source of the look one sees in the eyes of the women of Madrid: part sarcasm and part Merimée.

The truth is that Madrid is a city that doesn't exist—despite the warriors and priests who left the capital and never came back, despite the women of Madrid, melancholy and practical in the meseta's least pragmatic region.

Or maybe Madrid is an imaginary city, to which one has to hitchhike, not fly, and to which one can only come when one is twenty-five, not nearly fifty.

To call someone the Bukowski of Havana might even be flattering in a way, more of a compliment than an insult, but to say such a thing about a writer, a Cuban writer, I don't know, it could be taken as an open or veiled expression of contempt, because Bukowski, who was an excellent poet, a drunken poet shaped by the reading of bad translations of Li Po, another legendary drunk, has fallen into discredit in recent years, which is something that for the most part seems unfair, since even if he never really shone as a novelist, as a writer of short stories in a tradition that stretches from Twain to Ring Lardner he's the author of some notable works.

The critics call Pedro Juan Gutiérrez the Bukowski of Havana, and in fact the Cuban writer and the American writer have a number of things in common: a lifetime of odd jobs, most seemingly unrelated to literature; belated success; a simple style of writing (although here one has to be very careful); shared subjects like women, alcohol, and the struggle to live just one more week. Also, like Bukowski's, Gutiérrez's novels are notably inferior to his stories.

Simply put, Pedro Juan isn't taken seriously, which is something that I imagine he couldn't care less about, since on the one hand he's used to not being taken seriously and on the other hand I don't think that's quite what he wants anyway. His public image couldn't be more contradictory: there are those who see him as the ultimate priapic figure, the authentic Caribbean goods. In this sense Gutiérrez is like an unchained sexual Prometheus. His attraction to women knows neither age (though certainly no one has ever claimed he was a pedophile; on the contrary) or race (Gutiérrez flies the rainbow flag), or personal grudges (he could fall in love with the worst hellcats on Earth). I know readers who ask where this satyr finds the time to write, since he seems to be fucking all day long. I also know readers who think that Gutiérrez is a spy for Castro's regime and that his books are written by a team of literary commissars while he carries out his espionage duties. Castro's secret police would have to be truly deranged to invent a writer like this.

In Gutiérrez's stories, besides sex, drugs, and the survival instinct, the protagonist is Havana. A pitiful Havana in a state of coma, where the Revolution isn't even a joke anymore. Actually, Gutiérrez's Havana isn't comatose; it's anemic and feverish. Bucharest and Kiev or Sofia were comatose. But the fragility of the citizens of Havana resembles the fragility of the citizens of those formerly communist cities and also is not much different from the fragility of the citizens of any other big city in Latin America. Gutiérrez's stories, in this sense, insert themselves into the chaos of history (and not just into the chaos of the stories of individuals), and though Gutiérrez may be the Bukowski of Havana, they're more real and authentic and often much better written than the stories of authors dubbed serious by the critics, authors who are still struggling in the increasingly pestilent waters of the Boom, to give an example close to home, or who try, usually pathetically, to cross-dress in the garb of mandarin aloofness and aristocracy on a continent where there is no aristocracy and where the most terrible things happen inches from our wan faces (if they can be called faces).

Cuba is in bad shape. Latin America is in bad shape. Gutiérrez doesn't seem to be in much better shape. But I fear he remains faithful to his principles or to his nature. Whoever wants to judge for himself should read *Dirty Havana Trilogy* or the three paperback volumes in which Anagrama has collected all of his published stories.

A few years ago, my friends in Mexico got tired of me asking for information—more and more detailed information,
too—about the killings of women in Ciudad Juárez, and they
decided, apparently by common accord, to hand the job over
to Sergio González Rodríguez, who is a novelist, essayist, reporter, and probably all kinds of other things besides, and
who, according to my friends, was the person who knew most
about this case, a unique case in the annals of Latin American
crime: more than three hundred women raped and killed in
an extremely short period of time, between 1993 and 2002, in
a city on the U.S. border with a population of just under one
million.

I don't remember now what year it was when I began to
correspond with Sergio González Rodríguez. All I know is that
my fondness and admiration for him have only grown with
time. His technical help—if I can call it that—in the writing of
my novel, which I have yet to finish and don't know whether I'll
ever finish, has been substantial. Out just now is his book *Huesos en el desierto* [Bones in the Desert] (Anagrama), a book that
delves directly into the horror. Sergio is here in Barcelona to celebrate its publication, and soon there will be more celebrations
in Mexico City and then in Guadalajara, during the Book Fair.
And the book will be distributed throughout Latin America.
And surely translated into other languages. But before all that,
other things happened. Among them, an assassination attempt
that Sergio escaped by a hair. And various stalkings. And threats
and tapped phones. Things that would have frightened off anyone else, but that Sergio, with stunning calm, has experienced
like someone watching the rain fall.

In fact, what Sergio has observed and in some sense lived is less like a rain storm than a hurricane. His book, published as part of the Anagrama collection "Crónicas" that includes books by Wallraff, Kapuscinski, and Michael Herr, not only stands up to these legendary works but like them even breaks the rules of journalism as soon as it gets the chance in order to venture into the anti-novel, into first-person narrative, into open wounds, and even, in the last part, into lament. Thus instead of being just an imperfect snapshot of wrongdoing and corruption, as of course it must be, *Huesos en el desierto* becomes a metaphor for Mexico and the Mexican past and the uncertain future of all of Latin America. It's a book not in the adventure tradition but in the apocalyptic tradition, which are the only two traditions still alive on our continent, maybe because they're the only ones that draw us closer to the abyss that surrounds us.

Yesterday, however, Sergio was at my house and the conversation was about lighter things. My daughter took ownership of Paola, the girl who came with him. Carolina served ham and cheese. We opened a bottle of wine. As a gift, Sergio brought me half a pound of coffee from my yearned-for and loathed coffee shop La Habana, on Calle Bucareli. Paola and Carolina smoked unfiltered Delicados. We remembered the old Pegaso buses of Mexico City's public transportation system and we laughed. Then I was quiet and I thought that if ever I was in deep shit I would be all right so long as I had Sergio González Rodríguez by my side. Viva Mexico.

84, CHARING CROSS ROAD

Not many years ago I saw a movie on TV based on this book, although at the time I had no idea the book existed. It was very late, around four in the morning, and I only started watching partway through. Even so, I thought it was wonderful. To say that it was simple and restrained is too easy: it was, and the acting was excellent, but those clearly weren't the most important things about it. Its main virtue, or at least so it seemed to me in that single viewing, was its open-endedness, a sketch-like quality that encouraged the viewer to fill in the blanks with two or three or ten imaginary movies that had nothing (or seemingly nothing) to do with what was happening on screen.

A little while ago I came across the book—*84, Charing Cross Road* (Anagrama, 2002)—on which the movie was based, and despite expectations, I thought the book was even better. Its author is Helen Hanff and the volume in question, which isn't even one hundred pages long, is composed of the real letters that Miss Hanff, a poor Jewish New Yorker and would-be writer, sent to a bookseller in London in the years after World War II. At first the letters deal exclusively with book-related matters, but Miss Hanff soon gets herself involved in the lives of the clerks at the bookshop. How does she do this? By sending practical gifts, things like powdered eggs (news to me: I had no idea that powdered eggs were ever a popular item), ham, sugar, coffee; and even, in time, less practical gifts, like nylon stockings for the female clerks and the bookseller's wife.

These are gifts that touch the English (who are living under rationing) and touch the reader and establish a kind of kinship between Miss Hanff and her epistolary friends. Of course, the English also begin to send gifts to Miss Hanff: bedspreads or tablecloths, rare books, photographs. By this point, the reader, so as not to be left out, starts to cry, and if one wants to waste time examining one's own tears, which isn't advisable, one may discover a mysterious mechanism that also drives certain works by Dickens: the best tears are those that make us better and at the same time come closest to laughter.

This book by the admirable Miss Hanff (Philadelphia 1918 - New York 1997) contains a few other curious details. For example, the demonstrable fact that she never bought a book without having first read it at the Public Library; which is to say that she was an even better re-reader than reader. And another: her absolute disdain for fiction, which was only tempered as she got older. Good evidence of this is *84, Charing Cross Road*, in which all the letters written by her as well as those by her London correspondents are completely authentic, despite what is often the case in similar instances.

A final detail: the bookshop Marks & Co., which dealt in used books and welcomed customers at 84 Charing Cross Road, doesn't exist anymore. But its fair prices, its good practices in all matters bibliophilic, and the kindness of its employees survive in this book as an example for future booksellers and bookshops, two endangered species.

JAUME VALLCORBA AND THE PRIZES

Happy days for Jaume Vallcorba, founder of the Catalan-language publishing house Quaderns Crema and the Spanish-language publishing house El Acantilado, who has received good news. Imre Kertész was awarded the Nobel Prize, and until now no one had paid any attention to him except for Vallcorba, who is an expert in discovering hidden restaurants and strange books and writers. Actually, Vallcorba is an expert in many things.

Once we were talking about Guiraut de Bornelh—a Provençal troubadour I thought I knew something about—and also Jaufré Rudel, and possibly even Marcabrú, when suddenly Vallcorba began to recite the three troubadours in the original Provençal and Occitan—even, I would say, with the proper period accents and regional variants in each case. This is the kind of thing that, suddenly sprung on someone, can be terrifying.

I mean: his exhaustive knowledge of medieval and Latin literature, the tip of the massive iceberg that turns (sometimes harmoniously and sometimes chaotically) on that thing called European culture. But it's enough to meet him for any wariness or fear to be dispelled. Culture, Jaume Vallcorba tells us in everything that he does, is play and risk (the play and risk of intelligence), and if in the end we don't laugh, it's frankly not worth the effort.

That's the only way to explain his list and the prestige that El Acantilado has attained in just a few years. Who if not Vallcorba would dare to publish Stefan Zweig or Schnitzler? Lafcadio Hearn, Braque, Satie? Who could have the fun of publishing Guido Ceronetti's *Song of Songs*, or of reissuing Juan Ferraté's *Líricos griegos arcaicos* [Archaic Greek Lyrics] when it was clear, or seemed clear, that the only people interested already owned the first edition, published ages ago by Seix Barral, and therefore wouldn't buy his? Or most outrageous of all, Francesco Colonna's *Hypnerotomachia Poliphili*? But as I think about him now, while he's in Stockholm as Kertész's guest, the really amazing thing about Vallcorba is his attitude toward books, his tireless curiosity, his incredible modesty.

This modesty only grew, if possible, when he was awarded this year's prize for best editor in Spain. Which has done nothing to prevent him from continuing to visit bookstores as bizarre as the restaurants where he eats, or from talking to unpublished writers who other houses would write off in half a minute, or from embarking (stealthily but also boldly) on ventures of the sort that are only embarked upon, to the best of my knowledge, by Catalans, some Catalans. In fact, I'd go even further and say: some Catalan publishers.

I've had the satisfaction of meeting three of them. One has taught me a lot. The other is an enchanting person, in the medieval sense of the term, as the long-suffering Rudel would have it. The third is Jaume Vallcorba. I can't predict his fate, but I thank God for his presence. Not for my own sake, because I don't believe in God and I've already done the reading I was meant to do, but for the sake of all readers. Though also for my own sake.

TITIAN PAINTS A SICK MAN

At the Uffizi, in Florence, is this odd painting by Titian. For a while, no one knew who the artist was. First the work was attributed to Leonardo and then to Sebastiano del Piombo. Though there's still no absolute proof, today the critics are inclined to credit it to Titian. In the painting we see a man, still young, with long dark curly hair and a beard and mustache perhaps slightly tinged with red, who, as he poses, gazes off toward the right, probably toward a window that we can't see, but still a window that somehow one imagines is closed, yet with curtains open or parted enough to allow a yellow light to filter into the room, a light that in time will become indistinguishable from the varnish on the painting.

The young man's face is beautiful and deeply thoughtful. He's looking toward the window, if he's looking anywhere, though probably all he sees is what's happening inside his head. But he's not contemplating escape. Perhaps Titian told him to turn like that, to turn his face into the light, and the young man is simply obeying him. At the same time, one might say that all the time in the world stretches out before him. By this I don't mean that the young man thinks he's immortal. On the contrary. The young man knows that life renews itself and that the art of renewal is often death. Intelligence is visible in his face and his eyes, and his lips are turned down in an expression of sadness, or maybe it's something else, maybe apathy, none of which excludes the possibility that at some point he might feel himself to be master of all the time in the world, because true as it is that man is a creature of time, theoretically (or artistically, if I can put it that way) time is also a creature of man.

In fact, in this painting, time—sketched in invisible strokes—is a kitten perched on the young man's hands, his gloved hands, or rather his gloved right hand which rests on a book: and this right hand is the perfect measure of the sick man, more than his coat with a fur collar, more than his loose shirt, perhaps of silk, more than his pose for the painter and for posterity (or fragile memory), which the book promises or sells. I don't know where his left hand is.

How would a medieval painter have painted this sick man? How would a non-figurative artist of the twentieth century have painted this sick man? Probably howling or wailing in fear. Judged under the eye of an incomprehensible God or trapped in the labyrinth of an incomprehensible society. But Titian gives him to us, the spectators of the future, clothed in the garb of compassion and understanding. That young man might be God or he might be me. The laughter of a few drunks might be my laughter or my poem. That sweet Virgin is my friend. That sad-faced Virgin is the long march of my people. The boy who runs with his eyes closed through a lonely garden is us.

I'd like to buy all the books by Tolstoy and Dostoevsky that I've read but I don't own. Also everything by Daudet. And Victor Hugo. Sometimes I ask myself what I did with those books, how I could have lost them, where I lost them. Other times I ask myself why I want them if I've already read them, when reading books is the only way to hold on to them forever. The only plausible answer is that I want them for my children. But I know that's not a fair answer: you have to leave home to find the books that are waiting for you.

I still remember my old copy of *Crime and Punishment*, published in two columns (by Thor, of Buenos Aires) as if it were a work of pulp fiction, and maybe it was; a cheap book to read and then leave in a bus station or some café that doesn't close until four in the morning. What did I do with that book? I don't know. Probably the minute I read the last page it suddenly seemed less important and then I abandoned it somewhere. I didn't treasure it the way I treasure my books now. But I read it when I was very young and I couldn't lose Raskolnikov even if I wanted to.

I had the same problem with Petrus Borel and De Quincy. And also Baudelaire (of whose *Fleurs du mal* I've owned more than ten copies) and Mallarmé. If I could find an old Argentine or Mexican edition of *Igitur* again, I know it would make me happy. I didn't have the same problem with Rimbaud, or at least I didn't want to have the same problem with Rimbaud, or Lautréamont, but in the end I lost those books too.

To search for those copies or similar copies, the same font, the same layout, the same plot, the dark or bright syntax, somehow forces me to remember a time when I was young and poor and careless, though I know that the same copies, the exact same ones, will never be found, and to set myself such a task would be like marching into Florida in search of El Dorado.

Even so, I often browse used bookstores, sorting through stacks of books left behind by others or sold in a dark moment, and in corners like these I try to find the books that I lost or forgot more than thirty years ago on another continent, with the hope and dedication and bitterness of those who search for their first lost books, books that if found I wouldn't read anyway, because I've already read them over and over, but that I would look at and touch just as the miser strokes the coins under which he's buried.

But books have nothing to do with greed, though they do have something to do with coins. Books are like ghosts. Another tray of empanadas! Happy 2003! Music, maestro!

TRANSLATION IS AN ANVIL

What is it that makes an author, so beloved by those of us who speak Spanish, a figure of the second or third rank, if not an absolute unknown, among those who speak other languages? The case of Quevedo, as Borges reminds us, is perhaps the most flagrant. Why isn't Quevedo a living poet, by which I mean a poet worthy of being reread and reinterpreted and imitated in spheres outside of Spanish literature? Which leads directly to another question: Why do we ourselves consider Quevedo to be our greatest poet? Or why are Quevedo and Góngora our two greatest poets?

Cervantes, who in his lifetime was disparaged and looked down upon, is our greatest novelist. Regarding this there is almost no debate. He's also the greatest novelist—and according to some, the inventor of the novel—in lands where Spanish isn't spoken and where the work of Cervantes can for the most part only be read in translation. The various translations may be good or they may not be, which hasn't prevented the essence of *Don Quixote* from being imprinted on or filtered into the imagination of thousands of readers, who don't care about the verbal riches or the rhythm or force of Cervantine prose, a prose that any translation, no matter how good, obviously distorts or dissolves.

Sterne owes much to Cervantes, and in the nineteenth century, the century of the novel par excellence, so does Dickens. Neither of the two, it almost goes without saying, spoke Spanish, by which one can deduce that they read the adventures of *Don Quixote* in English. The wonderful thing—and yet also the natural thing, in this case—is that those translations of *Don Quixote*, good or not, were able to convey what, in the case of Quevedo or Góngora, wasn't conveyable and probably never will be: the quality that distinguishes an absolute masterpiece from an ordinary masterpiece, or, if such a thing exists, the quality that distinguishes a living literature, a literature that belongs to all mankind, from a literature that's only the heritage of a certain tribe or a part of a certain tribe.

Borges, who wrote absolute masterpieces, explained it once already. Here's the story: Borges goes to the theater to see a production of *Macbeth*. The translation is terrible, the production is terrible, the actors are terrible, the staging is terrible. Even the seats are uncomfortable. And yet when the lights go down and the play begins, the spectators, Borges among them, are immersed once again in the fate of characters who traverse time, shivering once again at what for lack of a better word we can call magic.

Something similar happens with the popular Passion plays, in which the eager amateur actors who once a year stage the crucifixion of Christ manage to transcend the most dreadful absurdity or unconscious heresy on the wings of divine mystery, which isn't actually divine mystery but art.

How to recognize a work of art? How to separate it, even if just for a moment, from its critical apparatus, its exegetes, its tireless plagiarizers, its belittlers, its final lonely fate? Easy. Let it be translated. Let its translator be far from brilliant. Rip pages from it at random. Leave it lying in an attic. If after all of this a kid comes along and reads it, and after reading makes it his own, and is faithful to it (or unfaithful, whichever) and reinterprets it and accompanies it on its voyage to the edge, and both are enriched and the kid adds an ounce of value to its original value, then we have something before us, a machine or a book, capable of speaking to all human beings: not a plowed field but a mountain, not the image of a dark forest but the dark forest, not a flock of birds but the Nightingale.

HUMOR IN THE WINGS

Cortázar complained that there was no tradition of erotic literature in Latin America. He could have just as well have complained about the lack of a comic tradition. The classics, for lack of a better name—I mean the classics of our developing countries—sacrificed humor in favor of saccharine romanticism and pedagogy, or in some cases protest. None of these works stand the passage of time very well and if they survive, they owe their endurance to the efforts of the bibliophile rather than to any real value or substance.

In the work of some early modernists or vanguardists, however, one can find instances of genuine humor. They're scarce, but they're real. I'm thinking about Tablada, a few obscure texts by Amado Nervo, fragments of prose by Darío, tales of horror and comedy by Lugones, the first forays of Macedonio Fernández. It's possible—especially in the case of Nervo—that this humor is involuntary. There are also excellent prose writers and poets in whose work humor is striking for its absence. Martí is the great example of this kind of writer, despite *The Golden Age*.

It could be said that in rural, provincial Latin America humor was an exercise in decadence and that it was only reborn with the mass arrival of immigrants at the beginning of the twentieth century. Our forbears, who in intellectual matters were almost always boors, were unfamiliar with Voltaire and Diderot and Lichtenberg, and, even worse, they had never read—or scarcely read, or only claimed to have read, lying through their teeth—the Archpriest of Hita, Cervantes, Quevedo.

It was the twentieth century when humor timidly assumed a place in our literature. Its practitioners, of course, are a minority. Most writers turn out lyric or epic verse or revel in imagining the superman or the ideal leader of the proletariat or in plucking the petals from the little flowers of the Holy Mother Church. Those who laugh (and their laughter is often bitter) can be counted on the fingers of two hands. There's no question that Borges and Bioy wrote the best humorous fiction, in the guise of H. Bustos Domecq, a pseudonymous creation often more real, if that makes sense, than the pseudonymous creations of Pessoa, and whose stories, from the *Six Problems for Don Isidro Parodi* to the *Chronicles of Bustos Domecq* should be part of any anthology that isn't just trash, as Don Honorio himself might put it. Or not.

Few writers follow the same course as Borges and Bioy. Cortázar, of course, but not Arlt, who, like Onetti, opts for the parched and silent abyss. Vargas Llosa in two books and Manuel Puig in two, but not Sábato or Reinaldo Arenas, who contemplate spellbound our collective fate. In poetry, once a refuge for laughter, the situation is much worse: one might say that all Latin American poets, whether naïve or flat-out idiots, vacillate between Shelley and Byron, between Darío's impossible fluency and Nerudian career aspirations. Intoxicated with lyricism, intoxicated with otherness, Latin American poetry is marching rapidly toward destruction. The camp of what in Chile is very fittingly called *serious fools* grows ever larger. If we reread Paz or Huidobro we notice the absence of humor, an absence that in the end is a comfortable mask, a mask of stone. Thank goodness we have Nicanor Parra. Thank goodness Parra's tribe has yet to lay down arms.

4.
SCENES

TOWN CRIER OF BLANES

First of all I have to thank the mayor, Ramón Ramos, and all those who had the foolish idea of asking me to deliver the holiday address for the new year, 1999, which as far as I'm concerned is the last year of the millennium, no matter what people who know something about mathematics say. Whether we've changed centuries or millennia or not, the coming year will be something new. It'll be the year 2000 and it will be different. A year is like a coat or a cape, sometimes a shirt, even a handkerchief. In fact: sometimes a year is like a Kleenex. And when we wrap ourselves in the year 2000 or blow our noses into the year 2000, our perception of time will somehow have changed. So I'm very happy to be bringing in the year 1999, a year that I've come to know very well and that I don't see as a handkerchief (much less a Kleenex), or even a coat, but rather a T-shirt, a big old T-shirt in which I feel completely comfortable. But I was saying something else.

I was saying that I'm grateful for the mayor's invitation. Of course I'm grateful. I'll try to say it without self-dramatizing: I'm grateful. It's an honor for me. An undeserved honor, as it happens, because I'm sure there are better qualified people to call in the new year. A few years ago, Àngel Planells, the most modest of the Catalan surrealist painters, spoke these words in his Blanes holiday address: "*També vull demanar perdó a tots vosaltres perquè aquí han vingut persones de molta memòria, de molta categoria y de molt valer, i jo sóc un nouvingut només.*"* The Planells who said what you've just heard me say in my atrocious Catalan was eighty-six-years old and he was without a doubt someone who did honor to the post of town crier. And even so, wise old Planells said: "*sóc un nouvingut només.*" And he also said: "*Us adverteixo que no vull fer cap conferència, sinó només una petita xerrameca el més informal possible. Encara que, tractant-se de mi, ja se sap que ha de ser una cosa informal, perquè de formalitat jo només en vaig tenir el dia que em vaig casar.*"† And two years later he died in Barcelona as quietly as he had lived. I hope that my address will be worthy of such an illustrious predecessor. I hope my *petita xerrameca* won't be too formal and that if Àngel Planells could hear it he would say "*no està mal, jove.*"

I came to this town by chance, many years ago now. I came one summer to open a store in Los Pinos and I stayed. Of course, I knew nothing about stores. And my time as a salesman was brief and in a way it brought an end to the cycle

* "And I'd like to beg everyone's pardon because there are people here with long memories, people of high standing, people of great worth, and I'm just a novice."—tr.
† "I warn you that instead of a lecture this will be a little chat, nothing formal. This being me, it couldn't be anything else, since the only formal occasion in my life will be the day I get married."—tr.

of all my countless extra-literary jobs. But I had heard of Blanes before. In fact, the first time I read its name was in Mexico, in the early 1970s, in a novel by Juan Marsé. I even remember the color of the Mexican sky during the two days it took me to read the novel. In it, a migrant laborer from Murcia, an interloper called Pijoaparte, who makes a living in part by stealing motorcycles, falls in love with a rich girl from Barcelona (she's stunningly beautiful too) whose name is Teresa. Teresa's parents have a house in Blanes, where the family spends the summers. The novel is called *Ultimas tardes con Teresa* [Last Afternoons with Teresa] and I advise those who haven't read it to go to the bookstore right now and buy it. It's Blanes in there. Not a real Blanes, but the spirit of Blanes or one of the spirits of Blanes, the paradise unattainable by the Murcian transplant Pijoaparte and the paradise attained by the Chilean transplant Bolaño. A paradise that doesn't call too much attention to itself, with a magnificent slice of sea, the sea that I discovered the first season I spent here, when I wasn't married yet, *"perquè de formalitat jo només en vaig tenir el dia que em vaig casar,"* as Àngel Planells says, and I walked along the Paseo Marítimo looking for the house of Teresa's parents, from the mouth of the Tordera to the coves near Lloret, and of course I couldn't find it, because the urban geography of Blanes as described in *Ultimas tardes con Teresa* is the urban geography of the soul, the geography of an exceptional writer like Marsé, and maps like those are made so that the heart doesn't get lost, but they're not much use if you're trying to find a real house in a real town. All of this I knew beforehand, of course, but I still went out walking when I had a break at the store, and since walking is tiring I stopped for beers at different bars and I talked to people and in the process I didn't find Marsé's house but I did make some friends. My first friends in Blanes were almost all drug addicts. That sounds like an exaggeration, but it's true. Today most of them are dead. Some died of overdoses, others of AIDS. When I met them they were young, good-looking kids. They weren't good students, none of them went to college, but they lived their lives—short lives, as it turned out—as if they were part of a vast Greek tragedy. As if they had read Euripides or Sophocles. As if they had read Aristophanes and laughed, though his name meant nothing to them. They weren't good students. They worked as waiters in the summer, or as construction workers. But they were generous with me and they didn't ask me where I was from or what I was doing or anything. They were the ghostly children of Pijoaparte. The children that Pijoaparte never had in Blanes with Teresa. Now they're dead, and almost no one remembers them, naïve kids who thought they were dangerous but who were a danger only to themselves. They welcomed me, gave me my official welcome to the town, you could say, and then I was welcomed by their mothers and fathers, who'd come to Blanes seeking a future for their children, and the tourists who each summer brightened my store, and some wonderful *botiguers*, straight out of *Lazarillo de Tormes* or the wildest chapters of Anselm Turmeda, and other kids, like Sebastián, who were princes, but not the reckless kind, because they didn't shoot up hard drugs, though Sebastian, who really was a prince, could have been killed any number of times in a car or a motorcycle accident and wasn't killed, and today Sebastián, Sebas, is a king and is married to a queen and has a little prince who I hope will grow up in a tolerant and open-minded Blanes, which is the greatest happiness to which a man can aspire. And I also met many other people in Blanes, by which I mean people who haven't died, like my friend Waldo, who's a policeman now and would surely win every shooting competition he entered if he had a decent gun, but who doesn't win because his gun isn't a precision instrument like his competitors' guns. Anyway, Waldo doesn't care, and he participates, and always places respectably. I hope these words won't be taken as a tribute to the police but as a tribute to my friend who is a policeman and also the best marksman in Blanes and the surrounding area. And then there's Narcís Serra, who ran and still runs a video rental store in Los Pinos and who was and I imagine still is one of the funniest people in town and also a good person, with whom I spent whole afternoons discussing the films of Woody Allen (whom Narcís recently spotted in New York, but that's another story) or talking about thrillers that only he and I and sometimes Dimas Luna, who back then was just a kid doing his military service and who now runs a bar, had seen. And to think of them all at once, Sebastián, Waldo, and Narcís, all three of them married now, all three of them fathers, is a little bit frightening because it means that the years have gone by, it means that all of us, but especially me, are leaving our youth behind, and it brings to mind yet again the word *tolerance*, which for me is the word that defines Catalonia but especially the word that defines Blanes, a town or small city that despite its problems, despite its defects, is tolerant, is lively and civilized, because without tolerance there is no civilization, without tolerance there are repressive-cities, robot-cities, cities that resemble the mechanical orange of our late lamented Kubrick and our late lamented Burgess, but that will never in any way be cities where we can live. And that's what Catalonia has taught me and what Blanes has taught me among many other things that I've learned here, the most important of which is to take care of my son, who is a citizen of Blanes and a Catalan by birth and not by adoption, like me: a tolerance that can sometimes be mistaken for timidity, but that knows how to be forceful when necessary. And I've learned many other things in Blanes, things I might have learned elsewhere but that I had the good fortune of learning here, like eating shrimp, for example, the best in the Mediterranean, according to my friend Jordi, who is a fisherman; and I've also learned, or learned again, because one can never let down one's guard in this respect, not to be embarrassed about being poor (which is something that's unfortunately common in Latin America where there are so many poor people), and this is important, because in Catalonia one is ashamed of not working, not of being poor. For a writer like me, who hasn't accumulated wealth or possessions, and who as Àngel Planells says *"vaig passar unes dificultats tremendes, vaig haver de fer una mica de tot,"** it's very important. But back to the *festa major.* To be honest, I have no idea what saint we're celebrating. I've lived in Blanes for more than fifteen years and I still don't know. Nor do I want to know. It might be Sant Bonosi or Sant Maximià. It might be Sant Pere. Or Santa Anna. Or Sant Joan. Who knows. Or Eolus, the lord of the winds. Or Vulcan, who is a smith but who if necessary could also be the god of fireworks. As far as I'm concerned, we're celebrating Blanes itself, which is older than New York. And we're celebrating all of those who were born here, all of those who at some point came here, all of those who passed through, even if it was only for a day, or a fleeting night, to watch the fireworks, for example. The *festa major* is no more than that. A symbol that unites us all: Blanenses and Barcelonans, Basques and Andalusians, Gambians and South Americans. A symbol that reminds us that we're alive and that every day is a treasure. A symbol that reminds us of our individuality, because when it comes down to it all symbols remind us of our individuality and our solitude, but that also reminds us of our need for others: because for there

* "Will experience all kinds of hardship, will have to do a bit of everything."—tr.

to be a *festa* there must be friends, family, neighbors, foreigners, strangers in whom we can see ourselves reflected and recognize ourselves or recognize a part of the mystery. And since I began by remembering the dead, I think I should end by remembering the living, the people I see every day or once a week, like the magnificent Mr. Ponsdomènech, the bard of Blanes, who knows how to enjoy people and enjoy each day as it passes, or like Rosa de Trallero, who just lost her husband, my friend Santiago Trallero, or like Santi, who works at Joker Jocs and is a minimalist philosopher, or like the girls at the Bitlloch stationery store, all of them pretty and nice without exception, or like the clerks at the Oms pharmacy, who have a kind word for everyone, and so many other friends that it would be hopeless to try to name them, and to whom I'd like to say that in three days I'm going to South America, but a month from now I hope to be back in Blanes and I also hope that by then no one will remember this clumsy New Year's speech. And if anyone does remember it, then I hope he'll be polite enough not to remind me of it. *Bones festes a tothom!!*

THE MARITIME JUNGLE

The name evokes a giant aquarium. But it isn't an aquarium, it's the home of the brave. Sometimes: the winter headquarters where the brave go to wait—and despair. More often: the dormitory city where the brave sleep and dream. A strip of land along the sea, and three towns or small cities—the first three cities of the Costa Brava, to the right of the main road from Barcelona—that couldn't be more different from one another: Blanes, which is older than New York and sometimes seems like a rabid mix of Tyre, Pompeii, and Brooklyn; Lloret de Mar, which resembles nothing but itself, or in other words Flaubert's Carthage; and Tossa, where there's a Chagall and the statue of a woman that on foggy days wanders off in search of a nice man. For those coming from elsewhere, it's hard to reach, that is, there's a *semblance* of difficulty about the approaches to the Maritime Jungle, especially if one doesn't have a car, but the traveler, once he's here or nearby, realizes with a feeling close to astonishment that this difficulty is basically an illusion. The train only stops in Blanes and the Blanes station isn't even close to Blanes, properly speaking. The Blanes station is near a factory. Years ago it was explained to me what the factory makes, but by now I've managed to forget. All I know is that the factory brought many immigrants to Blanes, and that most of those immigrants went to live in Los Pinos, which was nothing but a pine forest back then and is now a neighborhood of white single-story houses by the sea. Beyond Los Pinos there are campgrounds, a hotel or two, apartment buildings, all kinds of new construction, and beyond that is the Tordera River, and on the other side of the river is the province of Barcelona. But when one reaches Blanes by train all one finds is the station, surrounded by fields, and a bit further on, the barracks of the Guardia Civil, empty most of the time, and the factory that is now a very modern factory and where workers are almost never seen, as if the factory were an office full of clerks and all the hard work was done by machines, though I know that's not true, because if there aren't any workers then where did the people come from who settled and built Los Pinos and later La Plantera? But the sense one gets from the factory is of isolation. And that's what you find when you arrive by train, which is the cheapest way to get to the Maritime Jungle: an empty space, the space of childhood hula-hooping, the timeless space of the Mediterranean, which means fields, trees, and a proud and inscrutable silence. At the Blanes station (which doesn't resemble a church, like the Toledo station, or a surrealist puzzle, like the Perpignan station, but rather a doorway hidden in the shrubs), the travelers, a single unit until a minute before, go their separate ways, and some catch the bus to Blanes and others the bus to Lloret. If you want to go to Tossa you have to get off in Lloret and take a taxi or ask for directions to the place where the buses leave for

Tossa. The three towns of the Maritime Jungle are like three sisters who stopped talking to one another long ago. Let's start with the one in the middle.

Lloret, and this is one of its main virtues, resembles nothing but Lloret. There is no town on the Costa Brava, no town on the Catalan seaboard, no town or city on the Spanish coast that is anything like it. Lloret built itself and then burned the plans (or burned the architects, which amounts to the same thing). Of course, for lovers of antiquities there are still the second-century Roman ruins of Avellaners, as well as Iberian remains that date back to 250 BC at the Puig Castellet, a settlement of warriors whose function was probably to keep watch over the land. But Lloret is something else: it's the dream of the European proletariat, it's alcohol and sex and an architectural mish-mash that will delight the archeologists of the year 4500 (A.D.). Lloret is like Delphos. Lloret is like Alexandria without the library. Lloret is the song of summer translated into cement and bricks and streets that look like a blend of all the streets of Europe, democratic and rapturous streets where young blue-collar Germans meet young blue-collar Dutch girls, where sad English divorcés meet sad French divorcées, where hooligans chant melancholy songs at five in the morning like the Vienna choirboys they never were and always wanted to be, because life is beautiful, yes, but also terrible, and terribly short, and that (too) is Lloret: the mirror of our brevity, our fragility, our well-bred or ferocious happiness. Do I have to say that I think Lloret de Mar is wonderful? There, the last surviving waiters of Spain work their hardest. And the prettiest Spanish girls let themselves be seduced by the most insistent Italian men. Lloret is full of altars, and it doesn't look like any other city (except perhaps Flaubert's Carthage), though other cities run the risk of looking like Lloret. Months ago, as I was riding along one of the great boulevards of Berlin, a section of it—some fifteen yards at most—was suddenly transformed into a section of a street in Lloret de Mar. When I told this to the friend of mine who was driving, she replied, with German imperturbability, that it was impossible. We turned around and went looking for that slice of Lloret along the austere avenue. We couldn't find it. It was just a vision. Or maybe it was the postcards, the flowers, the café tables, the sparkle in the eyes and on the skin of some passersby who were no longer there. To watch day break in Lloret is an exhausting privilege.

Daybreak in Tossa is different. To begin with, in Tossa there's a Chagall (*The Blue Violinist*), and that sets a place apart. Chagall himself described Tossa as a *paradis bleu*. From celeste to blue there's only a blink, a slight shift or fading of the light, and that's Tossa: a luminiferous expansion and contraction. In other words, Tossa is a miracle. In other words, Tossa is the outcome—always uncertain—of a specific notion of beauty. With scarcely 4,000 inhabitants (Lloret has 15,000 and Blanes 30,000), Tossa is the little sister of the Maritime Jungle, the pretty one, the thin one, and the only one that, in addition to a Chagall, has a statue of Ava Gardner and a ghost. The statue of Ava is life-size and visitors often have their picture taken with her. They're surprised by her height: she's short, a bit over five feet, and sometimes one is struck by the suspicion that the statue isn't really as true to life, especially height-wise, as it claims to be. But it's Ava, Saint Ava, and she's in Tossa, where she was as happy as a clam, and at night her ghost rises up from the statue and strolls along the bay of Tossa and along the Moltó and Bona coves, and on moonlit nights it reaches the coves of Giverola and Senyor Ramon. And this isn't a legend. It's absolutely true. One rainy spring afternoon I saw Ava walking the slopes of the massif of Cadiretes (behind Tossa).

Tossa has a ghost. Blanes doesn't. What Blanes has instead is pure energy. I can't remember when it was that I first came here. All I know is that it was by train and many years ago. Juan Marsé, in *Ultimas tardes con Teresa* [Last Afternoons with Teresa], turned Blanes into the unattainable paradise of all Spain's Julien Sorels. I read the novel in Mexico and the sonority of the word Blanes (which comes from the Latin *blanda*) enthralled me. We're all Pijoaparte, but I never guessed that one day I would come to Blanes and that I'd never want to leave. As a desert guidebook (a guide to the desert of the mind) would put it, there are many sights of interest: the Mar I Murtra botanical garden, founded by Karl Faust in 1924, where one can admire more than 4,000 species of trees and plants; the Gothic fountain, the town jewel, built at the end of the fourteenth century by Violante de Cabrera, daughter of the Count of Prades, in the shape of a hexagon with six jets of water and six gargoyles, a fountain so beautiful and modest, there next to the old movie theater, that one asks oneself how it occured to the lovely Violante, where the master craftsmen who built it came from, how we can possibly pass it each day without weeping. And as if that weren't enough, there's the Pinya de Rosa botanical garden, founded by Riviere de Caralt and furnished with more than 7,000 species, a garden that definitely makes Blanes a town with a high index of exotic trees and plants; the chapel of Our Lady of Hope, where in the old days the chaplain taught grammar to the town's children; the twelfth-century chapel of Santa Bárbara from whose bell tower the Blanenses were alerted of the presence of enemy ships; and the chapel of San Juan, built at the highest point in town by Grau de Cabrera in the mid-thirteenth century, which is the first thing one sees when one arrives by train from Barcelona, the tower of San Juan, tall and outlined against the sky and the Mediterranean. But there's another type of monument or attraction that may be the kind I like best. The black rice at Can Tarrés, for example, or the black rice at Dimas's restaurant, or the market that every day, except for Sundays, stretches from one end to the other of Calle de Dentro, or the fish market, where the fish are auctioned every day, or the faint presence of the great writer Josep Maria de Sagarra, who in the '50s summered in Blanes with his young son Joan, or the big old house where Ruyra lived, or the rhapsode Ponsdomènech who still today, as he nears ninety, strolls the town reading his poems to those who need or want to hear them. Blanes is like Ponsdomènech. Blanes is like Violante de Cabrera, who instead of building fortifications or walls, like the rest of her clan, built a "Gothic civil fountain," in the middle of the street, for the use and benefit of all. Blanes is like the Catalans of the town who went off to fight in Cuba and the Andalusians who came here to work and later left to fight on the fronts of Aragón and the Ebro. Blanes is like its beaches, where each summer Europe's bravest come to lie in the sun, people from here and from the other side of the Pyrenees, the fat, the ugly, the skeletal, the prettiest girls of Barcelona, children of all kinds, the old, the terminally ill, the hung over, all half naked, all exposed to the Mediterranean sun and the sympathetic gaze of the tower of San Juan, and the smell that rises from the beaches (it's nice to remember this now, in the dead of winter) is the smell of body lotion, of tanning cream, of sunscreen, a smell that is what it is, of course, but that is also the smell of democracy, history, civilization.

BEACH

I gave up heroin and went home and began the methadone treatment administered at the outpatient clinic and I didn't have much else to do except get up each morning and watch TV and try to sleep at night, but I couldn't, something made me unable to close my eyes and rest, and that was my routine until one day I couldn't stand it anymore and I bought myself a pair of black swim trunks at a store in the center of town and I went to the beach, wearing the trunks and with a towel and a magazine, and I spread my towel not too far from the sea and then I lay down and spent a while trying to decide whether to go into the sea or not, I could think of lots of reasons to go in but also some not to (the children playing at the water's edge, for example), until at last it was too late and I went home, and the next morning I bought some sunscreen and I went to the beach again, and at around twelve I headed to the clinic and got my dose of methadone and said hello to some

familiar faces, no friends, just familiar faces from the methadone line who were surprised to see me in swim trunks, but I
acted as if there was nothing strange about it, and then I
walked back to the beach and this time I went for a dip and
tried to swim, though I couldn't, and that was enough for me,
and the next day I went back to the beach and put on sunscreen all over and then I fell asleep on the sand, and when I
woke up I felt very well-rested, and I hadn't burned my back
or anything, and this went on for a week or maybe two, I can't
remember, the only thing I'm sure of is that each day I got
more tan and though I didn't talk to anyone each day I felt
better, or different, which isn't the same thing but in my case
it seemed like it, and one day an old couple turned up on the
beach, I remember it clearly, it looked like they'd been together
for a long time, she was fat, or round, and must have been
about seventy, and he was thin, or more than thin, a walking
skeleton, I think that was why I noticed him, because usually
I didn't take much notice of the people on the beach, but I did
notice them, and it was because the guy was so skinny, I saw
him and got scared, fuck, it's death coming for me, I thought,
but nothing was coming for me, it was just two old people,
the man maybe seventy-five and the woman about seventy, or
the other way around, and she seemed to be in good health,
but he looked as if he were going to breathe his last breath any
time now or as if this were his last summer, and at first, once
I was over my initial fright, it was hard for me to look away
from the old man's face, from his skull barely covered by a thin
layer of skin, but then I got used to watching the two of them
surreptitiously, lying on the sand, on my stomach, with my
face hidden in my arms, or from the boardwalk, sitting on a
bench facing the beach, as I pretended to brush sand off myself, and I remember that the old woman always came to the
beach with an umbrella, under which she quickly ducked, and

she didn't wear a swimsuit, although sometimes I saw her in a swimsuit, but usually she was in a very loose summer dress that made her look fatter than she was, and under that umbrella the old woman sat reading, she had a very thick book, while the skeleton that was her husband lay on the sand in nothing but a tiny swimsuit, almost a thong, and drank in the sun with a voracity that brought me distant memories of junkies frozen in blissful immobility, of junkies focused on what they were doing, on the only thing they could do, and then my head ached and I left the beach, I had something to eat on the Paseo Marítimo, a little dish of anchovies and a beer, and then I smoked a cigarette and watched the beach through the window of the bar, and then I went back and the old man and the old woman were still there, she under her umbrella, he exposed to the sun's rays, and then, suddenly, for no reason, I felt like crying and I got in the water and swam and when I was a long way from the shore I looked at the sun and it seemed strange to me that it was there, that big thing so unlike us, and then I started to swim toward the beach (twice I almost drowned) and when I got back I dropped down next to my towel and sat there panting for quite a while, but without losing sight of the old couple, and then I may have fallen asleep on the sand, and when I woke up the beach was beginning to empty, but the old man and the old woman were still there, she with her novel under the umbrella and he on his back in the sun with his eyes closed and a strange expression on his skull-like face, as if he could feel each second passing and he was savoring it, though the sun's rays were weak, though the sun had already dipped behind the buildings along the beach, behind the hills, but that didn't seem to bother him, and then I watched him and I watched the sun, and sometimes my back stung a little, as if that afternoon I'd burned myself, and I looked at them and then I got up, I slung my towel over my shoulders like a cape and went to sit on one of the benches of the Paseo Marítimo, where I pretended to brush non-existent sand off my legs, and from up there I had a different vision of the couple, and I said to myself that maybe he wasn't about to die, I said to myself that maybe time didn't exist in the way I'd always thought it existed, I reflected on time as the sun's distance lengthened the shadows of the buildings, and then I went home and took a shower and examined my red back, a back that didn't seem to belong to me but to someone else, someone I wouldn't get to know for years and then I turned on the TV and watched shows that I didn't understand at all, until I fell asleep in my chair, and the next day it was back to the same old thing, the beach, the clinic, the beach again, a routine that was sometimes interrupted by new people on the beach, a woman, for example, who was always standing, who never lay down in the sand, who wore a bikini bottom and a blue T-shirt, and who only went into the water up to the knees, and who was reading a book, like the old woman, but this woman read it standing up, and sometimes she knelt down, though in a very odd way, and picked up a big bottle of Pepsi and drank, standing up, of course, and then put the bottle back down on the towel, which I don't know why she'd brought since she never lay down on it or went swimming, and sometimes this woman scared me, she seemed too strange, but most of the time I just felt sorry for her, and I saw other strange things too, all kinds of things happen at the beach, maybe because it's the only place where we're all half-naked, though nothing too important ever happened, once as I was walking along the shore I thought I saw an ex-junkie like me, sitting on a mound of sand with a baby on his lap, and another time I saw some Russian girls, three Russian girls, who were probably hookers and who were talking on cell phones and laughing, all three of them, but what really interested me most was the old couple, partly because I had the feeling that the old man might die at any moment, and when I thought this, or when I realized I was thinking this, crazy ideas would come into my head, like the thought that after the old man's death there would be a tsunami and the town would be destroyed by a giant wave, or that the earth would begin to shake and a massive earthquake would swallow up the whole town in a wave of dust, and when I thought about all this, I hid my head in my hands and began to weep, and while I was weeping I dreamed (or imagined) that it was nighttime, say three in the morning, and I'd left my house and went to the beach, and on the beach I found the old man lying on the sand, and in the sky, up near the stars, but closer to Earth than the other stars, there shone a black sun, an enormous sun, silent and black, and I went down to the beach and lay on the sand too, the only two people on the beach were the old man and me, and when I opened my eyes again I realized that the Russian hookers and the girl who was always standing and the ex-junkie with the baby were watching me curiously, maybe wondering who that weird guy was, the guy with the sunburned shoulders and back, and even the old woman was gazing at me from under her umbrella, interrupting the reading of her interminable book for a few seconds, maybe wondering who that young man was, that man with silent tears running down his face, a man of thirty-five who had nothing at all but who was recovering his will and his courage and who knew that he would live a while longer.

IN SEARCH OF THE TORICO OF TERUEL

I left Blanes for Teruel, where I was going to be on the jury for a short-story prize, without knowing very well whether Teruel exists (as they like to claim in Teruel) or not. Of course, I was inclined to think that it existed, but an inner voice—the rapturous voice of desire, which frightens us all—told me that it was possible that Teruel, in fact, didn't exist. The trip along the highway from Barcelona to Valencia was uneventful. The driver—whose name I unfortunately can't recall, just as I'm unable to recall the names of anyone else I met on that trip, except Ana María Navales, who more than anything else is a force of nature—talked to me about how good life was in Teruel, about its 30,000 inhabitants (Teruel is the same size as Blanes), about the unemployment rate (notably low), about the happy and well-documented possibility of crossing the whole city from end to end in twenty minutes. The driver was an exemplary citizen of Teruel, an excellent driver, and one could tell that he loved his city. The problems began when we turned off the highway and began to climb towards Teruel. The landscape was very beautiful, with that austere and mocking beauty of certain parts of Aragón; but there were also curves, and for a while now curves have made me sick to my stomach, which meant that several times we had to take breaks at roadside restaurants, places that vaguely reminded me of another time, when my father was a truck driver and we pulled into lost truckstops to eat fried eggs, because the roads of Teruel are lost in time and I began to feel that all zigzagging roads somehow led to Teruel, no matter where they were situated geographically or whether the roads were Chilean or Mexican or even Central American, which was rather disturbing, because everyone knows that nausea plus melancholia tends to be the harbinger of impending illness, and that made me a little sad, because not only did we have to stop at roadside restaurants, we also had to stop out in the open, which gave us the chance to gaze at the towns along the way to Teruel, sad, beautiful little towns, towns that are gradually being abandoned, the driver told me, as I gagged and retched at the side of the road, because the young people are leaving for the cities, for Valencia, Barcelona, Zaragoza, and Madrid, as if the battle of Teruel hadn't ended and the winter in which the battle was enveloped hadn't ended either.

So I was still sick when I caught a glimpse of the towns just outside Teruel and I continued to be sick when we got to the city, crossed a bridge, and looked down into a very deep gorge, like the dry bed of an enormous river, but with houses and buildings where the river once flowed, something which now that I'm no longer sick and able to think more clearly, strikes me as suspiciously wonderful. How could anything have been built there, in that giant ravine? It was an astonishing sight. Like the favelas of Rio de Janeiro, but the mirror image, with a bridge even passing over the houses. It was like Aragonese cubism in an age when no one makes cubist art anymore, let alone so obstinately. And at the other end of the bridge, Teruel rose like a minimalist labyrinth on a promontory or hill or mesa. This city is much better than people say, was what I thought. I was also thinking that I was sick, and that when I got to the hotel I'd better go straight to bed.

Then two friends appeared as I got out of the car and they took me to see several Mudejar towers, one after the other, and some of the towers were fake and others were real, and they were saying: this one is fake and this one is real, but so fast that I was never sure which were the fake ones and which were the real ones, which is odd anyway, because the name Teruel (Tirwal) means watchtower, and those giant watchtowers were used to sight enemy armies or parties coming from the west or the east, depending: if you climb to the top of an authentic Mudejar tower, you'll surely spy a dream, and if you climb to the top of a fake Mudejar tower, you'll surely spy a nightmare. And then there was Ana María Navales, a chain-smoker with a pronounced limp, and she sent me straight to my room in a hotel that has rooms of utter luxury in branches in other provincial capitals, but that in Teruel only has very sad and dignified rooms, as if in the rooms of that hotel—whose name I choose to forget—the din and silence of the battle of Teruel were still something real and terrifying. And it wasn't only the room that was modest, even timid, but also the receptionist and the men who strolled idly (or so it seemed) along the corridors and looked at you as if to inquire about the course of the battle. A cubist battle, evidently, in which time and space, at least as we understand them, didn't count for much.

When I came out of my room—still slightly feverish, I think, and feeling as sick as I had during the car trip—Ana María Navales was waiting for me, and we went off with the rest of the jury to decide which story should win the contest. As I expected, the winning story was about the civil war. Then we went out for a walk around the city, upon which night had already fallen. I remember the Mudejar towers, which appeared and disappeared in the most unlikely places. I remember streets with the names of saints. I remember priests rubbing their hands together or clasping them tight as they walked, as if they'd just received news of Buñuel's death. I remember Aragonese voices coming from the most surprising places (even from beneath the cobblestones). I remember fortress-churches and I remember a girl with short hair, no more than twenty, who passed me without a glance. I remember the Calle de los Amantes and the Plaza del Seminario, which is crammed with ghosts. I remember the faces of two colonels, Rey d'Harcourt, who surrendered, and Colonel Barba, who didn't. I remember the 20th corps of the Republican army, and the 18th and the 22nd, which launched the offensive in December 1937. And I remember Buñuel's brother, Alfonso Buñuel—few people rememember him; he made disturbing collages—who was born in 1915 and died in 1961, and whose work was shown to me in Teruel, where they have the custom of remembering precisely those who are remembered by no one, or hardly anyone. I also remember a warm cardoon salad and Ana María Navales talking to me about English women writers until three in the morning, both of us chain-smoking. And I remember that Juan Villoro, in Barcelona, had told me his family came from Teruel, and I remember my vain efforts, as a result, to buy him a bottle of wine to take back to Mexico to drink with Margarita.

But the main thing, the thing I remember best, I had yet to see. I saw it that night. All of a sudden we were in the Plaza del Torico. And there, on a column sturdy enough to hold a Greek hero or Franco's horse, was the Torico. Here was

Teruel, I knew it right away, and here also was the skeptical and indomitable spirit of Aragón. The Torico is tiny, as its name indicates, a toy for an eight-year-old child; but it isn't a toy, it's a miniature bull. It possesses a calm elegance not devoid of pride and indifference. It's one of the most beautiful statues I've seen in my life, if not the most beautiful. On the way home I got sick again and then I fell asleep. I dreamed that the Torico was walking along beside me. "Did you like Teruel?" it asked me, though only to be polite, because in reality the Torico couldn't care less whether I had liked his city or not. "Very much," I said. "And does it exist or not, do you think?" it asked me. Just as I was about to answer that I thought it did, the Torico turned away and I heard it say: "No, I'd rather not know." Then I dreamed that someone in a huge dark dance hall put on an album of the pasodoble *Suspiros de España*, and by the time the music began, the ghost that had set it playing was gone.

VIENNA AND THE SHADOW OF A WOMAN

I don't know what was best about Vienna: whether it was Vienna or Carmen Boullosa. Everyone knows that Vienna is a beautiful, cultured city, the capital of a country that flirts (and its flirting may have reached the feeling-up stage) with neofascism. But few in Spain know who Carmen Boullosa is.

The first reports I had of her told of a very beautiful woman who was causing the Mexican lyrical poets to lose their heads. Carmen, who at the time hadn't yet begun to write novels, was also a Mexican lyrical poet. I didn't know what to think. All those poets head-over-heels in love with a poet struck me as excessive. On top of it all, the poets who had been dumped by Carmen (or by themselves) got to be friends, or were already friends, and had formed a de facto group or club that met once a week or once a month at bars in the center of Mexico City or in Coyoacán to revile their former beloved.

I also learned, always from third parties, that in response Carmen had started a club or society or commando group of women writers who met in secret, just like their male counterparts.

One day, in a book about contemporary Mexican literature, I saw a picture of her. She was definitely a beautiful woman, dark, tall, with huge eyes and hair down to her waist. I thought she was very attractive, but I also imagined that she must write like one of the many imitators of a magic realism made for the consumption of zombies.

Then I read something she had written and my opinion changed: Boullosa had nothing to do with imitators or imitators of imitators. I read just a few pages, but I liked what I read. And then I received an invitation to come to Vienna, where we would both give readings.

One of the good things about going to Vienna is that you can fly Lauda Air, the airline founded by the mythic Formula 1 driver, with stewardesses who dress like racetrack mechanics. The food is good, too. If you're lucky (or unlucky) the plane may even be flown by Nikki Lauda himself. And a little while later, in the time it takes to pray three Our Fathers, you're sitting in a taxi in Vienna, and if you're lucky you might even be staying at the Hotel Graban, a little place on the Dorotheergasse, next to St. Stephen's Cathedral, or in other words right in the center of the city. Though the most important thing about the Hotel Graben isn't its location, but the fact that it's the place where Max Brod and Franz Kafka stayed when they came to Vienna.

Outside of the hotel there's a huge bronze plaque that says this, but I arrived at night and didn't see the plaque, so when the receptionist told me that she was going to give me Brod's room or Kafka's room (I wasn't sure which), I thought she was recommending that I read both Prague writers, which, given the country's political situation, seemed very timely. Then, gathering my courage, I asked whether she had any information about the arrival of Frau or Fraulein Boullosa, which the receptionist pronounced Bolosa, and which made me think that even though Carmen was Mexican and I was Chilean, we shared the same Galician roots. Her answer disappointed me deeply. Not only was *Frau* Bolosa not at the hotel, she didn't have a reservation, and nothing was known about her.

So I went for a walk nearby, along Graben (curious: my hotel was called Graben but it wasn't on Graben), through the cathedral square, past the Stephansdom, the Figarohaus, the Franziskanerkirche, the Shubertring and the Stadtpark, the places that my friend Mario Santiago had roamed by night, stealthily, and then I returned to the hotel and went to bed and spent a strange night, as if there really were someone else in my room, Kafka or Brod or one of the thousands of guests who've stayed at the Graben and are now dead.

In the morning I met Leopold Federmair, a young Austrian novelist, and together we walked around the city some more, visiting the cafés that Bernhard had frequented when he was in Vienna, one place that was very close to my hotel, on the Lobkowitzplatz or the Augustinerstrasse, I can't remember which, and then the Café Hawelka, across from my hotel, where the owner, a little old woman out of a medieval folktale, offered us free buns for which she later charged us, and then we walked some more and visited other cafés, until it was time for my reading, and time for me to meet or to not meet Carmen Boullosa, who was nowhere to be found.

When we got to the hall—late, because Federmair got lost twice—she was already there. I recognized her easily, though in person she's even prettier than in pictures. She seemed shy. Smart and nice. After a party at a restaurant with a Turkish cannonball still embedded in the wall, palpable proof of the Viennese sense of humor, which is somewhere between naïve and twisted, we were left alone. Then she told me that St. Stephen's Cathedral was secretly consecrated to the devil and then she told me all about her life. We talked about Juan Pascoe, who was her first editor in Mexico, and also mine; about Verónica Volkow, Trotsky's great-granddaughter; about Mario Santiago, who had been to her house a few times; about our respective children.

After leaving her at her hotel I walked back to the Graben and that night I was visited or dreamed that I was visited by Kafka, or Brod, and I saw both of them, one in my room and the other in the room next door, packing or unpacking suitcases and whistling a catchy tune that the next morning I was whistling too.

Our next excursion was to the Danube, which we reached by metro. Boullosa was even more beautiful than the night before. We set out walking toward Hungary and along the way we saw a couple of skaters, a woman sitting and watching the river, a woman who stood and cried without making a sound, and some very strange ducks, some black and others light brown, and each black duck was paired with a light brown one, which led Boullosa to muse that opposites attract, unless the black ducks were parents and the light brown ones babies.

And then everything went as well as it could have gone. Kafka and Brod abandoned the hotel; Helmut Niederle, a wonderful Viennese man, told me the story of the famous shoemaker of Vienna, which I included in a book; we had dinner at the Mexican embassy, where the ambassador (at Boullosa's urging, I imagine) kindly treated me as if I were Mexican; I insulted a Nazi without meaning to; I didn't dare set foot in St. Stephen's Cathedral; I met Labarca, an excellent

Chilean novelist, and two Latin American girls who organize an annual beatnik festival in Vienna; and most of all I walked and talked endlessly with Carmen Boullosa, the best woman writer in Mexico.

THE LAST PLACE ON THE MAP

Ushuaia, the southernmost city in the world, located on the north edge of the Beagle Channel and at the foot of the Martial Mountains, is the dazzling, natural, and untamed heart of the province of Tierra del Fuego.

For a long time, first in the South American imagination and then in Europe and America, in part due to the books by certain meticulous travelers, and most especially English travelers, and most especially Chatwin, Patagonia was something like what the vast and restless territory of the U.S.-Mexican border has been and continues to be. Instead of desert, pampa; instead of sleepy sun-baked towns, farmhouses swept by the wind and southern rain; instead of crowds of strange people singing strange songs, just a few scattered inhabitants and almost uninterrupted silence. And yet both the Mexican border region and the provinces that make up the territory of Patagonia constituted, along with the jungle, the fabled last place, the sacred place of the individual, the space where one goes to die or to watch the time pass, which amounts to essentially the same thing. The jungle, perhaps because of its profusion of mosquitos and the inevitable illnesses they carry, has gone out of fashion: travelers, even terminally ill travelers, want to die in peace, that is cradled and lulled by a specific aesthetic that excludes, one can safely say, dengue fever, irksome insect bites, and even more irksome diarrhea. The Mexican border region and Patagonia, in this sense, have much to offer: tequila, cocaine, and women to the north; maté, good barbecue, and temperatures worthy of any scholastic philosopher in the far south. One travels to Patagonia but one also flees to Patagonia. The literature chronicling this kind of flight isn't only Anglo-Saxon. At the end of Ernesto Sábato's *On Heroes and Tombs*, when all the protagonist's dreams have been dashed and he seems doomed, he decides to get on a bus and set off for the south. Other writers have followed Sábato's example.

In fact, the voyage to Patagonia has long transcended the bounds of literature. There are paintings in which artists, with more enthusiasm than talent, present their vision of the plain, the glaciers, the barren land. There are musical compositions in which the word *Patagonia* rhymes with *Celedonia*. There's even a movie, the director of which I can't recall, that tells the story of a dentist, English or maybe Canadian, played by Daniel Day Lewis, who rides a motorcycle across Patagonia on a personal crusade against cavities.

For a while Patagonia replaced the tropics as a source of landscapes suitable for magic realism. And I even seem to remember a proposal—this was some time ago—to cede a big piece of Patagonia's unoccupied territory to either the League of Nations or the United Nations (the former, I think) for the founding of a Jewish republic, or for the settlement of some wandering Asian nation, probably Chinese refugees fleeing

Japanese aggression, a proposal that outraged the Argentines of the day and that, if it had taken effect, would surely have given rise to the most civilized and prosperous country in all of South America.

Where does the name Patagonia come from? From its primitive inhabitants, the Patagon Indians, who were described by the Spanish explorers as giants, and giants with enormous feet too, bigger than any European's, which was perhaps only logical considering that they were giants. The first to spot them (and also the last, it's said) were Magellan's brave sailors, bent on sailing around the globe, which in the end, after many hardships, they succeeded in doing, leaving more than half of the crew in their wake, dead of disease, starvation, and various kinds of exposure. A chronicler of the trip, the Italian Pigafetta, describes these giants as ten feet tall. He was probably exaggerating. In the nineteenth century, less fanciful travelers claimed to have seen Patagons who were six and a half feet tall. Today, the few that remain are well under six feet.

The border of Patagonia isn't something that everyone can identify with utter certainty, least of all Argentines. According to the novelist Rodrigo Fresán, whom I consulted, Patagonia begins when you cross the Río Negro. Meanwhile, some bus drivers from Buenos Aires who drive the southern routes think that Patagonia begins where the province of Buenos Aires ends. According to an Argentine friend, Patagonia begins when you cross over into the province of Chubut, quite a bit further south than most people believe. According to another Argentine friend, Patagonia doesn't exist at all. I considered putting the question to Alan Pauls, one of my favorite Argentine writers, but I was afraid to.

Beyond debate is the fact that Patagonia is huge and full of its own particular kind of ghosts. No traveler can see everything, partly because Argentina isn't cheap and partly because there's so much land to cover, which means that it takes at least six months to visit what the tour guides call its hidden gems, even in the most superficial way.

For example, Neuquén. Not only is Neuquén the only Patagonian province with no outlet to the sea, it's also the the only one to share a border with Chile, which makes it a kind of Bolivia in the geostrategic imagination of the Chilean military, who might just as well be Prussian. Neuquén is like Jurassic Park, South America's lost world of dinosaurs. In Neuquén, one bumps into tyrannosauruses and pterodactyls on every corner. The ranchers of Neuquén no longer speak of heads of cattle but of velociraptors. Pilgrimages of paleontologists are notable in the spring and summer months.

The tourist generally gets around by plane, which makes sense. But the best way to travel in Patagonia is by hitchhiking. For example, one can take a bus to Choele Choel or fly to Bahía Blanca, and then hitchhike. That, at least, was how the cash-strapped Argentines who couldn't make it to Europe in the 1960s traveled, and that's how some Patagon Indians still travel when curiosity or some urgent errand brings them to the capital or to La Plata, that sinister city that Bioy pondered in his old age. Once in Choele Choel the traveler must ask himself a crucial question: Which way? The two routes into Patagonia are very different. Either you head for Bariloche or you head for Puerto Madryn. In Bariloche, the unsuspecting tourist will find the Andes and a legion of skiers, snow fanatics with perfect tans and serious psychological and sexual issues who stay at the Llao-Llao, a 1940s hotel vaguely reminiscent of a thermal spa. In Puerto Madryn, on the other hand, he'll come upon the Atlantic, which at these latitudes (though it depends on the time of year, of course) is a distinctly horrible shade, like the color of some rotting animal or the skin of a rotting carcass, something from an abandoned tannery, although the sea, as always, smells good. And from here one can visit the Valdés Peninsula, which is the northern edge of the Golfo Nuevo, or, better yet, leave Puerto Madryn and head for Trelew and Rawson, which are nearby, and where, at daybreak, if one climbs up on a certain rock out in the country called the Rock of Yanquetruz, one can hear the cries carried on the wind from both cities, cries that speak vaguely of young recruits, young prisoners, nausea, and herds of pigs.

After this it's best to hop on the first bus out of Trelew, and also Rawson. But here the indefatigable traveler is presented with another dilemma. Either he must take the road west, toward the mountains, toward Trevelín and Esquel, and visit Leleque and El Maitén, mountain towns of the province of Chubut, with stops at Los Alerces National Park or Lago Puelo National Park or even, if the traveler is unusually curious, the Cochamo Pass, where he can look over into Chile without knowing exactly why or what for, or he must take the road south, toward Comodoro Rivadavia and the Petrified Forest. South of the Petrified Forest anything can happen. Between the road that runs along the foot of the mountains and the road that runs along the Atlantic, there lies a vast expanse of land, the last place, the land toward which the hitchhiking Patagons are headed, crossed every so often by secondary roads or dirt tracks that first demoralize the traveler and then make him lose his way and finally plunge him into a kind of mystical delirium that hunger and good breeding manage to allay. The two roads meet in Río Gallegos, the last city in Patagonia. Beyond it, across the Straits of Magellan, is the Argentine and Chilean Tierra del Fuego, but that's another story.

FATEFUL CHARACTERS

What is clarity in photography? Is it seeing what needs to be seen and not what doesn't? Is it keeping one's eyes always open and seeing everything? Is it choosing what to see, making what one sees speak? Is it seeking, amid an avalanche of empty images, the thing the eye perceives as beauty? Is it the vain search for beauty?

The killer sleeps as the victim photographs him. This sentence, spoken with weary calm in a near whisper, has been haunting me or my shadow for years. The killer sleeps. The victim takes pictures. In images: a cheap single bed in a room neither bright nor dark, an unsuspecting man on the bed, asleep on his stomach or his side, wearing undershorts and a T-shirt, dark socks, no sheet to cover him, in the sleeper's customary state of abandon, and a shadow, neither man nor woman, just a shadow, an androgynous silhouette at the foot of the bed, pitched toward the left, toward the center of the room, who holds aloft a little camera and peers through the lens, as intently focused as the sleeping man, but (and this is another sign of horror and normality) in a different way. The camera that the shadow holds—it's important to emphasize this—appears to be fixed on a tripod, an imaginary tripod in the middle of a slightly messy room, a room that may or may not be a hotel room. Either way, it seems to be the sleeper's (or killer's) room, not the photographer's (or victim's) room, though the latter moves around it with a kind of familiarity, a growing familiarity, in which one senses equal degrees of perseverance and pain, rebellion and resignation, as if reality had curved, and time, if only for an instant, were gazing backward.

The person taking the picture wins, but victory can lead to a death without hope of appeal. The person with open eyes wins, but whom does he beat? And what good does it do to win when we know that in the end everybody loses, that we all lose?

The vagabond children of Santiago and the ghosts of London. The wet and the dry in the work of Larraín.

I'd like to say that I've lived in one of his photographs. Maybe I have. What I know for certain is that I've strolled through one: I've walked the streets that Larraín photographed, I've seen those floors like mirrors (mirrors in which only the most unstable objects or nothing at all is reflected), I've been gazed at by the same people who were gazed at by Larraín.

He's the accidental photographer, or so it seems; the playful photographer, the Chilean kid let loose. He appears to be many things that he isn't. At times I think he seeks harmony or a simulacrum of harmony: the instant at which everything stops and men come to resemble objects. Nothing moves. The rain freezes in the air. The man with the umbrella grows to look like the equestrian statue in the background. The eye opens until it's the size of a mouth.

I have the feeling that Larraín is the perfect tourist, the Medusa tourist who, as the result of years buried in the only corridor-country in the world and of generations of misspent, squandered, or forgotten Chilean lives, has been granted a gaze that is also a way of moving. Swift, agile, young, and vulnerable, Larraín scans a labyrinthine city and as he does so he scans us. The gaze of Larraín: an arborescent mirror.

Larraín photographs a line of people—waiting for the bus. This is in London but it might as well be on the fringes of hell. A perfectly orderly line, perfectly normal. When the bus comes everyone will get on and then the bus will go and the space where the people stood will remain empty for an instant. The sequence can be infinitely repeated. Incidentally, the people who get on the bus aren't going to hell. Fate has determined that they'll wander forever in the margins of the photograph.

Larraín photographs people walking in Hyde Park. The photograph seems very English and ordinary: it captures the same fragile harmony as the photograph of the queue. And yet, if I examine it carefully, on the right side I spot a parochial native of Santiago de Chile, a government or bank official, clerk or bureaucrat, a good man who has never left Chile, his little hat says as much, startled as he walks through Hyde Park with a stern look on his face (though his sternness is of the most helpless variety), as if he were thinking abstruse thoughts. On the left side of the picture a girl, possibly a nanny, pushes a baby carriage that isn't seen: only the handle appears in the frame. This girl is English: her eyes gaze at the carriage that I can't see and the child who I can't see, but by the expression on her face it's clear that she's elsewhere, a much warmer place, the tropic of geometric forms, the tropic of geometric exiles. The photograph doesn't end with these two figures, who actually only frame it and thereby give it a twist; between the Luciferian nanny and the parochial Chilean from Santiago, but further in the distance, a couple stroll arm in arm toward the photographer and the foreground, which thus becomes a promise of the future, as if the fate of that ideal (and eminently British) couple were the peripatetic Chilean and the baby we can't see and the baby's questionable caretaker. But even here the photograph doesn't end (because this photograph and maybe all photographs have a beginning and an end, though as a general rule we never know for sure what they are), or the staging of the scene doesn't end: in the background there are three tiny silhouettes, this time in the exact center of the lens, three silhouettes poised at the point where the placid Hyde Park path merges with the horizon, silhouettes that may either be approaching Larraín's camera or moving away from it, probably approaching, three silhouettes that are like three black holes or like three tiny scratches in the fateful serenity (and clarity) of this photograph.

Larraín photographs a man who has just come down the stairs of the Baker Street tube station. The composition is like a commentary on a painting by the Belgian Delville. In the painting, people rise from hell or descend into it and their naked bodies glisten like a whirlwind. In Larraín's photograph, people go up and down the stairs into the tube with the same pomp and circumstance, with the same remoteness, with the same half-thoughtful, half-sad expressions on their faces.

From this perspective, London Bridge, complete with doubledecker bus and monstrous columns that plunge into the cold dark water, assumes the guise of hell-bridge: a bridge along which shadows scurry and beneath which water flows (water is almost always disturbing when photographed by an artist) with the majesty and arrogance of death. I say *monstrous, hell, shadows, majesty, death*, though none of these words should be read with emphasis, but instead in a casual tone, just as Larraín photographs them.

Anyway, disquieting chance flits across the photograph more than once, as if to allow us to discover it, to glimpse its face composed of air, its smile composed of air, the sovereign robes in which it's wrapped, and in which, magnificent and cold, it wraps us. As if chance were a synonym of hell. Or worse yet: as if chance were the essence of hell, its inner workings, its walls, its holes that swell like eyes.

Sometimes one has the sense that Larraín operates in the midst of indifference, feigning indifference, though he's positively disposed toward any accident. Sometimes one has the sense that his strength (a *youthful* strength) is close to failing. But his strength never fails because it stems from grace. The gracefulness of chance.

Larraín photographs seven men walking along a sidewalk. Some are wearing bowler hats. They probably work in the City. The one in the middle of the photograph vaguely resembles or reminds one of Winston Churchill. Six of the men are in focus. The seventh, the one on the far right, is out of focus, and one might say he stepped into the frame at the last minute. But that's impossible. The other six are walking at a good clip, so if someone suddenly stepped into the picture it couldn't have been any of them. The seventh, though I can't say for sure, looks like a doorman or a maintenance man. The seventh looks like ectoplasm gone astray, gazing at Larraín's photograph from *behind* the photograph. On the opposite sidewalk, other men (whom we don't see head on) are walking toward their banks or offices. The seventh man is therefore a kind of mirror. A living (and empty) mirror able to appear at any point in the story and comment on chance from the vantage point of chance itself.

But the men in bowler hats, and even those without bowler hats, also know how to be alone. To be alone is essentially to travel and Larraín shows them on their urban journeys: fearsome beings who make their way through the fog, men in coats, bowlers, and umbrellas who stride, majestic and stolid, through places where few venture to go, much less tourists, unless that tourist is Larraín. And here we can even conjecture wildly: those sad men, reasonably well-dressed, miraculous incarnations of an utter absence of doubt, are they accidental characters or has the young Chilean Larraín followed them, stealing along like a spy or haranguing them, from crowded streets to lonely streets, from the farthest and blackest corners of the river or the suburbs, with the intention, when the moment comes, of photographing them? Are they strangers to Larraín? Maybe. Most are seen from behind. All are absorbed in the contemplation of a scene that may be either exterior or interior: the immaculate room of a despondent I. And yet one of them, I think, is looking straight at Larraín at the moment he takes the photograph: this man, wearing bowler hat, coat, and tie, walks with the gravity of an astronaut. For an instant one has the sense of having arrived, years earlier, on a distant planet in our solar system, a distant and elusive planet. Hidden behind his dark glasses are probably reddened, sleepless eyes. It's likely that in Larraín this space traveler has recognized his equal.

In some photographs there seems to be no air. The atmospheric pressure is fierce. People move like sleepwalkers, hearts and lungs each going their own way, unbound. In some photographs I can imagine the young Chilean photographer in a polychromed aluminum wheelchair, navigating the streets of a dream that resembles a city called London but is less a city then an array of speeds. I can imagine Larraín, his face covered in tiny scars as if he had cut himself that morning shaving or as if he didn't know how to shave. In some photographs it's Larraín who seems to be inside a fishbowl photographing a vast and vaguely familiar planet.

This is off the subject, but when I was a boy and even an adolescent, people said that Chile was the England of South America (in the same way that Uruguay was the Switzerland, Buenos Aires, Chicago, etc.). Those who claimed this, of course, were Chilean. After 1973 the joke stopped being funny, or became what it had always been: sarcastic. But comparisons are never innocent and after a while they return or their ghosts return: in new trappings, with new frills, with new meaning. They return as doubts. They return as answers. In October 1998 the smug joke of our adolescence, that tedious joke, turned up again. Now England, in its leisure moments, dresses up as Chile and in those images of England, in that English hospitality, we Chileans seek our perfect adolescence (our laughter, in other words, and our carefree existence), but we find nothing. Or maybe we do find something: ugly shadows that belong to us, impossible images from the late 1950s or the mid-1960s, when we could still see things in a different way.

Larraín photographs a parked car and it seems to be going more than sixty miles an hour.

Larraín photographs deserted streets and those streets seem to be emerging from being or nothingness, noiselessly, as if in outer space.

The speeding parked car and the silent streets are simply metaphors of our own loneliness, a loneliness in motion. The mirror of our efforts and our endurance.

Larraín photographs the legs, the shoes, of a woman and a man. They've stopped, they're waiting, but the observer knows they'll keep walking, move apart, come together, move apart again in a series of irretrievable instants that eventually we'll call life, chance, nothingness.

One could say that in London the young Larraín found not a city but a universe.

5.
THE BRAVE LIBRARIAN

OUR GUIDE TO THE ABYSS

All American novelists, including those who write in Spanish, at some point get a glimpse of two books looming on the horizon. These books represent two paths, two structures, and above all two plots. Even sometimes: two fates. One is *Moby-Dick* and the other is the *Adventures of Huckleberry Finn*.

The first is the key to those realms that by convention or for the sake of convenience we call the realms of evil, those places where man struggles with himself and with the unknown and is generally defeated in the end; the second is the key to adventure and happiness, a lesser-known land, modest and unassuming, in which the character or characters set the quotidian in motion, start it rolling, and the results are unpredictable and at the same time recognizable and close at hand.

We know that not just anyone can be Ishmael and only one in fifty million can be Captain Ahab. We know it and it doesn't trouble us, although if we think about it, it should.

But we delegate. Huckleberry Finn, however, could be anyone, and though that should make him more lovable, if possible, it fills us with the kind of horror that strikes when we remember passages from our adolescence, an adolescence—Huck's and our own—full of strength, of curiosity, of ignorance and determination, when lying wasn't a habit more or less forbidden by some tenuous moral code, but the best way to survive, one way or another, on the Mississippi or on the turbulent and portable river of our inchoate lives, that is of our young lives, when like Huck we were still poor and free.

All American writers drink of these two galloping streams. All of us search these two forests, each looking for his own lost face. Courage, daring, the bliss of he who has nothing to lose or he who has much to lose but whose generosity or madness impels him to risk everything with an elegance that has nothing to do with European elegance (that is, with European perspectives or European literary forms): these are the attributes of men who are now American through and through, an impossiblity, no matter how you look at it, an act of the will, an entelechy that neither Melville nor Twain consciously constructs (at least not the latter), but that is automatically set up by the hunting of the whale from that terrible ship full of men of every stripe, and by that meandering voyage down the Mississippi. Here we have the founding fathers. From Homer to Whitman and from Whitman to the plight of a slave and the madness of a whaling captain. No transition, no method, in the manner of this new and untamed world.

What was Melville trying to tell us? This is an enigma that has yet to be solved because Melville is an enigma and also a writer of greater depth than Twain. What was Twain trying to tell us? Many things, all of them more or less plain: that life is only worth living in adolescence and that adolescence, the territory of immaturity, can extend as far as the freedom of the individual. At first glance it doesn't seem like much for a founding father. But it's plenty if the message (which is the message of Thoreau and Rousseau, who was a terrible father) is delivered with energy and humor, and here no one can beat Mark Twain, whose energy, fueled by dialogue and popular turns of phrase, is unique, as is his very black humor.

No one escapes when Twain takes up his pen, when Twain consigns his son Huck to a vagabond life, sending him down the Mississippi River that Twain loved so much in search of freedom for himself and for Jim, a black man who seeks to escape slavery, and the journey of these two characters, along with the voyage of Ishmael on the *Pequod*, is the quintessence of all trips, an absurd voyage, because instead of traveling upstream or turning at the mouth of the Ohio and heading for the free states, they travel downstream, straight toward the heart of the slave states, and though this would plunge anyone into despair or trigger a nervous breakdown, Huck, who is fleeing his father, and Jim, who is fleeing society, find their lives scarcely disrupted at all as they drift into adventure and meet incredible characters and are shipwrecked and rescued.

Survival. That's one of the kinds of magic to be found here. The ability to survive. If the novel is read carefully and read at least ten times, some of this magic might come off the page and begin to flow through the veins of the person reading it.

Then there's the magic of friendship. When Huck, after playing a joke on Jim, discovers with regret that he's offended him, or when each thinks back on the good things he left behind—Jim: his family; Huck: Tom Sawyer and little else—or when, more commonly, they spend their time lazing around the raft, sleeping or fishing or doing the chores necessary to keep their craft shipshape, or when they experience moments of danger, what persists in the end is a lesson in friendship, friendship that is also a lesson in the civilization of two totally marginal beings who have only each other and who look after each other without gentle words or tenderness, as outlaws or those outside the bounds of respectability look after each other, because the *Adventures of Huckleberry Finn* isn't a novel for respectable people, quite the contrary, which is odd, because the success of Twain's book among respectable people, who are after all the primary purchasers and consumers of fiction, was huge, and the novel sold (and still sells) in astronomical quantities, which says a lot about the secret urges of respectable or middle-class people, the kind of people we'll all be someday, as Borges dreamed, and without a doubt was little read in the circles most frequented by Huck, that is among adolescent children of alcoholic and abusive parents, runaways, swindlers and miscreants, or in black American circles, although according to Chester Himes the *Adventures of Huckleberry Finn* doesn't fare too badly in the prison libraries of the United States.

As I'm writing this I read in the paper that there's a movie on TV today called *Back to Hannibal: The Return of Tom Sawyer and Huckleberry Finn*. The plot reflects the unbridled American desire for happiness, or in other words the happiness offered by Walt Disney, the movie's producer, as well as the loneliness of us all. The listing in the paper describes it like this: Tom Sawyer has become a lawyer and Huck a reporter, and both return to Hannibal to help Jim, whose profession isn't revealed but who is probably no longer a slave. Maybe Jim has become a faith healer or owns a small farm. It's possible to see Tom Sawyer as a lawyer. In fact, very possible. But Huck a reporter? That's a stretch.

Who was Mark Twain, which in Mississippi pilot lingo means *two fathoms*? First he was Samuel Langhorne Clemens, his real name, and also Thomas Jefferson Snodgrass, a short-lived pseudonym, and he was born in Florida, Missouri, in 1835, although his childhood and adolescence were spent in Hannibal, a town on the banks of the Mississippi. From a very early age he worked at a printing press that belonged to his brother Orion, whose private secretary he would later become in Nevada, where Orion was in turn secretary to the governor, which paints Orion not only as an enterprising type but as a schemer, that is, a politician. Twain was a river pilot on the Mississippi until the beginning of the Civil War and from that period comes a book that owes something to its day but also transcends its times, a strange book, *Old Times on the Mississippi*, whose first paragraph can be read as the kind of statement of principles that Tom Sawyer might have made, though not Huckleberry Finn: "When I was a boy, there was but one permanent ambition among my comrades in our village on the west bank of the Mississippi River. That was, to be a steamboatman. We had transient ambitions of other sorts, but they were only transient. When a circus came and went, it left us all burning to become clowns; the first negro minstrel show that came to our section left us all suffering to try that kind of life; now and then we had a hope that if we lived and were good, God would permit us to be pirates. These ambitions faded out, each in its turn; but the ambition to be a steamboatman always remained."

The ambition to be a steamboatman turned into a passion for the Mississippi and for traveling: to the west, first Nevada, with his canny brother, and to California, from which he sailed to Hawaii, a singular trip in his day, although in fact all of Twain's trips were singular, even those he took around New England as the new husband of Olivia Langdon, a pretty girl with money who never understood him and whom he, meanwhile, never made the least effort to understand, their marriage the kind that in those days was called odd (or singular, like his trips) and that these days is usually called disastrous, not to mention that it was touched by adversity, a kind of adversity that no other writer could have withstood and that Twain may not have withstood either. A more sensitive man would have killed himself, but Twain believed that suicide was redundant: his scorn for the human race grew into something like a shield, a protective shell, all kinds of bad things could happen and it wouldn't trouble him, because he expected it and had predicted it and he lived like the gladiators whose motto was *nec spe, nec metu* ("without fear or hope").

Writing about a photograph of Twain, Javier Marías says: "In nightshirt or shirt, he's writing in bed, and unlike Mallarmé or Dickens it seems likely that he's not even pretending but actually earnestly spelling out some word, because he wasn't one to waste time. He must have known that his picture was being taken, but the impression he gives is that he doesn't know or doesn't care. The bed is tidy. It doesn't look like a sickbed, which is always rumpled and sunken in the middle, the pillows flat. The viewer has therefore no choice but to wonder whether Mark Twain lived in bed."

Marías's fond description misses some important details. Twain really was sick. His mane (one can't call that mop hair) is exactly the same as it was in his youth, just a different color, which says a lot about Twain's self-image. And finally, the wrists, those enormous lumberjack wrists, out of all proportion to his relatively small hands, prodigious wrists, like a cartoon character's. Writers write with their hands and their eyes. Twain, old and sick, skeptical of everything, even his own work, writes with his wrists and his eyes, as if all his strength as a perpetual traveler were centered in them.

But these aren't Huckleberry Finn's wrists, they're Tom Sawyer's. And that's Mark Twain's primary misfortune and also our delight, hypocritical readers, because it seems clear that if Twain had become Huck at some point in his eventful life, he would surely have written nothing or almost nothing, because boys and men like Huck don't write, they're too busy, satiated by life itself, a life in which one fishes not for whales but for catfish in the river that splits the United States in two, to the east the dawn, civilization, everything that strives desperately to be history and to be storied, and to the west the clarity of blindness and myth, everything that lies beyond books and history, everything that we fear in our innermost selves. To one side the land of Tom, who will settle down, who may even triumph, and who will surely have descendents, and on the other side the land of Huck, the wild man, the loafer, the son of an alcoholic and abusive father, in other words the ultimate orphan, who will never triumph, and who will disappear without leaving a trace, except in the memory of his friends, his comrades in misfortune, and in the ardent memory of Twain.

No, Mark Twain didn't have much regard for the rest of mankind. There's a passage from the *Adventures of Huckleberry Finn* that should be inscribed in golden letters on the wall of every bar (and school) in the world. This passage foreshadows half the complete works of Faulkner and half the complete works of Hemingway, and it foreshadows especially what both of them, Faulkner and Hemingway, wanted to be. The passage is simple. It describes a duel and its consequences. It begins with a drunk who likes to go around cursing and threatening people. One morning he goes to challenge the town's storekeeper.

Boggs rode up before the biggest store in town, and bent his head down so he could see under the curtain of the awning and yells:

"Come out here, Sherburn! Come out and meet

the man you've swindled. You're the houn' I'm after, and I'm a-gwyne to have you, too!"

And so he went on, calling Sherburn everything he could lay his tongue to, and the whole street packed with people listening and laughing and going on. By and by a proud-looking man about fifty-five—and he was a heap the best dressed man in that town, too—steps out of the store, and the crowd drops back on each side to let him come. He says to Boggs, mighty ca'm and slow—he says:

"I'm tired of this, but I'll endure it till one o'clock. Till one o'clock, mind—no longer. If you open your mouth against me only once after that time you can't travel so far but I will find you."

Then Sherburn, who's a colonel, old Colonel Sherburn, as we've just been informed, goes back into his store and Boggs rides around town cursing him at the top of his lungs. People aren't laughing anymore. When Boggs goes back to the store (where he no longer needs to bend his head down to see whether Sherburn is inside), he continues his tirade. Some people try to make him be quiet. They warn him that it's a quarter to one. But Boggs ignores them. Earlier he's seen Huck Finn and asked him: "Whar'd you come f'm, boy? You prepared to die?" Huck doesn't answer. And now some people try to convince the drunk man to go home, but Boggs "throwed his hat down in the mud and rode over it, and pretty soon away he went a-raging down the street again, with his gray hair a-flying," a description that while perfectly vulgar, as the situation merits, also soars to epic heights, because Twain knows that all epics are vulgar and that the only thing that can somewhat relieve the immense sadness of all epics is humor. And so Boggs keeps slandering Sherburn up and down the street, with no one able to get him to dismount or shut up, until someone remembers his daughter, the only person who might be able to reason with him, and they go off in search of her and then Boggs disappears for a few minutes and when Huck sees him again he has dismounted and he's on foot, not striding along but stumbling a bit, and two friends have him by the arms: "He was quiet, and looked uneasy; and he warn't hanging back any, but was doing some of the hurrying himself." Then a voice is heard shouting Boggs's name and everyone turns and it's Colonel Sherburn, and Twain describes him standing motionless in the middle of the street, a pistol raised in his right hand, a pistol that he doesn't aim at anyone but at the sky, like a classic duelist, and then Boggs's daughter appears at the other end of the street, but Boggs and the men with him don't see her, they've turned around, and the only thing they see is Sherburn with his pistol raised, a pistol "with both barrels cocked," that is a duelist's pistol, with just two bullets, and the men with Boggs jump to one side and only then is Sherburn's pistol lowered and aimed at the unfortunate drunk and the latter manages to raise both hands in a gesture more of entreaty than of surrender, saying "Oh Lord, don't shoot," and then, without transition, the shot is heard and Boggs stumbles backward, "clawing at the air" and then Sherburn shoots again and Boggs "tumbles backwards on to the ground." Now chaos reigns, Boggs's daughter cries, the crowd swarms around the dying man, Sherburn has tossed his pistol down and gone, Boggs is carried into a drugstore and set down on the floor with a Bible under his head and another Bible open on his chest, and then he dies. And when Boggs dies people start to talk, mulling over the killing, telling what they saw, and after a while someone, an anonymous voice in the crowd, says they should lynch Sherburn, and almost immediately they're all in agreement, the whole town is in agreement, and they head for

Sherburn's house "mad and yelling, and snatching down every clothes-line they come to to do the hanging with."

And that's the end of Chapter XXI, in which the reader has the sense of being in the presence of something completely real, not literary, or in other words deeply literary, a high point of the *Adventures of Huckleberry Finn*, and Chapter XXII begins where the previous chapter leaves off, with Twain going on to speak eloquently about bravery and crowds, as if the day before he'd read Canetti's *Crowds and Power*, and in the same chapter he also talks about loneliness and the most desperate pride in the world, and he cross-dresses as Captain Ahab.

It's a spare scene, though set in the middle of the chaos of a lynching. The mob reaches Sherburn's house. There's a small yard. The mob sets up camp, shouting ("you couldn't hear yourself think for the noise") from the other side of the fence. There's a call to tear down the fence. "Then there was a racket of ripping and tearing and smashing, and down she goes, and the front wall of the crowd begins to roll in like a wave." Only then does Sherburn appear. He's on the porch roof and he's carrying a double-barrelled rifle and he's "perfectly ca'm and deliberate," watching as his fence is torn down, and when the crowd sees him up above, they in turn stop and stare. For a while nothing happens. The stillness is perfect. The mob below and Colonel Sherburn above, watching. At last Sherburn laughs and says:

> "The idea of *you* lynching anybody! It's amusing. The idea of you thinking you had pluck enough to lynch a *man!* Because you're brave enough to tar and feather poor friendless cast-out women that come along here, did that make you think you had grit enough to lay your hands on a *man?* Why, a *man's*

safe in the hands of ten thousand of your kind—as long as it's daytime and you're not behind him.

"Do I know you? I know you clear through. I was born and raised in the South, and I've lived in the North; so I know the average all around. The average man's a coward. In the North he lets anybody walk over him that wants to, and goes home and prays for a humble spirit to bear it. In the South one man all by himself, has stopped a stage full of men in the day-time, and robbed the lot. Your newspapers call you a brave people so much that you think you *are* braver than any other people—whereas you're just *as* brave, and no braver. Why don't your juries hang murderers? Because they're afraid the man's friends will shoot them in the back, in the dark—and it's just what they *would* do.

"So they always acquit; and then a *man* goes in the night, with a hundred masked cowards at his back and lynches the rascal. Your mistake is, that you didn't bring a man with you; that's one mistake, and the other is that you didn't come in the dark and fetch your masks. You brought *part* of a man—Buck Harkness, there—and if you hadn't had him to start you, you'd a taken it out in blowing.

"You didn't want to come. The average man don't like trouble and danger. *You* don't like trouble and danger. But if only *half* a man—like Buck Harkness, there—shouts 'Lynch him! lynch him!' you're afraid to back down—afraid you'll be found out to be what you are—*cowards*—and so you raise a yell, and hang yourselves on to that half-a-man's coat-tail, and come raging up here, swearing what big things you're going to do. The pitifulest thing out is a mob; that's what an army is—a mob; they don't fight with courage that's born in them, but with courage that's borrowed from their mass, and from their officers. But a mob without any *man* at the head of it is *beneath* pitifulness. Now the thing for *you* to do is to droop your tails and go home and crawl in a hole. If any real lynching's going to be done it will be done in the dark, Southern fashion; and when they come they'll bring their masks, and fetch a *man* along. Now *leave*—and take your half-a-man with you"—tossing his gun up across his left arm and cocking it when he says this.

The crowd washed back sudden, and then broke all apart, and went tearing off every which way.

There's no question that Mark Twain had little regard for people's bravery. He knew a coward when he saw one. He held a similarly low opinion of other writers, in whom he scented imposture. Colonel Sherburn, who is a patient man, is also a cool killer, someone who doesn't hesitate to shoot a foolish drunk who even raises his hands at the crucial moment ("Oh Lord, don't shoot") as if it had all been a joke, a stage play spun out of control. Sherburn is afflicted with a kind of inflexibility that today we would consider politically incorrect. But he's a man and he behaves like one, while everyone else behaves like a mob or like actors, the former including the townspeople who intend to lynch him and the latter including the unfortunate Boggs, who's ready to recite his lines but not to keep his word, the same Boggs who, without getting off his horse, asks Huck, "Whar'd you come f'm, boy? You prepared to die?"

Twain was always prepared to die. That's the only way to understand his humor.

THE MAD INVENTORS

The Temple of Iconoclasts is one of the best books of the twentieth century. Its author, Rodolfo Wilcock, is a legendary writer.
Born in Buenos Aires in 1919, he died in Lubriani, Italy in
1978, and he was a friend of Jorge Luis Borges and Adolfo
Bioy Casares. His first books were of poems: *Primer libro de
poemas y canciones* [First Book of Poems and Songs] (1940), *Los
hermanos días* [The Kindred Days] (1942), *Paseo sentimental*
[Romantic Stroll] (1945). At the age of thirty-nine he went
to live in Italy and began to write in Italian. Notable works
from his Italian period, which was his richest, are the novel
El templo etrusco [The Etruscan Temple] (1973), the prose of
El estereoscopio de los solitarios [The Stereoscope of the Lonely]
(1972), *El Caos* [The Chaos] (1974), and *El libro de los mon-
struos* [The Book of Monsters] (1978), and several volumes of
poetry and plays.

His greatest work, however, is the book that has just been reissued by Anagrama. It was first published in 1982. The copy I have in my hands was published in 1999. If one considers the span between the dates of the first and second Spanish editions, it's frankly disheartening. *The Temple of Iconoclasts*, which was originally published in Italian in 1972, is without a doubt one of the funniest, most joyful, irreverent, and most corrosive books of the twentieth century. Owing a debt to Borges, Alfonso Reyes, and Marcel Schwob, who in turn owe a debt, in the manner of funhouse mirrors, to the prose of the encyclopedists, *The Temple of Iconoclasts* is a collection of biographies of mad inventors, adventurers, scientists, and the odd artist. According to the Argentine writer Héctor Bianciotti, the book can be read "as a human comedy in which a bitter rage like Céline's is disguised in the form of Marx Brothers gags." I don't think a bitter rage lurks in Wilcock's prose, much less a bitter rage like Céline's. When his characters are bad, they're bad because they're so good, and when they're good they're oblivious, and then they're frightening, but only as frightening as the rest of humankind. Wilcock's prose—methodical, always confident, unassuming even when it deals with lurid or over-the-top subject matter—tends toward understanding and forgiveness, never bitterness. From his humor (because *The Temple of the Iconoclasts* is essentially a comic novel) no one is safe.

Some of his characters are real historical figures, like Hans Hörbiger, the Austrian scientist who advanced the theory of successive moons and counted Hitler among his disciples. Others might as well be, like André Lebran, who is "remembered, occasionally remembered, or in fact not remembered at all, as the inventor of the pentacycle or the five-wheeled bicycle." Some are heroic, like the Filipino José Valdes y Prom, telepath and hypnotist. Others are wholly innocent creatures or saints, like Aram Kugiungian, an Armenian immigrant in Canada, who is reincarnated or *transmigrated* into hundreds, maybe thousands of people, and who always says, when confronted with the evidence, that he feels "nothing unusual, in fact nothing at all, at most a vague sensation of not being alone in the world." Not to mention Llorenç Riber, the Catalan theater director capable of wearing down not only the most brutal censors but also his occasional audiences by staging an adaptation of Wittgenstein's *Philosophical Investigations*. Or the Canarian inventor Jesús Pica Planas, father of the revolving grill turned by four turtles or of elastic underwear for dogs in heat or of a photoelectric mouse trap complete with guillotine, to be placed in front of mouseholes. Thirty-five biographies like these make this a festive, laugh-out-loud read, a book by one of the greatest and strangest (in the revolutionary sense of the word) writers of this century, a writer whom no good reader should miss.

WORDS AND DEEDS

He was a great writer. A great man. That's how one must always begin, said a medic from the Red Cross. The bandage before the wound. But it's suffocating, in a way, this avalanche of praise on the day of his death. So he died in a state of perfect repose, not a single muscle of his face twitching? A statement like that, ridiculous and trivial, adds nothing to a reputation based as much on words as on deeds.

How did Luis Martín-Santos die? Screaming in agony, with the faintest of whimpers? How did Juan Benet die? Lost in a labyrinth, watching the ghosts of Spain file past through a cascade of tears or dandruff or piety? It's suffocating, this avalanche of praise. Today I read that Arrabal, along with two distinguished friends, considered Cela to be the world's greatest living writer. I want to think that the pain must be impairing his judgement. What impels or sustains this unanimous accord? The Nobel? Is it Benavente's hordes, returning on crutches of oblivion? Such unanimity is frankly sickening. All this impromptu literary criticism, all these mediocre professors, all these bureaucrats on the loose.

Not even Cela, who did so many things—some of them, I want to believe, done independently and done well—deserves this. No real writer deserves this. Literature, unlike death, lives out in the open, exposed to the elements, far from the rule of government and law, except for the law of literature which only the best of the best are capable of breaking. And after all, literature doesn't exist anymore, only the example of it.

Between the old macho and the bewildered knight, between the fleshy Dalí and the lifeless academic, between the champion prize-winner and the man with lofty contempt for all faggots, there is a secret slot for Cela at his best, as one of the great prose stylists, plural, of Spain in the second half of the twentieth century, as a human being happy with his wife Marina, as a man dangerously like us.

VILA-MATAS'S LATEST BOOK

Everything about this book is disturbing, beginning with the cover, an August Sander photograph of three young peasants dressed in their Sunday best, all three with hat and cane, gazing proudly at the camera, their pride tinged with a kind of elegance and indifference and aloofness, as if they know something about literature that the rest of us don't. These peasants, who are as good-looking as they are young, are walking along a dirt road, what appears to be a narrow road, between sown fields or fallow fields, and they've turned their faces toward the camera, a pause on the road, a pause that scarcely alters those proud faces, faces sculpted for the abyss and vertigo. And that's what awaits readers inside of *Bartleby & Co.* (Anagrama), Vila-Matas's latest effort, a brief stroll, composed in the form of footnotes, through the abyss and vertigo not only of literature (though at moments that might seem to be the only subject) but of life, of the thin slice of life that each human being is dealt. In that sense this is a defiant book: defiant in its depiction of those who at a certain moment decided to give up writing, and defiant in its forays into territory where the possibility and impossiblity of writing is disputed with the not always infallible weapons of elegance and humor. Once we've reached this point it's necessary, out of courtesy, to ask ourselves an increasingly rhetorical question: Is the book we have before us a novel, a collection of literary or anti-literary offerings, a miscellaneous volume that doesn't fit any set category, a diary of the life of the writer, an interweaving of newspaper pieces? The answer, the only answer that occurs to me just now, is that it's something else, something that might be a blend of all the preceding options, and we might have before us a twenty-first-century novel, by which I mean a hybrid novel, a gathering together of the best of fiction and journalism and history and memoir. In a way, it reminds me of another book by Vila-Matas, *Para acabar con los números redondos* [An End to Round Numbers], published in 1997, a wonderful book, one of the happiest I've ever read, which went almost unnoticed when it was clearly the best thing published in Spain that year. The spirit is the same. The poetic force is the same. Even the levity is similar. But what in *Para acabar con los números redonodos* was certainty and therefore an accumulation of felicities and clarities, in *Bartleby & Co.* is the laybrinth of the belated, like the labyrinths of the symbolist painters, and it's also the fevered search for exits and sometimes the song or honk of the swan, and most of all it's the courage of a writer who collects and catalogues pocket-size hells or invisible hells, which when viewed from a global perspective are pieces of a larger hell, fragments that say something not only about those writers who at a certain moment in their lives (a moment of clarity or desperation or madness) gave up writing but also about those writers who, like Vila-Matas himself, will never give up writing, and, beyond that, say something about death, and about vain gestures that may not stave off death but that save us (or can save us) nonetheless, and none of this is just about writers, as the reader only realizes toward the end, but actually about readers, about human beings of every ilk, about people who live and one day stop living, about adventurers and the dying, about people who read and people who one day stop reading, and all of it—which put this way could make us think that we're up against the wall—is presented to us in a book of scarcely 179 pages, a book moderated by the humor and grace of Vila-Matas, a writer who has no equal in the contemporary landscape of the Spanish novel, and whose defiant attitude resembles that of the peasants on the cover in their Sunday best, though Vila-Matas is the furthest thing from a peasant I know, and Vila-Matas works on Sundays.

He started out as a poet. He admired German expressionist literature (he learned French out of obligation and German out of something that might be called love, and he learned it without teachers, on his own, the way one learns all the most important things), but he may never have read Hans Henny Jahnn. In photographs from the 1920s he looks haughty and sad, a young man with few rough edges, someone whose body tended toward plumpness, softness. He cultivated friendships, and he was loyal. His first friends, from Switzerland and Mallorca, lived on in his memory with adolescent fervor or the fervor of innocent adolescent memory. And he was lucky: he got to know Cansinos-Assens and he gained a unique perspective on Spain that he never lost. But he returned to the country of his birth and encountered the possibility of destiny. The destiny of his dreams, in a country shaped by his dreams. In the American vastnesses he dreamed of courage and its shadow, the immaculate loneliness of the brave, days perfectly fitted to the contours of life. And he was lucky again: he met Macedonio Fernández and Ricardo Güiraldes and Xul Solar, who were worth more than most of the Spanish intellectuals he had gotten to know, or so he believed, and he was hardly ever wrong. And yet his sister married a Spanish poet. It was the age of the Argentine Empire, when everything seemed within reach and Buenos Aires could call itself the Chicago of the southern hemisphere without blushing. And the Chicago of the southern hemisphere had its Carl Sandburg (a poet, incidentally, admired by our writer), and his name was Roberto Arlt. Time brought them together and then drove them apart forever, when one of the two plunged into the abyss and the other set off in search of the word. From Arlt's abyss was born the most demented kind of utopia: a story of sad gunmen that anticipated, like Sábato's *Abaddón, el exterminador* [Abaddón, the Exterminator], the horror that much later would hover over the country and the continent. From the search for the word, meanwhile, came patience and a modest certainty of the joys of literature. Boedo and Florida were the names of the groups that grew up around the two men. The first refers to a poor neighborhood, the second to a main street, and today the two names march together toward oblivion. Arlt, Gombrowicz: he might have been friends with them and he wasn't. This lack of dialogue left a great void that is also a part of our literature. Of course, Arlt died young, after a tumultuous life full of hardships. And he was essentially a writer of prose. Not our man. He was a poet, and a very good one, and he wrote essays, and only when he was well into his thirties did he begin to write fiction. It must be said that the reason he did was because he realized he couldn't be the greatest poet in the Spanish language. There was Neruda, for whom he never felt much affection, and the shadow of Vallejo, whom he didn't often read. There was Huidobro, who was a friend and later an enemy of his sad and inevitable Spanish brother-in-law, and Oliverio Girondo, whom he considered to be superficial, and then there was García Lorca, whom he called a professional Andalusian, and Juan Ramón, at whom he laughed, and Cernuda, to whom he paid scarcely any attention. Actually, there was only Neruda. There was Whitman, there was Neruda, and there was the epic. The thing he thought he loved. The thing he loved best. And then he began to write a book in which the epic is simply the flip side of misfortune, in which irony and humor and a few human beings, valiant and adrift, replace the epic. The book is indebted to *Retratos reales e imaginarios* [Real and Imaginary Portraits], by his friend and teacher Alfonso Reyes, and, through the Mexican writer's book, to *Imaginary Lives*, by Schwob, whom they both loved. Many years later, now blind and more celebrated than his teacher, he visited Reyes's library in Mexico City, officially dubbed the "Alphonsine Chapel" and he couldn't help imagining how Argentines would react to the indecorous notion of calling Leopoldo Lugones's house the "Leopoldine Chapel." This inability to keep quiet, his perpetual readiness to engage, was something he always lost in the company of idiots. He claimed to have read *Don Quixote* for the first time in English, and said that it had never seemed as good to him since. The caped avengers of Spanish criticism rent their cloaks. And they forgot that the truest words about *Don Quixote* were written not by Unamuno, or by any of Unamuno's flock of motheaten followers, like the regrettable Ramiro de Maeztu, but by our man. After his book on pirates and other outlaws, he wrote two story collections that are probably the best written in Spanish in the twentieth century. The first appeared in 1941, the second in 1949. From that moment on our literature was forever changed. Then he wrote indisputably superb books of poetry that went unremarked in the midst of his own glory as a teller of fantastic tales and amid his tremendous number of muses, male and female. And yet his poetry has many merits: clarity of language, a response to Whitman unmatched by any other contemporary response, a dialogue and monologue with history, an honest tribute to English verse. And he gives us classes in literature that everyone ignores. And lessons in humor that everyone claims to understand and no one does. At the end of his life he asked for forgiveness and he confessed that he liked to travel. He admired courage and intelligence.

BOMARZO

During the first half of the twentieth century, in Buenos Aires, there lived a generation of writers of the stature of Roberto Arlt, Ernesto Sábato, Julio Cortázar, Adolfo Bioy Casares, José Bianco, Eduardo Mallea, Jorges Luis Borges. Some learned their craft under the tutelage of Macedonio Fernández. As if that weren't enough, one day Witold Gombrowicz came to Argentina and decided to stay. To this diverse group belonged Manuel Mujica Láinez, at first glance the least professional of them all, in the sense that it's hard for us to imagine Mujica Láinez as a writer living for the sake of literature and making a living from literature. It's easier to see him as a man of independent means who devotes his free time, of which he has very little, to writing novels with the sole ambition that they be read by his wide circle of friends. And yet Mujica Láinez was perhaps the most prolific Argentine novelist of his day. Not the most ambitious or the most seminal (roles probably reserved for Cortázar or Sábato), or the closest to Argentine reality (a role assigned to Arlt, Cortázar, Sábato, or Bioy, depending on the degree of madness), or the most forward-looking in devising literary structures that could make strides into undiscovered territory (like Borges and Cortázar), or the one who forged deepest into the mystery of language (the undisputed realm of Borges, who, it must be remembered, wasn't just a great prose writer but also a great poet). Mujica Láinez, in this sense, was a modest figure. In fact, when viewed in the company of such exceptional writers and literary giants as Borges, Cortázar, Arlt, Bioy Casares, and Sábato, he seems to shrink and seek quiet refuge in Argentine literature, in provincial literature, but upon even the most cursory reading of his work, this impression turns out to be completely mistaken.

From the beginning, in his first novel, *Don Galaz de Buenos Aires* (1938), two traits became evident that would prove constant in Mujica Láinez's life as a writer. On the one hand, there's his exquisite command of a precise, rich, and dextrous Spanish that manages never to lapse into grandiosity or stiff formality. On the other hand, and this may be what really matters, there's his cheerful approach to the act of writing. It's true that he never took huge risks and that, compared to the great Latin American novelists of the twentieth century, his work is in some sense that of a minor writer. But what a wonderful minor writer! Capable of producing, for example, *Misteriosa Buenos Aires*, or *El viaje de los siete demonios* [The Voyage of the Seven Demons], or *The Wandering Unicorn*, or *Los viajeros* [The Travelers], all of them enjoyable to read, all of them modest (and rather jittery) books, like their author, and enough to assure him a place alongside other minor writers like Mallea or José Bianco.

But Mujica Láinez's great surprise was yet to come, and that surprise is *Bomarzo*. Published in 1962, the novel won

Argentina's National Literature Prize and then the John F. Kennedy Prize in 1964, shared with Cortázar's *Hopscotch* (or *Rayuela*), which (as Marcos Ricardo Barnatán reminds us) gave Mujica the idea of publishing both novels in a joint edition under a single title, either *Ramarzo* or *Boyuela*.

My generation, it goes without saying, fell in love with *Hopscotch*, because it was exactly what we needed, our salvation, and we only read *Bomarzo* years later, almost as an exercise in archeology. Despite what we expected, we didn't emerge unscathed, among other things because no one or almost no one can emerge unscathed from reading any book, much less if it's the more than six hundred pages of *Bomarzo*, a happy novel, or a novel that will make any reader happy, and that will teach the young writer absolutely nothing. The life and adventures of the Duke of Orsini, his thousand adventures and countless mishaps and feats, are a stage for the unfolding of a kind of writing, an art of storytelling, that at once recalls the classics of the nineteenth century and introduces apocryphal luxuries of the sixteenth century, the century of the monstrous and angelic Orsini.

At first glance *Bomarzo* seems to be a novel of conflict, a novel of survival, a historic novel, a novel of intrigue, a bodice-ripper. It may in fact be all those things. But it's also many other things: it's a novel about art and a novel about decadence, it's a novel about the luxury of writing novels and a novel about the exquisite uselessness of the novel. Between the lines, it's also Mujica Láinez's commentary or playful epilogue on himself and his family. And of course it's also a novel to be read aloud, with the whole family gathered around, although in the latter case there's always the risk that the children will flee en masse.

After *Bomarzo* Mujica didn't have much left to say. He traveled frequently and in high style all over the planet. He wrote *De milagros y melancolías* [Of Miracles and Sorrows] and *El gran teatro* [The Great Theater], with what appeared to be the greatest of ease. And before he died, in 1984, at the age of seventy-four, he had time to write the 500-page novel *El escarabajo* [The Scarab] (1982), which tells of the vicissitudes of the possessors of an Egyptian talisman through time, and which is an intelligent, well-written work, pleasing to read (possibly pleasing to write), with measured doses of humor, suffering, and travel. A happy novel, like most of his books.

TWO NOVELS BY MARIO VARGAS LLOSA

THE CUBS, AGAIN

Among the books I read in my youth, I remember four short novels written by authors who mostly wrote long novels, four novels that years later still retain all of their original explosive charge, as if after exploding on a first reading they had exploded again on a second and a third and so on, without ever being depleted. Beyond question, they are perfect works. All four are about defeats, but they turn defeat into a kind of black hole: the reader who ventures in will emerge trembling, ice-cold or dripping with sweat. They are perfect and they are caustic. They are precise: the hand that wields the pen is that of a neurosurgeon. And they are also a celebration of movement: the speed at which they move was something unprecedented at the time in Spanish-language literature. These novels are García Márquez's *No One Writes to the Colonel*, Julio

Cortázar's *The Pursuer*, José Donoso's *Hell Has No Limits*, and Vargas Llosa's *The Cubs.*

I don't think it's a coincidence that the four authors knew each other and were friends, that each kept a curious eye on what the others were writing, and that these four books were written, if I'm not mistaken, in the 1960s (though *The Pursuer* may date from the 1950s), a prodigious decade for Latin Americans, with all the good and bad implied by that adjective.

From these four novels (if their authors had written nothing else, which isn't the case), one could create a literature. Of the four, *The Cubs* is probably the most caustic, the most fiendishly paced, and the one in which the voices—the multiplicity of forms of speech—are most alive. It's also the most complicated, at least from a formal perspective. The first version was written in 1965, that is, when Vargas Llosa was twenty-nine, the youngest of the Boom authors; the definitive version dates from 1966 and was originally published by Lumen with photographs by Xavier Miserachs. On the surface, *The Cubs* couldn't be simpler. In a variety of voices, from a variety of angles (one is tempted to say *torsions*, maneuvers performed by the writer that often become practical and masterful demonstrations of the many things that can be done with the Spanish language), it tells the story of the life of P. P. Cuéllar, an upper-middle-class boy from Lima, and the story is told in the voices of his childhood friends, boys like P. P. Cuéllar, residents or citizens of the Lima neighborhood of Miraflores, a place that leaves its stamp on these future lords of Peru.

But P. P. Cuéllar has an accident that will mark him for the rest of his life and make him different: the novel is the exploration of that *difference*, a collective attempt to explain Pichula Cuéllar's progressive distancing from his peers until they are light years apart, a horror tale mixed with social realism. The distance between them, incidentally, is something that oscillates, that shrinks and grows, because Cuéllar may gradually become estranged from his peers but that doesn't mean he stops trying to be part of the group, and his efforts to draw near are more painful, more revealing of the overall picture, than his radical distancing. His descent into hell, told in cries and whispers, is in a sense a foretelling of the narrators' own descents into another kind of hell. In fact, what terrifies the narrators is that P. P. Cuéllar is one of them and that he never stops trying to be one of them, and it's only fate that makes him different. In his difference, the narrators can see themselves in their true guises, the hell to which they could have been relegated and weren't.

Anomaly is unbearable, although after the destruction of Cuéllar the storytelling voices find themselves faced with the flatness of adulthood, the quiet devastation of their bodies, the hopeless and complete acceptance of a bourgeois mediocrity from which Cuéllar has removed himself through horror, a price doubtless too high to pay and yet the only possible price, as the young Vargas Llosa at moments seems to suggest.

I previously mentioned the speed of *The Cubs* and its three twin sisters. I made no mention of their musicality, a musicality based on colloquial speech, on the voices that punctuate the story, and that are woven through by the speed of the text. Speed and musicality are two constants in *The Cubs* and in some way this brilliant exercise in speed and musicality serves Vargas Llosa as a practice run for the novel he would write soon afterwards, one of his great works and one of the best Spanish-language novels of the twentieth century: *Conversation in the Cathedral* (published in 1969), whose bold, original structure bears a strong resemblance to that of *The Cubs*.

Vargas Llosa's first book was *The Leaders*. Among the stories in it is one that features the first appearance of Sergeant Lituma, who pops up like a chameleon throughout Vargas

Llosa's fiction; other stories are about the loose ends of a be-
trayal, the cruel joke of an old man, a double duel, a local
tyrant. All are cold and objective. All show glimpses of a desperate pride.

THE PRINCE OF THE APOCALYPSE

The Real Life of Alejandro Mayta, like almost all of Vargas Llosa's novels (except for his erotic fiction), lends itself to more
than one or two readings. It can be read as the dream-turned-
nightmare of some poor naïve youths and it can also be read
as the relentless unfolding of a nightmare that to everyone's
surprise becomes gradually more bearable, more ordinary, less
sad, and more inevitable. It's also possible to read it—because
of its structure and thesis or subject matter—as a footnote to
Vargas Llosa's masterpiece *Conversation in the Cathedral*, and
it can even be read as a note or additional study or growth on
another of his great works, *The War of the End of the World*, a
novel which, read today, seems—at least to me—more revela-
tory than Conrad's *Heart of Darkness*, which Vargas Llosa himself recommends to us as an aide to understanding the clash
between East and West, between civilization and barbarism.

Of course, it can also be read as a portrayal of a certain cultural and social age, Latin American as well as Peruvian, dating
from the first armed struggles in the name of revolution (and
therefore Enlightenment) in the late 1950s and early 1960s to
the era of the Shining Path and the millenarian guerrillas in
the 1980s, during which—especially in Peru—the thing that
came to be known as the Latin American terror was unleashed.

The Real Life of Alejandro Mayta plunges us into the worst
of times. The guerrillas are advancing everywhere, sweeping
everything away, the representatives of the right as well as those

of the non-dogmatic left, against a backdrop that resembles certain paintings by Brueghel or an alien invasion. The scene is broadly sketched, to be sure, but in no way implausible. The citizens of Lima live in something like a state of permanent siege, and extreme violence is exercised not only by the millenarian guerrillas but also by the Police and the Army and also the death squadrons. In the midst of this chaos, a writer or a reporter, possibly Vargas Llosa or possibly not, decides to write the story of the first Peruvian guerrilla movement, founded in 1958, even before Fidel Castro seized power.

This is where Mayta comes in, and the portrait of Mayta is perhaps Vargas Llosa's greatest achievement in this novel. Mayta isn't a boy, but he acts like a boy, or in other words he lingers in a kind of deliberate adolescence, though one can't say whether it's intentionally sought or accepted with resignation. Objectively speaking, Mayta is maladjusted, but he isn't violent or manipulative, much less a nihilist. Mayta belongs to a Trotskyist party with seven members, a splinter group of a Trotskyist party of twenty, but before that he belonged to the communist party and before that to the anti-imperialist, Marxist-influenced APRA, and he left each because of his natural tendency toward dissent and doubt. Mayta would like to shower every day but there's no shower in the room that he rents and he has to content himself with going to the public baths once every three days. Mayta is fat and no one would call him attractive and he's also gay at a time when being gay in Peru and Latin America was seen as despicable deviant behavior.

As a result, Mayta hides his homosexuality, especially from his comrades (because in matters of sexuality the Left and the Right march in lockstep in Latin America, like Siamese twins), and he sublimates it or crushes it under a mountain of propaganda work or activism or quartermaster duties that he takes on with the patience of a saint. To a great extent, that's what Mayta is: a modern-day saint, tempted by the devil in the desert, whose commitment to others (or his pure faith) is so great that it seems monstrous.

That alone would make this a memorable novel. But there's more: the young lieutenant who inspires Mayta, a naïve and impetuous leader whose fragility, sensed from the very beginning as a mambo or bolero plays, is conveyed in strokes that signal the end of innocence; Mayta's recycled comrades and their different accounts of him; the small stories that the reporter gathers and that seem extraneous to the novel but that taken together weave a rich narrative web; the story of Professor Ubilluz, a model of the provincial Latin American intellectual; the composition of the novel, which is so much like a puzzle pieced together in the abyss; Vargas Llosa's sense of humor, which leaps, in Balzacian fashion, even over his own political convictions; political convictions that give way in the face of literary convictions, which is something that only happens to real writers. And finally the kindness and compassion—which others might call objectivity—that Vargas Llosa shows his own characters.

NOTES ON JAIME BAYLY

There are words in Bayly's novels that pop up all the time but still seem mysterious to me. *Sassy* for example. I've always wanted to know exactly what that means. In Bayly's novels I understand it, of course, but not entirely. And his characters are always *sassy**! As often as they're *spoiled rotten*†, which is an activity to which all of Bayly's characters devote themselves wholeheartedly: in his books everyone is *spoiled rotten* or tries to be *spoiled rotten* by other people or is *spoiled rotten* by the wrong people and, on top of it all, at the worst possible moment.

There's a scene in *Yo amo a mi mami* [I Love My Mommy], the last scene in the Annie chapter, that gives us a good sense of Bayly's talent as a storyteller. In this scene Jimmy and his

---

* *Disforzados* —tr.
† *Engreído* —tr.

mother are driving to the airport to say goodbye to Annie, who is going to live in the United States. The scene begins with Jimmy asking his mother to take him to the airport. His mother makes him beg. She says that first she has some exercises to do (aerobic, though possibly also spiritual), then she'll take a shower, and after that she'll drive him. Suddenly, time is short and mother and son get in the car and speed off. The way from their house in a suburb called Los Cóndores to the airport is a drive through Latin American impossibility, that is: through the desert, through the barren spaces of a continent with no exit. The description of Jimmy's mother's car and of the highway is like a mirage projected by other mirages.

Along the way not much happens. Jimmy's mother accelerates, but she accelerates in third, because a lady never uses fourth gear. At a certain point they hit a dog. When they get to the airport a policeman wants to see Jimmy's mother's *brevete*—I assume that *brevete* means driver's license—and she doesn't have it and she ends up bribing the policeman by the expeditious method of buying him all the numbers in an imaginary lottery. By then Annie and her parents are already in the departure lounge and Jimmy can only say his goodbyes from the terrace, with waves and shouts. Strangely, the one who shouts most is Jimmy's mother (Annie's mother was her best friend, and for reasons beside the point the friendship has been deteriorating) and in this woman's exaggerated cries we suddenly glimpse all her fear, her warmth, and her frustrations.

Where does Bayly come from? At first glance his literary antecedents are clear. Bayly comes directly from Vargas Llosa, especially from *Conversation in the Cathedral*, a novel that is, among many other things, an extremely comprehensive sampler of Peruvian Spanish. Vargas Llosa's ear finds in Bayly's ear its most talented disciple. *Yo amo a mi mami*, on the other hand, reminds me of Bryce Echenique's *A World for Julius*. Of course, Vargas Llosa's prose is weightier than Bryce Echenique's, though the weightiness of the latter isn't insignificant. Bayly shares with Bryce the impulse to launch himself headlong, leaving the formal plotting of the novel for later, or for right this minute, to be embarked upon in the very act of writing: Bryce and Bayly are devourers of blank pages. This isn't the only thing they have in common: they both possess an apparently incorrigible sense of humor, they're both autobiographical writers (or so it seems, though it doesn't pay to trust some autobiographies), both have English last names, which is saying a lot in a country like Peru, and both are "men and sentimental," as the song goes.

Of course, there are things that make them different and even distance them from each other, but I don't think this is the moment to make an inventory of those dissimiliarities. In fact, another similarity occurs to me: tenderness, a kind of compassionate gaze that some see in Bryce but refuse to see in Bayly. About Baylian compassion, however, which is sometimes disguised as fierceness and cynicism, I'll have more to say later.

A clarification, possibly unnecessary. One has to be very brave to write about homosexuality in Peru. One has to be very brave to write *from* homosexuality in Peru. Especially if one does it without begging the pardon of anyone, whether of those on the Right or those on the Left, who in these matters are as identical as two peas in a pod, which should lead us to the conclusion that the Left isn't the Left it claims to be, though the Right really is the Right.

A while ago, talking to Jesús Ferrero, I was told the story of a trip he took to Guatemala. Ferrero arrives in Guatemala, gets a taxi since no one has come to pick him up at the airport, and heads into the strange city. Night is falling and the streets flow into each other as if the taxi were moving through a labyrinth, the effect magnified by the darkness and the public lighting, which we should presume deficient or possibly excessive. Suddenly the taxi driver stops, whether confused or frightened we don't know, to consult a map of the city and Ferrero looks out the window at a group of transvestites gathered around a fire in the middle of a side street. This is it, says the driver: you can get out here. Ferrero gets out with his suitcase in his hand, and is left alone in the middle of the street without another soul in sight. The taxi leaves and the fiercest transvestites in the world come up to him. They're Indians or mestizos. Indians, yes, or urban mestizos swept into the capital by the country's convulsions. They're prostitutes in the bodies of raped men. They're men in strange bodies and in a strange city that they try vainly to remake in their own image: an alien city within a Central American capital with a bloody past. In any case, they look nothing like European transvestites. They are to European transvestites what a velociraptor is to a heron. And these barbarians moved in on Ferrero like urban guerrillas, they circled him, surrounded him, cut off any possible escape routes, and then, when things looked blackest for the novelist, they began to *talk* to him, exchanging remarks about colonial architecture, for example, or about Guatemala City's maze of streets, and they ask him where he comes from, and then, with a graciousness that I can only call Mayan graciousness or pre-Colombian courtesy, they show him the right way to go, and they even walk with him for a while, because at that time of night and in that part of the city everything is dangerous, though for them *nothing* is dangerous.

Bayly's words. In the same way that there is *sassy* behavior in Bayly's novel, there are also lots of *patas*. This word has always seemed mysterious to me. A *pata* is a friend. Where does the word *pata* come from? It's crisp, easy to pronounce, and the only word that measures up to it is the Mexican *cuate*, which also means friend and of whose etymology I'm equally ignorant, though everything indicates that *cuate* means "twin."

Bayly's *patas* aren't like Rulfo's *cuates*, clearly, or like the *patas* of Salvador Bondy, who I don't think ever used the term, though they share the same shadowy provenance, because *patas* and *cuates* can both come to seem like creatures straight out of hell, but they're all we've got, all we can trust.

Bayly's characters. In *Yo amo a mi mami*, there's a return appearance of the character I think is his most lovable, El Papapa, who previously appeared in *Los últimos días de La Prensa* [The Last Days of *The Press*]. One of El Papapa's traits is that when he goes to the bathroom to defecate he says "I'm going to feed the Chileans." Extremely offensive and at the same time playful. I think he said the same thing in *Los últimos días de La Prensa*. As a Chilean, I find it a charming expression. His son-in-law, Jimmy's father, meanwhile, is an admirer of Pinochet. This means that when Jimmy's father goes to the bathroom he isn't feeding the Chileans, at least not consciously.

There are those who reproach Bayly for his neglect of form. On rare occasions, I've been one of them. But actually I don't think that Bayly neglects the formal aspect so much as it might seem at first glance. Especially beginning with his third novel, I think he tries to seek a form that suits his narrative strength, his inexhaustible verbal flow. Because let's be clear: Bayly's strength as a storyteller, his strength as a writer of dialogue, his ability to escape from any predicament, is extraordinary. Enough to satisfy any writer. No one asks Balzac to be Stendhal. All anyone asks of Balzac is that he be God. What we should demand of Bayly isn't formal perfection but worlds, crowds, soap operas of real life, torrents of humor, what we should demand of Bayly is what he's already giving us: the most wonderful ear in new Spanish fiction, an often poignant gaze that turns inward without complacency and that is turned on others with humor and irony and also tenderness, the tenderness of a survivor of a time that's already past and that probably only existed in the narrator's dreams, a Peru in its death throes or a Peru that is now only a glimmer of what it once was.

What a relief to read Bayly after so many inscrutable or pathetic figures who confuse realism with dogmatism, information with proclamation. What a relief Bayly's writing is after the interminable lineup of talentless Latin American chest-thumpers, of snobs with their corseted prose, of pontificating bureaucratic heroes of the proletariat. What a relief to read someone who has the narrative will not to avoid almost anything.

Machiavellian Bayly, or naïve Bayly. These words were written a few hours ago, after reading in today's *El País*, Thursday March 25, what Bayly said the day before yesterday to the Madrid press, which is that *Yo amo a mi mami* was a gift for his mother. With gifts like this, one can be assured of making enemies for life. Thank goodness it's for his mother, although if fifteen years from now my son were to give me a gift like this, I think we'd have a problem. Anyway, it could also be argued that Bayly presents his mother with a portrait of his grandfather, which really is a splendid gift. And ultimately, yes, it can be said that this is a genuine gift for his mother: a true if terrible mirror, a mirror in which the lady from Lima circles, across which she bumps and bounces, all in a frighteningly coherent way, a mirror in which the lady from Lima trembles, lost in limbo but still alive, somehow alive, with all her contradictions and obsessions, her vices and her small virtues, and all thanks to her son, the son, the family idiot.

Bayly's prose, which I wouldn't hesitate to call luminous (luminous and brave, though not luminous like the desert or the forest, but luminous like urban afternoons, and not reck-lessly brave or somberly brave but brave like someone who has to struggle with himself and not lose his happiness), isn't an isolated phenomenon in Spanish-language literature. Bayly must be read in this context, too: that of a literature in which for the first time novels produced on opposite sides of the At-lantic are, in a certain sense, walking hand in hand. Unlike the group of Boom writers, made up solely of Latin Americans, in the still undefined sphere of the end-of-the-millennium novel there's room for Spaniards and Latin Americans alike, for ex-ample, the work of Enrique Vila-Matas, César Aira, and Javier Marías, a Catalan, an Argentine, and a writer from Madrid, probably the three authors farthest out ahead in the new ter-ritory to explore. What is this new territory? The same as it always is, but different, which is a way of saying that I don't know. Anyway, it's the territory where the bones of Cervantes and Valle-Inclán lie buried, and it's the undiscovered territory, the territory of the dead and the territory of adventure. And advancing toward it, I think, are at least ten writers whose books can be called alive, and one of them is Jaime Bayly.

A STROLL THROUGH THE ABYSS

Of the many novels that have been written about Mexico, the best are probably the English novels and the odd American one. D. H. Lawrence takes a stab at the agonist novel, Graham Greene the moral novel, and Malcolm Lowry the total novel, by which I mean the novel that plunges into chaos (which is itself the subject of the ideal novel) and tries to order it and make it legible. Few contemporary Mexican writers, with the possible exception of Carlos Fuentes and Fernando del Paso, have embarked on such an undertaking, as if they were barred from it from the outset or as if what we call Mexico, which is also a jungle or a desert or a faceless crowd, were a territory reserved solely for foreigners.

Rodrigo Fresán more than fulfills this and other requirements for writing about Mexico. *Mantra* is a kaleidoscopic novel, shot through with fierce, occasionally over-the-top humor, written in a prose of rare precision that allows itself to oscillate between anthropological document and the delirium of late nights in a city—Mexico City—that superimposes itself on the subterranean cities beneath it like a snake swallowing itself.

The novel, or so it appears (and I say *appears* because everything in this novel can come to seem only apparent, though its parts are assembled with mathematical exactitude), is divided into three long chapters. The first is narrated by an Argentine boy and takes place in Argentina, upon the arrival at school of a new student, a Mexican boy who goes from potential victim to leader of the group in less than a minute by the clever (and dangerous) trick of playing Russian roulette with a real gun in front of the other students when the teacher leaves them alone. The boy, Martín Mantra, is the ultimate incarnation of the enfant terrible: son of two soap opera actors, he comes to school accompanied by his Mexican bodyguard, a former masked wrestler, and he plans to revolutionize the world of film and television. The novel's vision of Mexico, the place where this incredible boy comes from, is projected through the boy and the Argentine narrator's memories of his own childhood, and through something that is never clearly stated but that at times resembles an illness or societal collapse and that may just be the irremediable end of childhood.

The symbolic figure who presides over this first section is a hero of the past, the (*post-mortem*) General Gervasio Vicario Cabrera, a mixed-up Mexican who fought in Argentina's war of independence and was executed by firing squad, by all accounts too hastily, just as the symbolic figure who presides over the novel's third part is a robot whose shadow seems to mingle with the first words of *Pedro Páramo*.

The second chapter—the best, in my opinion—is organized alphabetically, like a dictionary of Mexico City or a dictionary of the abyss. It's also the longest section of the novel, beginning on page 144 and ending on page 509. It's open-ended: it can be read linearly or the reader can begin with any letter he wants. The narrator this time is a French man, a man who knows Martín Mantra only by reputation, and who travels to Mexico to kill and be killed. And even to continue killing after death. Among the multiple plotlines that criss-cross like lightning bolts is the story of Joan Vollmer, killed in Mexico City while playing William Tell with her husband, William Burroughs; and the story of the Mexican masked wrestlers and the nouvelle vague film that one of them wants to make in France; and the story of LIM, the international language of the dead; and the story of Mexican monsters and Mexican pornography; and the story of the female rock group Anorexia & The Skinny Chicks; and the story of Martín Mantra as a millenarian and media-savvy guerrilla; and even the love story (though it's set in Paris) of the French narrator and a Mexican girl.

Words from *Mantra* selected at random. From the section "Soap Operas," for example: "Soap operas are like mutant newscasts." And the section "Television Sets": "You ask what brand those dead television sets are, the kind the dead watch, and I say [. . .] those zombie boxes where zombies feed their eyes to other zombies are Sonbys." From the section "Vomit": "That's how Joan Vollmer talks, and here's what she says as she chain-smokes invisible cigarettes. She tells me that her cigarettes are a strange brand: some make her speak in the first person and others in the third person, in that choked and spasmodically seismic language that is the International Language of the Dead."

So the dead speak a language of tremor-like cadences. And *Mantra*, or so we discover as we progress through the different superimposed layers of the novel, gradually fills up with the dead, all the dead of Mexico, from the eminent to the anonymous. And the tremor that the reader feels is the tremor of LIM, a language that can also be used to write novels so long as they're organized alphabetically.

The third and last part of the novel is a futurist fable. Mexico City no longer exists, destroyed by perpetual earthquakes, and amid the ruins rises a new city called New Tenochtitlán of the Tremor. A robot returns to the heart of that strange city to search for his creator-father, Mantrax, thus keeping a promise made to his computer mother. Clearly, we have here a new version of *Pedro Páramo* or the perilous encounter of Rulfo's *Pedro Páramo* and Kubrick's *2001* at the foot of a sacrificial altar, with a surprise ending.

Mantra is one of the most exciting books I've read in recent years. It made me laugh more than any other book, and it seemed more virtuous and at the same time more roguish; it's steeped in melancholy, but always to some aesthetic end, never lapsing into the preciousness or sentimentality always in vogue in Spanish-language literature. It's a novel about Mexico, but like all great novels it's really about the passage of time, about the possibility and impossibility of dreams. And on an almost secret level it's about the art of making literature, though very few may realize it.

SEVILLA KILLS ME

1. *The title.* In theory, and with no input from me whatsoever, the title of my talk was supposed to be "Where does the new Latin American novel come from?" If I stay on topic, my answer will be about three minutes long. We come from the middle classes or from a more or less settled proletariat or from families of low-level drug traffickers who're tired of gunshots and want respectability instead. As Pere Gimferrer says: in the old days, writers came from the upper classes or the aristocracy, and by choosing literature they chose—at least for a certain period that might be a lifetime or four or five years—social censure, the destruction of learned values, mockery and constant criticism. Now, on the other hand, especially in Latin America, writers come from the lower middle classes or from the ranks of the proletariat and what they want, at the end of the day, is a light veneer of respectability. That is, writers today seek recognition, though not the recognition of their

peers but of what are often called "political authorities," the usurpers of power, whatever century it is (the young writers don't care!), and thereby the recognition of the public, or book sales, which makes publishers happy but makes writers even happier, because these are writers who, as children at home, saw how hard it is to work eight hours a day, or nine or ten, which was how long their parents worked, and this was when there was work, because the only thing worse than working ten hours a day is not being able to work at all and having to drag oneself around looking for a job (paid, of course) in the labyrinth, or worse, in the hideous crossword puzzle of Latin America. So young writers have been burned, as they say, and they devote themselves body and soul to selling. Some rely more on their bodies, others on their souls, but in the end it's all about selling. What doesn't sell? Ah, that's an important consideration. Disruption doesn't sell. Writing that plumbs the depths with open eyes doesn't sell. For example: Macedonio Fernández doesn't sell. Macedonio may have been one of Borges's three great teachers (and Borges is or should be at the center of our canon) but never mind that. Everything says that we should read him, but Macedonio doesn't sell, so forget him. If Lamborghini doesn't sell, so much for Lamborghini. Wilcock is only known in Argentina and only by a few lucky readers. Forget Wilcock, then. Where does the new Latin American literature come from? The answer is very simple. It comes from fear. It comes from the terrible (and in a certain way fairly understandable) fear of working in an office and selling cheap trash on the Paseo Ahumada. It comes from the desire for respectability, which is simply a cover for fear. To those who don't know any better, we might seem like extras from a New York gangster movie, always talking about respect. Frankly, at first glance we're a pitiful group of writers in our thirties and forties, along with the occasional fifty-year-old, waiting for Godot, which in this case is the Nobel, the Rulfo, the Cervantes, the Príncipe de Asturias, the Rómulo Gallegos.

2. *The lecture must go on.* I hope no one takes what I just said the wrong way. I was kidding. I didn't mean what I wrote, or what I said. At this stage in my life I don't want to make any more unnecessary enemies. I'm here because I want to teach you to be men. Not true. Just kidding. Actually, it makes me insanely envious to look at you. Not just you but all young Latin American writers. You have a future, I promise you. Sorry. Kidding again. Your future is as a gray as the dictatorship of Castro, of Stroessner, of Pinochet, as the countless corrupt governments that follow one after the other on our continent. I hope no one tries to challenge me to a fight. I can't fight without medical authorization. In fact, when this talk is over I plan to lock myself in my room to watch pornography. You want me to visit the Cartuja? Fuck that. You want me to go see some flamenco? Wrong again. The only thing I'll see is a rodeo, Mexican or Chilean or Argentine. And once I'm there, amid the smell of fresh horse shit and flowering Chile-bells, I'll fall asleep and dream.

3. *The lecture must plant its feet firmly on the ground.* That's right. Let's plant our feet firmly on the ground. Some of the writers here are people I call friends. From them I expect nothing but perfect consideration. The rest of you I don't know, but I've read some of you and heard excellent things about others. Of course, certain writers are missing, writers without whom there's no understanding this entelechy that we call new Latin American literature. It's only fair to list them. I'll begin with the most difficult, a radical writer if there ever was one: Daniel Sada. And then I should mention César Aira, Juan Vil-

loro, Alan Pauls, Rodrigo Rey Rosa, Ibsen Martínez, Carmen Boullosa, the very young Antonio Ungar, the Chileans Gonzalo Contreras, Pedro Lemebel, Jaime Collyer, Alberto Fuguet, and María Moreno, and Mario Bellatin, who has the fortune or misfortune of being considered Mexican by the Mexicans and Peruvian by the Peruvians, and I could go on like this for at least another minute. It's a promising scene, especially if viewed from a bridge. The river is wide and mighty and its surface is broken by the heads of at least twenty-five writers under fifty, under forty, under thirty. How many will drown? I'd say all of them.

4. *The inheritance.* The treasure left to us by our parents, or by those we thought were our putative parents, is pitiful. In fact, we're like children trapped in the mansion of a pedophile. Some of you will say that it's better to be at the mercy of a pedophile than a killer. You're right. But our pedophiles are also killers.

6.
THE PRIVATE LIFE
OF A NOVELIST

WHO WOULD DARE?

The books that I remember best are the ones I stole in Mexico City between the ages of sixteen and nineteen, and the ones I bought in Chile when I was twenty, during the first few months of the coup. In Mexico there was an incredible bookstore. It was called the Glass Bookstore and it was on the Alameda. Its walls, even the ceiling, were glass. Glass and iron beams. From the outside, it seemed an impossible place for shoplifting. And yet prudence was overcome by the temptation to try and after a while I made the attempt. The first book to fall into my hands was a small volume by Pierre Louÿs, with pages as thin as Bible paper, I can't remember now whether it was *Aphrodite* or *Songs of Bilitis*. I know that I was sixteen and that for a while Louÿs became my guide. Then I stole books by Max Beerbohm (*The Happy Hypocrite*), Champfleury, Samuel Pepys, the Goncourt brothers, Alphonse Daudet, and Rulfo and Areola, Mexican writers who at the time were still more or less practicing, and whom I might therefore meet some morning on Avenida Niño Perdido, a teeming street that my maps of Mexico City hide from me today, as if Niño Perdido could only have existed in my imagination, or as if the street, with its underground stores and street performers had really been lost, just as I was lost at the age of sixteen. From the mists of that era, from those stealthy assaults, I remember many books of poetry. Books by Amado Nervo, Alfonso Reyes, Renato Leduc, Gilberto Owen, Heruta and Tablada, and by American poets, like *General William Booth Enters Into Heaven*, by the great Vachel Lindsay. But it was a novel that saved me from hell and plummeted me straight back down again. The novel was *The Fall*, by Camus, and everything that has to do with it I remember as if frozen in a ghostly light, the still light of evening, although I read it, devoured it, by the light of those exceptional Mexico City mornings that shine—or shone—with a red and green radiance ringed by noise, on a bench in the Alameda, with no money and the whole day ahead of me, in fact my whole life ahead of me. After Camus, everything changed. I remember the edition: it was a book with very large print, like a primary school reader, slim, hardback, with a horrendous drawing on the jacket, a hard book to steal and one that I didn't know whether to hide under my arm or in my belt, because it showed under my truant student blazer, and in the end I carried it out in plain sight of all the clerks at the Glass Bookstore, this is one of the best ways to steal, which I had learned from an Edgar Allan Poe story. After that, after I stole that book and read it, I went from being a prudent reader to being a voracious reader and from being a petty book thief to being a book hijacker. I wanted to read everything, which in my innocence was the same as wanting to uncover or trying to uncover the hidden workings of chance that had induced Camus's character to accept his hideous fate. Despite what one

might expect, my career as a book hijacker was long and fruit-
ful, but one day I was caught. Luckily, it wasn't at the Glass
Bookstore but at the Cellar Bookstore, which is or was across
from the Alameda, on Avenida Juárez, and which, as its name
indicates, was a big cellar where the latest books from Buenos
Aires and Barcelona sat piled in gleaming stacks. My arrest
was ignominious. It was as if the bookstore samurai had put
a price on my head. They threatened to have me thrown out
of the country, to give me a beating in the cellar of the Cellar
Bookstore, which to me sounded like a discussion among neo-
philosophers about the destruction of destruction, and in the
end, after lengthy deliberations, they let me go, though not
before confiscating all the books I had on me, among them
The Fall, none of which I'd stolen there. Soon afterwards I left
for Chile. If in Mexico I might have bumped into Rulfo and
Arreola, in Chile the same was true of Nicanor Parra and Enrique Lihn, but I think the only writer I saw was Rodrigo Lira,
walking fast on a night that smelled of tear gas. Then came the
coup and after that I spent my time visiting the bookstores of
Santiago as a cheap way of staving off boredom and madness.
Unlike the Mexican bookstores, the bookstores of Santiago
had no clerks, each of them was run by a single person, almost
always the owner. There I bought Nicanor Parra's *Obra gruesa*
[Complete Works] and the *Artefactos*, and books by Enrique
Lihn and Jorge Teillier that I would soon lose and that were essential reading for me; although essential isn't the word: those
books helped me breathe. But *breathe* isn't the right word either. What I remember best about my visits to those bookstores are the eyes of the booksellers, which sometimes looked
like the eyes of a hanged man and sometimes were veiled by a
kind of film of sleep, which I now know was something else.
I don't remember ever seeing lonelier bookstores. I didn't steal
any books in Santiago. They were cheap and I bought them.

At the last bookstore I visited, as I was going through a row of old French novels, the bookseller, a tall, thin man of about forty, suddenly asked whether I thought it was right for an author to recommend his own works to a man who'd been sentenced to death. The bookseller was standing in a corner, wearing a white shirt with the sleeves rolled up to the elbows and he had a prominent Adam's apple that quivered as he spoke. I said it didn't seem right. What condemned men are we talking about? I asked. The bookseller looked at me and said that he knew for certain of more than one novelist capable of recommending his own books to a man on the verge of death. Then he said that we were talking about desperate readers. I'm hardly qualified to judge, he said, but if I don't, no one will. What book would you give to a condemned man? he asked me. I don't know, I said. I don't know either, said the bookseller, and I think it's terrible. What books do desperate men read? What books do they *like*? How do you imagine the reading room of a condemned man? he asked. I have no idea, I said. You're young, I'm not surprised, he said. And then: it's like Antarctica. Not like the North Pole, but like Antarctica. I was reminded of the last days of Arthur Gordon Pym, but I decided not to say anything. Let's see, said the bookseller, who would have the audacity to drop this novel on the lap of a man sentenced to death? He picked up a book that had done fairly well and then he tossed it on a pile. I paid him and left. When I turned to leave, the bookseller might have laughed or sobbed. As I stepped out I heard him say: What kind of arrogant bastard would dare to do such a thing? And then he said something else, but I couldn't hear what it was.

THE PRIVATE LIFE OF A NOVELIST

My literary kitchen is often an empty room, without even a window. Of course, I'd like it if there were something in it, a lamp, some books, a faint scent of courage, but the truth is that there's nothing.

And yet sometimes, when I succumb to irrepressible bouts of optimism (which lead, incidentally, to terrible allergy attacks), my literary kitchen becomes a medieval castle (with a kitchen) or a New York apartment (with a kitchen and incredible views) or a hut in the foothills of the mountains (without a kitchen, but with a campfire). In these circumstances, I do what everybody does: I lose my sense of proportion and imagine I'm immortal. I don't mean immortal in literary terms, because you'd have to be an idiot to believe that, but literally immortal, like dogs and children and good citizens who have yet to fall ill. Fortunately or unfortunately, every bout of optimism has a beginning and an end. If it didn't, it would become a political calling. Or a religious declaration. And from there it's just a short step to burying books (I won't say "burning books" because that would be an exaggeration). In my case, at least, the truth is that these bouts of optimism come to an end, and with them goes the literary kitchen, which vanishes into thin air, and all that's left is my convalescent self and a faint smell of dirty pots, unscraped plates, spoiled sauces.

The literary kitchen, I tell myself sometimes, is ruled by taste, by which I mean that it's a domain in which memory and ethics (or moral values, if I can call them that) play a game whose rules I don't know. Talent and excellence watch the game, mesmerized, but they don't take part. Daring and bravery do take part, but only at certain moments, which is to say not often. Suffering takes part, pain takes part, death takes part, but on the condition that they don't take the game seriously. They're just playing to be polite.

Much more important than the literary kitchen is the literary library (if you'll excuse the redundancy). A library is much more comfortable than a kitchen. A library is like a church, whereas a kitchen gradually begins to resemble a morgue. Reading, said Gil de Biedma, is more natural than writing. I would add (redundancy aside) that it's also much healthier, no matter what the ophthalmologists say. In fact, literature is a long struggle from redundancy to redundancy, until the final redundancy.

If I had to choose a literary kitchen to move into for a week, I would choose one that belonged to a woman writer, so long as that writer wasn't Chilean. I would live very happily in Silvina Ocampo's kitchen, or Alexandra Pizarnik's, or in the kitchen of the novelist and Mexican poet Carmen Boullosa, or of Simone de Beauvoir. Among other things, because they're cleaner.

Some nights I dream about my literary kitchen. It's huge, like three soccer stadiums, with vaulted ceilings and endlessly long tables at which all the living beings on earth crowd together, the extinct and those soon to be extinct; it's unevenly lit, in some places with anti-aircraft searchlights and in others with torches, and naturally there are plenty of dark sections where all that can be glimpsed are yearning or menacing shadows, and big screens on which, out of the corner of your eye, you can see silent films or slideshows, and in the dream or nightmare I stroll around my literary kitchen and occasionally I fire up a stove and make myself a fried egg, sometimes even a piece of toast. And then I wake up feeling utterly exhausted.

I don't know what you should do in a literary kitchen, but I do know what you shouldn't do. You shouldn't plagiarize. Plagiarists deserve to be hanged in the public square. Swift said so, and Swift, as everybody knows, was always right.

Just so we're clear on this point: no one should plagiarize, unless he wants to be hanged in the public square. Although today plagiarists aren't hanged. In fact, they're given scholarships, prizes, public office, and if very lucky, they become bestsellers and opinion makers. What a strange and ugly term: opinion makers. I suppose it means the same thing as shepherd, or spiritual guide of slaves, or poet laureate, or father of the nation, or mother of the nation, or uncle-by-marriage of the nation.

In my ideal literary kitchen there lives a warrior, whom some voices (disembodied voices, voices that cast no shadow) call a writer. This warrior is always fighting. He knows that in the end, no matter what he does, he'll be defeated. But he still roams the literary kitchen, which is built of cement, and faces his opponent without begging for mercy or granting it.

ADVICE ON THE ART OF WRITING SHORT STORIES

Now that I'm forty-four, I have some advice to offer on the art of writing short stories. 1) Never tackle stories one by one. Really, if you tackle them one by one you could be writing the same story until the day you die. 2) It's best to write stories three at a time, or five at a time. If you've got the energy, write them nine at a time, or fifteen at a time. 3) Careful: the temptation to write them in twos is as dangerous as deciding to write them one by one—it conceals the rather sticky game of mirrors in love, which yields melancholic reflections. 4) You must read Quiroga, you must read Felisberto Hernández, you must read Borges. You must read Rulfo and Monterroso. A short-story writer with any respect at all for his work will never read Cela or Umbral. He'll read Cortázar and Bioy Casares, but by no means Cela and Umbral. 5) Let me repeat, in case it's not clear: Cela and Umbral must be avoided like the plague. 6) A short-story writer must be brave. Sad to say, but it's true.

7) Short-story writers often boast of having read Petrus Borel. In fact, short-story writers are notorious imitators of Petrus Borel. Big mistake: they should imitate the way Petrus Borel dresses! But the truth is they hardly know anything about Petrus Borel! Or about Gautier, or Nerval! 8) Let's make a deal. Read Petrus Borel, dress like Petrus Borel, but also read Jules Renard and Marcel Schwob, especially Marcel Schwob, and after that Alfonso Reyes, and then Borges. 9) The honest truth is that if we read Edgar Allan Poe that would be more than enough. 10) Consider that ninth point. Consider and reflect. It's not too late. You must consider point number nine. If possible: on your knees. 11) Highly recommended books and authors: *On the Sublime*, by Longinus; the sonnets of brave, ill-fated Philip Sidney, whose biographer was Lord Brooke; the *Spoon River Anthology*, by Edgar Lee Masters; *Suicidios ejemplares* [Exemplary Suicides], by Enrique Vila-Matas; and *While the Women Are Sleeping*, by Javier Marías. 12) Read these books and also read Chekhov and Raymond Carver. One of the two of them is the best short-story writer this century has produced.

ABOUT THE SAVAGE DETECTIVES

There are some nice things—not many—about finishing a novel, and one of them is beginning to forget it, remembering a dream or a nightmare that gradually fades so that we can face new books, new days, without the constant reminder of what in all likelihood we could have done better and didn't. Kafka, this century's best writer, showed the way when he asked a friend to burn all his work. He assigned the task to Brod, on the one hand, and also to Dora, his lover. Brod was a writer and he didn't keep his promise. Dora was less educated and she may have loved Kafka more, and one *presumes* that she carried out her lover's request to the letter. All writers, especially on the flat day, which is the day after, or what we vainly believe is the day after, have two devils or angels inside called Brod and Dora. One is always bigger than the other. Usually Brod is bigger or more powerful than Dora. Not in my case. Dora is considerably bigger than Brod, and Dora helps me forget what I've written so that I can write something new, with no pangs of shame or regret. So *The Savage Detectives* is more or less forgotten. I can only venture a few thoughts about it. On the one hand I think I see it as a response, one of many, to *Huckleberry Finn*; the Mississippi of *The Savage Detectives* is the flow of voices in the second part of the novel. It's also the more or less faithful transcription of a segment of the life of the Mexican poet Mario Santiago, whose friend I was lucky enough to be. In this sense the novel tries to reflect a kind of generational defeat and also the happiness of a generation, a happiness that at times delineated courage and the limits of courage. To say that I'm permanently indebted to the work of Borges and Cortázar is obvious. I believe there are as many ways to read my novel as there are voices in it. It can be read as a deathbed lament. It can also be read as a game.

THE END: "DISTANT STAR"
(INTERVIEW WITH MÓNICA MARISTAIN)

On the lackluster literature scene in the Spanish-speaking world, a space where young writers turn up every day who care more about collecting grants than about contributing anything to artistic creation, the figure of a lean man stands out, blue backpack at the ready, huge glasses, eternal cigarette in hand, and subtle irony delivered rapid-fire.

Roberto Bolaño, born in Chile in 1953, is the best thing that's happened to the craft of writing in a long time. Since his monumental novel *The Savage Detectives*, perhaps the great contemporary Mexican novel, brought him fame and garnered him the Herralde Prize (1998) and the Rómulo Gallegos Prize (1999), he has continued to grow in influence and stature. Everything he says (with pointed humor and exquisite intelligence), and everything he writes (at great poetic risk and with deep creative commitment, his pen unerring) merits the attention of those who admire him, and, of course, of those who detest him.

The author, who appears as a character in the novel *Soldiers of Salamis*, by Javier Cercas, and who is paid homage in Jorge Volpi's latest novel, *El fin de la locura* [The End of Madness], is, like all brilliant men, a divisive figure, someone who inspires antipathy despite his gentle nature and despite his voice, somewhere between high-pitched and hoarse, in which he tells *Playboy* that he can't write a story for the magazine because he's still working on his next novel, which is already 900 pages long and will be about the killings of women in Ciudad Juárez.

Roberto Bolaño lives in Blanes, Spain, and he's very sick. He hopes that a liver transplant will give him the strength to live with the intensity lauded by those fortunate enough to know him personally. These people, his friends, say that when he's writing he sometimes forgets to go to doctors' appointments.

At fifty, this man—who backpacked across Latin America, who escaped the clutches of Pinochet's regime because one of his jailors was once a classmate, who lived in Mexico, who met the militants of the Farabundo Martí (future assassins of Roque Dalton) in El Salvador, who was a watchman at a campground in Catalonia, a seller of costume jewelry in Europe, and always a pilferer of good books, because reading demands action, not just attitude—has changed the course of Latin American literature. And he's done it suddenly and without begging anyone's leave.

PLAYBOY: Was it hard being born dyslexic?

BOLAÑO: No. Playing soccer was hard; I'm left-footed. Masturbating was hard; I'm left-handed. Writing was hard; I'm right-handed. But as you can see, no serious difficulties.

PLAYBOY: Is Enrique Vila-Matas still your friend after your fight with the organizers of the Rómulo Gallegos Prize?

BOLAÑO: My fight with the jury and the organizers of the

prize was basically due to the fact that they wanted me, from Blanes and sight unseen, to endorse a selection that I'd had nothing to do with. Their methods, which a Chavista pseudo-poet communicated to me by phone, reeked of the persuasive techniques of the Casa de las Américas in Cuba. I thought it was a huge mistake that Daniel Sada and Jorge Volpi were eliminated early on, for example. They said that what I wanted was a free trip with my wife and children, which was completely untrue. Out of my indignation about that lie came the letter in which I called them neo-Stalinists and worse, I guess. Actually, I was informed that from the very start they intended to give the prize to a different author, not Vila-Matas, as it happens, whose novel I thought was good, and who was definitely one of my candidates.

PLAYBOY: Why doesn't your office have air conditioning?

BOLAÑO: My motto isn't *Et in Arcadia ego* but *Et in Esparta ego*.

PLAYBOY: Don't you think that if you'd gotten drunk with Isabel Allende and Ángeles Mastretta you'd feel differently about their books?

BOLAÑO: I doubt it. First, because there's no way those two ladies would go out drinking with me. Second, because I don't drink anymore. Third, because even at my drunkest moments I never lost a certain basic clarity, a sense of style and rhythm, a horror of plagiarism, mediocrity, and silence.

PLAYBOY: What's the difference between an authoress and a writer?

BOLAÑO: Silvina Ocampo is a writer. Marcela Serrano is an authoress. A distance of light years separates them.

PLAYBOY: What makes you think that you're a better poet than novelist?

BOLAÑO: I judge by how much I blush when I open a book of my poetry or my prose. The poetry makes me blush less.

PLAYBOY: Are you Chilean, Spanish, or Mexican?

BOLAÑO: I'm Latin American.

PLAYBOY: What does *homeland* mean to you?

BOLAÑO: I'm afraid I have to give you a sappy answer. My two children, Lautaro and Alexandra, are my only homeland. And in second place, maybe a few instants, a few streets, a few faces or scenes or books that live inside me. Things I'll forget someday, which is the best remedy for homelands.

PLAYBOY: What is Chilean literature?

BOLAÑO: Probably the nightmares of Carlos Pezoa Véliz, who was the bitterest and grayest and perhaps most cowardly of Chilean poets. He died at the beginning of the twentieth century and wrote just two memorable poems, though they were truly memorable, and he still sees us in his dreams and is tormented. Maybe he hasn't actually died yet, and we're all a part of his long death throes. Or at least we Chileans are a part of them.

PLAYBOY: Why do you like to be so contrary?

BOLAÑO: I'm never contrary.

PLAYBOY: Do you have more friends than enemies?

BOLAÑO: My best friend was the poet Mario Santiago, who died in 1998. Right now three of my best friends are Ignacio Echevarría, Rodrigo Fresán, and A.G. Porta.

PLAYBOY: Did Antonio Skármeta ask you to be on his show?

BOLAÑO: One of his secretaries called me, or maybe it was the cleaning lady. I told her I was too busy.

PLAYBOY: Did Javier Cercas share the royalties for *Soldiers of Salamis* with you?

BOLAÑO: No, of course not.

PLAYBOY: Enrique Lihn, Jorge Teillier, or Nicanor Parra?

BOLAÑO: Nicanor Parra over everyone else, including Pablo Neruda and Vicente Huidobro and Gabriela Mistral.

PLAYBOY: Eugenio Montale, T. S. Eliot, or Xavier Villaurrutia?

BOLAÑO: Montale. If it were James Joyce instead of Eliot, then Joyce. If it were Ezra Pound instead of Eliot, then definitely Pound.

PLAYBOY: John Lennon, Lady Di, or Elvis Presley?

BOLAÑO: The Pogues. Or Suicide. Or Bob Dylan. But let's not split hairs: Elvis forever. Elvis wearing a sheriff's badge and driving a Mustang, popping pills. Elvis and his golden voice.

PLAYBOY: Who reads more, you or Rodrigo Fresán?

BOLAÑO: It depends. Rodrigo takes the West. I take the East. Then we tell each other about the books from our respective domains and it's as if we'd read them all.

PLAYBOY: What is Pablo Neruda's best poem?

BOLAÑO: Almost anything from *Residence on Earth*.

PLAYBOY: If you'd met her, what would you have said to Gabriela Mistral?

BOLAÑO: Mother, forgive me, I've sinned, but I was saved by the love of a woman.

PLAYBOY: And Salvador Allende?

BOLAÑO: Not much, if anything. Those in power (even if it's only for a little while) know nothing about literature, all they care about is power. And I'll play the fool for my readers, if I feel like it, but never for the powerful. That may sound melodramatic. It may sound like the declaration of an honest hooker. But it's the truth, in the end.

PLAYBOY: And Vicente Huidobro?

BOLAÑO: Huidobro bores me a little. Too much trilling and tra-la-la-ing, too much of the parachutist who sings Tyrolean songs as he falls. Better the parachutist who plummets in flames, or the parachutist whose parachute simply never opens.

PLAYBOY: Is Octavio Paz still the enemy?

BOLAÑO: Definitely not for me. I don't know about the poets who wrote like his clones when I lived in Mexico, what they think. It's been a long time since I knew anything about Mexican poetry. I do reread José Juan Tablada and Ramón López Velarde, I can even recite Sor Juana, if it comes to that, but I don't know anything about what's being written by the poets who are nearing fifty, like me.

PLAYBOY: Wouldn't Carlos Fuentes play that role now?

BOLAÑO: It's been a long time since I read anything by Carlos Fuentes.

PLAYBOY: How do you feel about the fact that Arturo Pérez-Reverte is currently the the most widely read writer in Spanish?

BOLAÑO: Pérez-Reverte or Isabel Allende, it makes no difference. Feuillet was the most widely read French writer of his time.

PLAYBOY: And the fact that Arturo Pérez-Reverte has been inducted into the Royal Academy?

BOLAÑO: The Royal Academy is a hotbed of genius. Juan Marsé isn't a member, Juan Goytisolo isn't a member, Mendoza and Javier Marías aren't members, Olvido García Valdés isn't a member, I can't remember whether Álvaro Pombo is a member (if he is it's probably a mistake), but there's Pérez-Reverte. Well, Paulo Coelho is a member of the Brazilian Academy.

PLAYBOY: Do you regret criticizing the dinner you were served by the writer Diamela Eltit?

BOLAÑO: I never criticized her dinner. If anything, I should have criticized her sense of humor, her vegetarian sense of humor, or better yet, her diet-starved sense of humor.

PLAYBOY: Does it trouble you that she considers you a bad person after your account of that ill-fated meal?

BOLAÑO: No, poor Diamela, that doesn't trouble me. Other things trouble me.

PLAYBOY: Have you shed any tears over all the times you've been criticized by your enemies?

BOLAÑO: Many tears. Every time I read that someone's said something bad about me I sob, I throw myself on the floor, I claw at myself, I stop writing for an unspecified length of time, I lose my appetite, I smoke less, I exercise, I go for walks along the shore, which as it happens is less than thirty yards from where I live, and I ask the seagulls, whose ancestors ate the fish that ate Ulysses, why me, when I've never done them any wrong.

PLAYBOY: Whose opinion of your work do you value most?

BOLAÑO: Carolina reads my books first, and then Herralde, and then I try to forget them forever.

PLAYBOY: What did you buy with the money from the Rómulo Gallegos Prize?

BOLAÑO: Not much. A suitcase, I seem to remember.

PLAYBOY: During the time when you made a living from story competitions, were there ever any that didn't pay up?

BOLAÑO: Never. In that regard, Spanish municipalities are above reproach.

PLAYBOY: Were you a good waiter, or were you better at selling cheap jewelry?

BOLAÑO: The job I was best at was being a night watchman at a campground near Barcelona. No one stole anything while I was there. I broke up some fights that could have turned ugly. I prevented a lynching (though afterwards I would happily have lynched or strangled the guy myself).

PLAYBOY: Have you experienced terrible hunger, bone-chilling cold, choking heat?

BOLAÑO: I quote Vittorio Gassman from a movie: In all modesty, yes.

PLAYBOY: Have you ever stolen any book and later discovered you didn't like it?

BOLAÑO: Never. The good thing about stealing books (as opposed to safes) is that one can carefully examine their contents before perpetrating the crime.

PLAYBOY: Have you ever walked in the desert?

BOLAÑO: Yes, and once even arm in arm with my grandmother. The old lady just kept going and I was afraid we wouldn't make it out alive.

PLAYBOY: Have you seen colored fish underwater?

BOLAÑO: Of course. In Acapulco, to begin with, in 1974 or 1975.

PLAYBOY: Have you ever burned yourself with a cigarette?

BOLAÑO: Never on purpose.

PLAYBOY: Have you ever carved the name of your beloved into a tree trunk?

BOLAÑO: I've done more outrageous things, but let's let them languish in oblivion.

PLAYBOY: Have you ever seen the most beautiful woman in the world?

BOLAÑO: Yes, when I was working at a store, sometime around 1984. The store was empty and a Hindu woman came in. She looked like a princess and maybe she was. She bought some earrings from me. I almost swooned, of course. She had copper-colored skin, long red hair, and everything else about her was perfect. A timeless beauty. When I had to ring her up I was incredibly embarrassed. She smiled as if to say that she understood and I shouldn't worry. Then she disappeared and I've never seen anyone like that again. Sometimes I think she was the goddess Kali, patron saint of thieves and goldsmiths, except that Kali is also the goddess of assassins, and not only was this Hindu woman the most beautiful creature on Earth, she also seemed to be a good person, very sweet and considerate.

PLAYBOY: Do you like dogs or cats?

BOLAÑO: Dogs, but I don't have pets anymore.

PLAYBOY: What do you remember about your childhood?

BOLAÑO: Everything. I have a good memory.

PLAYBOY: Did you collect trading cards?

BOLAÑO: Yes. Of soccer players and Hollywood actors and actresses.

PLAYBOY: Did you have a skateboard?

BOLAÑO: My parents made the mistake of giving me a pair of skates when we lived in Valparaíso, which is a city of hills. The results were disastrous. Every time I put on the skates it was as if I had a death wish.

PLAYBOY: What's your favorite soccer team?

BOLAÑO: I don't have one anymore. The teams that drop quickly through the divisions down to the regionals, and then are gone. The ghost teams.

PLAYBOY: What historical characters would you have liked to model yourself after?

BOLAÑO: Sherlock Holmes. Captain Nemo. Julien Sorel, our father; Prince Mishkin, our uncle; Alice, our teacher; Houdini, who is a mix of Alice, Sorel, and Mishkin.

PLAYBOY: Did you fall in love with older neighborhood girls?

BOLAÑO: Of course.

PLAYBOY: Did the girls at school pay attention to you?

BOLAÑO: I don't think so. At least I was convinced they didn't.

PLAYBOY: What do you owe the women in your life?

BOLAÑO: A lot. A sense of challenge and the ambition to aim high. And other things that I won't mention for the sake of decorum.

PLAYBOY: Do they owe you anything?

BOLAÑO: Nothing.

PLAYBOY: Have you suffered for love?

BOLAÑO: The first time I suffered terribly, then I learned to take things with more of a sense of humor.

PLAYBOY: What about hatred?

BOLAÑO: It may sound a little pretentious, but I've never hated anyone. At least, I know I'm not capable of sustained hatred. And if hatred isn't sustained, it isn't hatred, is it?

PLAYBOY: How did you woo your wife?

BOLAÑO: By cooking rice for her. In those days I was very poor and all I ate was rice, so I learned how to cook it lots of ways.

PLAYBOY: What kind of day was it when you became a father for the first time?

BOLAÑO: It was nighttime, a little before midnight, I was alone, and since you couldn't smoke in the hospital I smoked a cigarette practically perched on a ledge four floors up. It was a good thing no one saw me from the street. No one but the moon, as Amado Nervo would say. When I came back in a nurse told me that my son had just been born. He was very big, almost completely bald, and his eyes were open as if to ask who the hell this guy holding him was.

PLAYBOY: Will Lautaro be a writer?

BOLAÑO: I just hope he'll be happy. Which means it would be better if he were something else. A pilot, for example, or a plastic surgeon, or an editor.

PLAYBOY: In what ways do you see yourself in him?

BOLAÑO: Luckily he's much more like his mother than like me.

PLAYBOY: Do you care about the sales rankings of your books?

BOLAÑO: Not in the slightest.

PLAYBOY: Do you ever think about your readers?

BOLAÑO: Almost never.

PLAYBOY: Of all the things readers have said about your books, what has moved you?

BOLAÑO: I'm moved by readers in general, by those who still dare to read Voltaire's *Philosophical Dictionary*, which is one of the most entertaining and modern books I know. I'm moved by the fortitude of young people who read Cortázar and Parra, just as I once read them and as I try to read them still. I'm moved by young people who sleep with books under their heads. A book is the best pillow there is.

PLAYBOY: What things have made you angry?

BOLAÑO: At this point getting angry is a waste of time. And sadly, at my age time matters.

PLAYBOY: Have you ever been afraid of your fans?

BOLAÑO: I've been afraid of the fans of Leopoldo María Panero, who in my opinion, by the way, is one of the three best living poets in Spain. In Pamplona, during a series of readings organized by José Ferrero, Panero was the last on the program, and as the day of his reading approached, the city (or the neighborhood where our hotel was) filled up with freaks who seemed to have just escaped from a mental asylum, which incidentally is the best audience any poet can hope for. The problem is that some of them didn't look only like madmen. They looked like killers, and Ferrero and I were afraid that at some point someone would get up and say: I shot Leopoldo María Panero, and then plug four bullets into Panero's head—and then with one each for Ferrero and me for good measure.

PLAYBOY: Are you curious about the critical anthology your fellow Chilean Patricia Espinoza is putting together?

BOLAÑO: Not at all. I think Espinoza is an excellent critic, regardless of how I'll come off in her book, which I imagine won't be very well, but Espinoza's work is essential in Chile. In fact, the need for a new criticism—for lack of a better term—is something that's become urgent everywhere in Latin America.

PLAYBOY: And what about the Argentine Celina Manzoni's book?

BOLAÑO: I know Celina personally and I'm very fond of her. I dedicated one of the stories from *Putas asesinas* to her.

PLAYBOY: What things bore you?

BOLAÑO: The empty discourse of the Left. I take for granted the empty discourse of the Right.

PLAYBOY: What things do you enjoy?

BOLAÑO: Watching my daughter Alexandra play. Having breakfast at a bar on the beach and eating a croissant as I read the paper. The works of Borges. The works of Bioy. The works of Bustos Domecq. Making love.

PLAYBOY: Do you write by hand?

BOLAÑO: Poetry, yes. Everything else on an old computer from 1993.

PLAYBOY: Close your eyes: Of all the landscapes of Latin America you've seen, which comes to mind first?

BOLAÑO: Lisa's lips in 1974. My father's truck broken down on a desert highway. The tuberculosis ward of a hospital in Cauquenes and my mother telling my sister and me to hold our breath. A trip to Popocatépetl with Lisa, Mara, and Vera and someone else I can't remember, though I do remember Lisa's lips, her incredible smile.

PLAYBOY: What's paradise like?

BOLAÑO: Like Venice, I hope, somewhere full of Italians. Somewhere that's used well and used up and that knows that nothing lasts, not even paradise, and in the end it doesn't matter.

PLAYBOY: And hell?

BOLAÑO: Like Ciudad Juárez, which is our curse and our

mirror, the unquiet mirror of our frustrations and of our vile interpretation of freedom and of our desires.

PLAYBOY: When did you learn that you were gravely ill?

BOLAÑO: In 1992.

PLAYBOY: What parts of your character were changed by your illness?

BOLAÑO: Nothing changed. I discovered that I wasn't immortal, which—at the age of thirty-eight—it was about time I discovered.

PLAYBOY: What things would you like to do before you die?

BOLAÑO: Nothing in particular. Well, I'd rather not die, of course. But sooner or later the great lady makes her entrance. The problem is that sometimes she's no lady, let alone great. Instead, as Nicanor Parra says in a poem, she's a cheap whore, which is enough to make anyone's teeth chatter.

PLAYBOY: Who would you most like to meet in the afterlife?

BOLAÑO: I don't believe in the afterlife. If it exists, I'll be surprised. First thing, I'd sign up for whatever class Pascal was teaching.

PLAYBOY: Did you ever think about killing yourself?

BOLAÑO: Of course. At some point I survived precisely because I knew I could kill myself if things got worse.

PLAYBOY: Did you ever think you were going crazy?

BOLAÑO: Yes, but I was always saved by my sense of humor. I told myself stories that cracked me up. Or I remembered situations that made me roll on the ground laughing.

PLAYBOY: Madness, death, love: Which of the three has there been most of in your life?

BOLAÑO: I hope with all my heart that it's love.

PLAYBOY: What makes you laugh?

BOLAÑO: My own misfortunes, and other people's misfortunes.

PLAYBOY: What makes you cry?

BOLAÑO: The same thing: misfortunes, mine and other people's.

PLAYBOY: Do you like music?

BOLAÑO: Very much.

PLAYBOY: Would you cut anything from *The Savage Detectives*?

BOLAÑO: No. To cut anything I would have to reread it and that's against my religion.

PLAYBOY: Aren't you afraid that someone might make a movie of it?

BOLAÑO: Ay, Mónica, I'm afraid of other things. More horrific things, shall we say; much more horrific things.

PLAYBOY: Is "Mauricio ('The Eye') Silva" an homage to Julio Cortázar?

BOLAÑO: Not at all.

PLAYBOY: When you finished writing "Mauricio ('The Eye') Silva" didn't you feel that you had written a story on a par with "House Taken Over"?

BOLAÑO: When I finished writing "Mauricio ('The Eye') Silva" I stopped crying. Or something like that. I wish it *was* like a Cortázar story, though "House Taken Over" isn't one of my favorites.

PLAYBOY: Do you get along well with your editor?

BOLAÑO: Fairly well. Herralde is an intelligent and often charming person. It might be better for me if he weren't so charming. The truth is that I've known him for eight years now, and at least as far as I'm concerned the love just keeps growing, in the words of the bolero. Though it might be better for me if I weren't so fond of him.

PLAYBOY: What do you have to say about those who think *The Savage Detectives* is the great contemporary Mexican novel?

BOLAÑO: They say it because they feel sorry for me, they see me looking depressed or as if I'm on my last legs and the best they can come up with is a white lie, which in fact is only appropriate in cases like this and isn't even a venial sin.

PLAYBOY: Is it true that it was Juan Villoro who convinced you not to give your novel *By Night in Chile* the title *Storms of Shit*?

BOLAÑO: Villoro and Herralde.

PLAYBOY: Whose advice do you listen to most when it comes to your work?

BOLAÑO: I don't listen to anyone's advice, not even my doctor's. I give advice right and left, but I never take it.

PLAYBOY: What is Blanes like?

BOLAÑO: A pretty town. Or a small city of 30,000, quite pretty. It was founded two thousand years ago by the Romans, and then people came from all over. It's not a luxury resort, it's a place for the working class. People from Northern or Eastern Europe. Some end up staying forever. The bay is beautiful.

PLAYBOY: Do you miss anything about your life in Mexico?

BOLAÑO: My youth and my walks with Mario Santiago.

PLAYBOY: What Mexican writer do you deeply admire?

BOLAÑO: Of my generation I admire Sada, whose goals seem the most daring to me, Villoro, Carmen Boullosa. Among the younger writers I'm very interested in what Álvaro Enrigue and Mauricio Montiel are doing, or Volpi and Ignacio Padilla. I keep reading Sergio Pitol, who gets better every day. And Monsiváis, who, according to Villoro, gave Taibo II or III (or IV) the nickname "Pol Pit" which I think is a stroke of poetic genius. Monsiváis still keeps his talons filed. I also like what Sergio González Rodríguez is doing.

PLAYBOY: Does the world have a cure?

BOLAÑO: The world is alive and nothing alive needs a cure, which is lucky for us.

PLAYBOY: In what or in whom do you place your hopes?

BOLAÑO: My dear Maristaín, you propel me again into the realm of sappiness, which is my natural abode. I have hope in children. In children and warriors. In children who fuck like children and warriors who fight like brave men. Why? I refer you to the gravestone of Borges, as the illustrious Gervasio Montenegro, of the Academy, would say. And that's enough of that.

PLAYBOY: What does the word posthumous remind you of?

BOLAÑO: It sounds like the name of a Roman gladiator. An undefeated gladiator. Or at least that's what poor Posthumous imagines in order to give himself courage.

PLAYBOY: What do you think about the people who say that you'll win the Nobel Prize?

BOLAÑO: I'm sure I won't, just as I'm sure that some slacker from my generation will, and he won't even give me a nod in his speech in Stockholm.

PLAYBOY: What would you have liked to be instead of a writer?

BOLAÑO: I would much rather have been a homicide detective than a writer. That's one thing I'm absolutely sure of. A homicide cop, someone who returns alone at night to the scene of the crime and isn't afraid of ghosts. Maybe then I really would have gone crazy, but when you're a policeman, you solve that by shooting yourself in the mouth.

PLAYBOY: Do you confess to having lived?

BOLAÑO: I'm still alive, I'm still reading, I'm still writing and watching movies, and as Arturo Prat said to the sailors of the Esmeralda before their last stand, so long as I live, this flag will fly.

SOURCES

The references that follow don't pretend to be exhaustive. As is not uncommon, Bolaño occasionally submitted for publication pieces that had previously appeared elsewhere, especially if in a different country. To follow the trail of each and every one of the pieces gathered here through the many Spanish and Latin American newspapers and magazines to which Bolaño contributed is a task that lies outside the scope of this volume. In fact, the volume was assembled in the knowledge that some pieces that had been overlooked would inevitably turn up here and there after it was published. At least there won't be many of them, since access was had to the computer files where Bolaño himself kept most, if not all, of his contributions—in considerable disarray, it must be said. Which means that it's impossible to be sure whether a few of the pieces included here were ever previously published. When it's known that a certain piece was published in more than one place, the different sources are given. In just a few cases, and in fairly arbitrary fashion, some explanatory notes are included when judged to be of interest to the reader.

PREFACE

Self-Portrait. Brief autobiographical statement written at the request of the Rómulo Gallegos Center for Latin American Studies when, in 1999, Bolaño won the prize awarded by the Center.

THREE INSUFFERABLE SPEECHES

The Vagaries of the Literature of Doom. Read December 14, 2002 at the Kosmópolis International Festival of Literature hosted by the Centre de Cultura Contemporànea (CCCB) in Barcelona. Bolaño introduced the reading of the text with the following remarks (which are transcribed from a tape recording): "This piece is very limited in scope and hasn't been revised, which means that everything said in it is subject to subsequent rectification. Originally I wanted to discuss the literature of the Southern Cone of America, or Chile, Argentina, and Uruguay, but Argentine literature is so rich, so powerful, that in the end it seemed more fitting to focus exclusively on it; on Argentine fiction, basically. My initial idea was to talk about Argentine literature from Borges to Rodrigo Fresán, but I soon realized that in order to do that I would've needed one hundred pages, not ten, and I was no more prepared to write one hundred pages than you would've been to listen to them. The piece is therefore limited to the drift of Argentine literature since Borges's death; to its gangster drift since Borges's death, basically. Sadly, this gangster literature, or literature of doom is the most vital, the richest. Personally, it doesn't excite me much, mostly because I'm sick of the literature of doom, but there's no doubt that it's the most vital, and that it has the most influence on the rest of Latin American literature. The literature of doom, as I've said, is a kind of sub-world or infra-world outside the law." For his reading, Bolaño numbered the paragraphs of the text.

Caracas Address. Read August 2, 1999 at the award ceremony for the Rómulo Gallegos Prize, in Caracas. Published in *Diagonal* (cultural supplement of the newspaper *El Metropolitano*, Santiago de Chile), September 5, 1999 (under the title "Corriendo la línea" [Running the Line]). Also published in the Spanish edition of the magazine *Letras Libres*, Number 10, October 1999, and in the magazine *Lateral* (Barcelona), Number 59, November 1999, pp. 40–41. Collected by Celina Manzoni in *Roberto Bolaño: La escritura como tauromaquia* [Writing as Tauromachy], Buenos Aires, Corregidor, 2002, pp. 207–214.

Literature and Exile. Read April 3, 2000 as part of "Europe and Latin America: Literature, Immigration, and Identity," a symposium organized by the Austrian Society for the Literature of Vienna. Published in *sábado* (cultural supplement of the newspaper *unomásuno*, Mexico), October 7, 2000; also published in the magazine *Turia* (Teruel), number 54, November 2000, pp. 41–46.

FRAGMENTS OF A RETURN TO THE NATIVE LAND

Exiles. Possibly unpublished text, in any case written before Bolaño's first trip to Chile, in November 1998. It's likely that Bolaño wrote it for the lecture series "Literature and its Limits," organized by Jesús Ferrero as part of the Navarra Festivals, 1997. Bolaño gave his talk on August 13.

Fragments of a Return to the Native Land. Published in the magazine *Paula* (Santiago de Chile), Number 792, February 1999, pp. 98–101. The piece was preceded by the following editor's note: "Last November, when the writer Roberto Bolaño was in Chile as a juror for *Paula*'s story competition, we asked him to write his impressions of the country after 25 years away. Two months later he sent us what he'd written, begging us not to cut a thing or change a single comma. We obeyed, and here's his piece in full, exclusively for our readers."

The Corridor with No Apparent Way Out. Ajoblanco (Barcelona), Number 116, May 1999, pp. 54–57. The piece was accompanied by the following editor's note: "The writer Roberto Bolaño, winner of the Herralde Prize for *The Savage Detectives*, has returned to his native Chile after twenty-five years of exile. Three months ago he told us in these very pages that he hoped to find a 'tolerant country,' but that was 'just a dream.' This is the account of his bitter home-coming." As noted in the Introduction, the piece soon made the rounds in Chile, arousing feelings of resentment, so that when Bolaño returned to Chile in November 1999, he was the frequent target of hostile remarks and attitudes. By then, Bolaño had won the Rómulo Gallegos Prize and his growing fame and prestige did much to heighten the suspicions and offense fostered by his often defiant declarations about the culture, politics, and society of his native country. An unpublished text discovered among Bolaño's posthumous papers describes an incident that occurred during his first trip to Chile, in 1998: "The next year, in 1999, I traveled to Chile at the invitation of the Book Fair. Possibly to celebrate my recent receipt of the Rómulo Gallegos Prize, almost all the Chilean writers decided to attack me *en patota*, as they say in Chile, or en masse. I counterattacked. An older woman, who had lived all her life on the handouts that the State gives to artists, called me a lackey. I've never lived on the largesse of any country, so this accusation surprised me. It was also said that I was a *patero*, which doesn't mean the same thing as *patota*. A *patero* doesn't necessarily belong to a *patota*, as one might inadvertently assume, although in every *patota* there are always *pateros*. A *patero* is a flatterer, a smooth-talker, a bootlicker; an ass-kisser, in proper Spanish. The incredible thing about this is that the people who were calling me names were Chil-eans, left-wing as well as right-wing, who kissed ass incessantly to cling to their shreds of fame, whereas everything that I've achieved (which isn't much) I'd gotten without the help of anyone. What was it they didn't like about me? Well, someone said it was my teeth. There I have to say they were absolutely right." This isn't the place to explain the allusions that Bolaño makes here, though it's worth confirming that everything he reports is true, including the remark by a distinguished Chilean writer about his teeth.

Words from Outer Space. El Periódico (Barcelona), February 5, 1999. Bolaño alludes to some clandestine tape-recordings of telephone conversations between military commanders the day of the coup led by Augusto Pinochet, September 11, 1973.

A Modest Proposal. Text found among Bolaño's posthumous papers. It hasn't been possible to discover whether it was ever published, though by all indications it was. In any case, the text was written after Bolaño's first trip to Chile, in November 1998.

Out in the Cold. Text found among Bolaño's posthumous papers. As with the previous piece, it hasn't been possible to discover whether it was published, though by all indications it was.

Chilean Poetry Under Inclement Skies. Remarks commemorating the publication of a single-subject issue of the magazine *Litoral* (Málaga) titled *Chile: Contemporary Poetry (with a Glance at Contemporary Art)*, Numbers 223–224, November 1999, pp. 9–10. Also published as a stand-alone piece in *Las Últimas Noticias*, May 2000.

On Bruno Montané. Jacket copy for a book of poems by Bruno Montané, *El maletín de Stevenson. El cielo de los topos* [Stevenson's Suitcase: The Moles' Sky], Mexico, Ediciones El Aduanero, 2002.

Eight Seconds with Nicanor Parra. Remarks commemorating the publication of the catalogue for the exhibition *Artefactos visuales. Dirección obligada* [Visual Artifacts: Address Required], by Nicanor Parra, on display at the Telefónica Foundation of Madrid from April 25 to June 10, 2001.

The Lost. Text found among Roberto's posthumous papers. It hasn't been possible to discover whether it was ever published.

The Transparent Mystery of José Donoso. Hoja por Hoja (literary supplement of the Mexican newspaper *Reforma*, Mexico), special issue for the Guadalajara International Book Fair, November 1999.

On Literature, the National Literature Prize, and the Rare Consolations of the Writing Life. Published as a stand-alone piece in *Las Últimas Noticias*, August 27, 2002. Shortly after sending this article to *Las Últimas Noticias*, Bolaño sent me a copy of it by email, with the following message: "Dear Ignacio: Restif de la Bretonne on the barricades or how to make more friends in Chile. The neo-pamphlet will be the great literary genre of the 22nd century. In this sense, I'm a minor author, but ahead of my times." Soon afterward, in response to my questions and comments on the text, he wrote (August 26, 2002): "Friday is the national litherathure [sic] prize gala, tacky ceremony if ever there was one. I hope that my pamphlet won't be read solely in that context. Frankly, I don't give a damn what people think. Metaphor matters to me, meter matters to me. It's not a suicidal gesture—no sir, as the excellent and always under-appreciated Lute said: legitimate self-defense, your honor, legitimate self-defense." The National Prize that year was won by Teitelbaum.

BETWEEN PARENTHESES

As mentioned in the Introduction, the columns gathered in this section were published in the *Diari de Girona* (the early ones), and later on in the Chilean newspaper *Las Últimas Noticias*. The first *Diari de Girona* column appeared on January 10, 1999 ("The Best Gang") and the last on April 2, 2000 ("Hell's Angels"). Bolaño ended up publishing nearly forty columns in the *Diari de Girona*, at more or less weekly intervals. Here they're presented in the order in which they appeared, except for a few which have been impossible to date. The columns were published in Catalan translation, and in some cases the Spanish originals couldn't be found. Those pieces aren't reproduced here, since it seemed pointless to include texts by Bolaño translated from another language. During the months that he published his column in the *Diari de Girona*, Bolaño gradually began to contribute to other publications (especially *Diagonal*, the cultural supplement of the now-defunct *El Metropolitano* of Santiago, Chile, which was headed by his friend Roberto Brodsky), to which he occasionally sent the same pieces, sometimes simultaneously. The reasons why Bolaño chose to stop writing for the *Diari de Girona* are unknown, though it's easy to imagine that around this time, with his work in increasing demand, he might have grown tired of the weekly effort of writing a column that had a very limited readership and for which he couldn't have been paid a very enticing amount.

The first column in *Las Últimas Noticias* appeared on July

30, 2000 ("An Afternoon with Huidobro and Parra"). Bolaño began by recycling many of the columns already published in the *Diari de Girona*, sometimes lightly revised. The columns in *Las Últimas Noticias* were published once a week, with very few exceptions, until July 4, 2001 ("An Attempt at an Exhaustive Catalogue of Patrons"). Around this time, Bolaño informed Andrés Braithwaite that he wouldn't be able to send him new articles because he was so absorbed by the writing of *2666*. But behind this explanation lay a growing fatigue, due to health problems. In fact, beginning especially in January 2001, Bolaño's correspondence with Andrés Braithwaite begins to contain frequent references to the deterioration of his health. "My health is bad," writes Bolaño on January 16. "The long-awaited moment seems to have come or is imminent . . . Of course, now I don't feel like writing. In fact, I don't even answer letters anymore. But maybe all of this will pass, and it's caused by the fear or exhaustion that flare up in situations like this. Really, the situation has its humorous side." On January 24 he returns again to the same subject: "I don't feel much like working, it's true. In my current state, what the body craves is the reading aloud of the Tibetan book of the dead or the praying of the rosary, but I won't let you down." And on February 7, never losing his sense of humor, he writes: "Today I sent you a piece ["The Ancestor"] that I think is good. A year from now you might even have enough material to put together a posthumous book. I suggest the following title: *Thus Spake Bolaño*. I don't know, it seems tasteful and suggestive, as our friend Carlos Argentino Daneri from *El Aleph* would say."

A little more than a year later, Bolaño decided to start up his column in *Las Últimas Noticias* again. "Get ready, girls, because Bolaño's back. I'll be writing . . . weekly," he tells Braithwaite on August 28, 2002. And on September 9, 2002, "Jim" is published, which marks the beginning of the third and final stage of Bolaño as columnist. This new round would end on January 20, 2003 ("Humor in the Wings"), once again for health reasons. Around this time Bolaño writes to Braithwaite, apologizing for the delay in sending the final column: "I've had it up to here with all the tests. And now I'm on the transplant list. In other words, they could call me at any minute, since my blood group—B+—is rare, and according to the doctors, I'm not in a position to chivalrously give up my place in line. You know what this means. More Bolaño or *finis terrae* or *c'est tout*. I'm sorry to make things difficult for you, but ultimately that's what editors are there for." After he had stopped contributing to *Las Últimas Noticias*, as late as March 4, 2002, Bolaño promises Braithwaite that he'll keep writing for the newspaper "as soon as I recover." But as we know, that was not to be.

Like the columns for the *Diari de Girona*, the columns written for *Las Últimas Noticias* were eventually recycled by Bolaño for other publications, sometimes slightly recast, revised, or with new titles. On September 9, 2000, in *sábado*, the cultural supplement of the Mexican newspaper *unomásuno*, Bolaño published eight columns, under the title "Alfabeto de lecturas" [Alphabet of Readings] that had previously appeared in the *Diari de Girona* and were later reclaimed for *Las Últimas Noticias*. During the fall-winter of 2001–2002, in the same cultural supplement, Bolaño had a section titled "Carta de Blanes" [Letter from Blanes] that featured pieces that had generally been published before in one of the two newspapers. Later, in the summer of 2001, Roberto kicked off a short-lived new section titled "Ventana" [Window] in the Mexican weekly *Cambio*, for which he again used columns that he'd already written. And one can imagine the same thing happening here and there with whichever of the many publications, based in Spain or Chile, Mexico, Argentina, or any other Latin American country, that solicited contributions from Roberto.

At the same time, Roberto would occasionally appropriate pieces originally intended for other purposes for his columns. This was the case, for example, of the column titled "A Few Words for Enrique Lihn," published September 30, 2002 and originally written as the prologue to *Tigre de Pascua* [Easter Tiger], by Enrique Lihn, published by Calembé in Santiago de Chile in the fall of 2002.

SCENES

Town Crier of Blanes. Read at the opening ceremony of the holiday celebrations in Blanes, July 1999.

The Maritime Jungle. El Viajero (travel supplement of the newspaper *El País*, January 9, 2000.

Beach. El Mundo (Madrid), August 17, 2000. The piece was part of a section titled "The Worst Summer of My Life."

In Search of the Little Bull of Teruel [ch]. El Viajero (travel supplement of the newspaper *El País*, Madrid), March 25, 2001.

Vienna and the Shadow of a Woman. El País (Madrid), "Summer Magazine," August 25, 2000.

The Last Place on the Map. El Mundo (Madrid), November 2, 2001.

Fateful Characters. Remarks commemorating the publication of the catalogue of an exhibition of photographs by Sergio Larraín held at the IVAM [Valencia Institute of Modern Art] from July 1 to September 26, 1999.

THE BRAVE LIBRARIAN

Our Guide to the Abyss. Prologue to the *Adventures of Huckleberry Finn*, by Mark Twain, published by the Biblioteca Universal del Círculo de Lectores, Barcelona, 1999, pp. 11-21. Bolaño felt a great and enduring admiration for this novel. Later, in the text "About The Savage Detectives," he would write that his novel was "a response, one of many, to *Huckleberry Finn.*"

The Mad Inventors. El Periódico (Barcelona), February 29, 1999.

Words and Deeds. El País (Madrid), January 19, 2002. This article was written two days after the death of Camilo José Cela, and it is a response to the countless obituaries that portrayed him in a very admiring light.

Vila-Matas's Latest Book. Published as a review in the cultural supplement of the *Diari de Girona*, March 17, 2000. Also published in *sábado* (cultural supplement of the newspaper *unomásuno*, Mexico) on November 11, 2000.

The Brave Librarian. Diagonal (cultural supplement of the newspaper *El Metropolitano*, Santiago de Chile), August 22, 1999. Also published in the *Diari de Girona*, May 23, 1999.

Bomarzo. Prologue to *Bomarzo*, by Manuel Mujica Láinez, published by Biblioteca El Mundo (sold with the newspaper *El Mundo*), 2001.

The Cubs, Again. El Mundo (Madrid), August 11, 1999. Article published on the occasion of the publication of *The Cubs* in the collection "Las 100 Joyas del Milenio" [The 100 Gems of the Millennium], sold with the newspaper.

The Prince of the Apocalypse. Prologue to *The Real Life of Alejandro Mayta*, by Mario Vargas Llosa, published by the Biblioteca El Mundo in 2001.

Notes on Jaime Bayly. Lateral (Barcelona), Number 53, May 1999, pp. 37–38. Also in *Diagonal* (cultural supplement of the newspaper *El Metropolitano*, Santiago, Chile), May 23, 1999. Text of remarks commemorating the publication of the book *Yo amo a mi mami* (Barcelona, Anagrama, 1999), at an event at the Barcelona bookstore La Central on Thursday, March 25, 1999. In the magazine, the piece appears under the title "*Disforzados* Characters, *Patas* . . ."; here it's given Bolaño's original title.

A Stroll Through the Abyss. Published as a stand-alone story in *Las Últimas Noticias*, May 22, 2002. Later it was also published in the newspapers *Página 12* of Buenos Aires and *Reforma* of Mexico.

Sevilla Kills Me. Unfinished speech that Roberto Bolaño planned to read at the I Encuentro de Escritores Latinoamericanos [First Conference of Latin American Writers], organized by the publishing house Seix Barral and held in Sevilla during the month of June, 2003. In the end, Bolaño read the text "Los Mitos de Cthulhu" ["The Myths of Cthulhu"], previously presented in a course on his work offered by Cátedra de las Américas (Institut Català de Cooperació Iberoamericana de Barcelona) in November 2002. The text is collected in the volume *Palabra de América* [Word of America] (Barcelona, Seix Barral, 2003, pp. 17–21, which is a collection of the papers presented by the twelve participants in the conference.

THE PRIVATE LIFE OF A NOVELIST

Who Would Dare? Babelia (book supplement of *El País*, Madrid), January 31, 1998. The piece was part of a section titled "Mis lecturas" [Books I've Read].

The Private Life of a Novelist. Clarín (Buenos Aires), March 25, 2001. *Advice on the Art of Writing Short Stories. Quimera* (Barcelona), number 166, February 1998, p. 66. In the magazine, it was published under the title "Numbers."

About "The Savage Detectives." Text published as part of the program for the ceremony in which Roberto Bolaño received the 1999 Rómulo Gallegos Prize, held in Caracas, April 1999.

THE END

Roberto Bolaño. Interview with Mónica Maristain published in the Mexican edition of *Playboy*, Number 9, July 2003, pp. 22–30. Also published in the Buenos Aires newspaper *Página 12,* July 23, 2003, under the title "Distant Star," retained here.

INDEX